Prime Minister and Cabinet today

Politics Today

Series Editor: Bill Jones

Political ideology today
Ian Adams

Parliament today, 2nd edition
Andrew Adonis

Pressure groups today
Rob Baggott

Local government today, 2nd edition
J. A. Chandler

Political issues in Ireland today
Neil Collins (editor)

Irish politics today, 3rd edition
Neil Collins and Terry Cradden

General Elections today, 2nd edition
Frank Conley

East Central European politics today
Keith Crawford

Political issues in America today
Philip John Davies and Fredric A. Waldstein (editors)

British political parties today
Robert Garner and Richard Kelly

Political issues in Britain today, 4th edition
Bill Jones (editor)

British politics today, 5th edition
Bill Jones and D. Kavanagh

Trade unions in Britain today, 2nd edition
John McIlroy

American politics today, 3rd edition
Richard Maidment and Michael Tappin

French politics today
Peter Morris

Britain in the European Union today
Colin Pilkington

Representative democracy in Britain today
Colin Pilkington

European politics today
Geoffrey Roberts and Particia Hogwood

Government and the economy today
Graham P. Thomas

Political communication today
Duncan Watts

Prime Minister and Cabinet today

Graham P. Thomas

Manchester University Press
Manchester and New York
Distributed exclusively in the USA by St. Martin's Press

Published by Manchester University Press
Oxford Road, Manchester M13 9NR, UK
and Room 400, 175 Fifth Avenue, New York, NY 10010, USA

Distributed exclusively in the USA by
St Martin's Press, Inc., 175 Fifth Avenue, New York,
NY 10010, USA

Distributed exclusively in Canada by
UBC Press, University of British Columbia, 6344 Memorial Road,
Vancouver, BC, Canada V6T 1Z2

British Library Cataloguing-in-Publication Data
A catalogue record for this book is available from the British Library

Library of Congress Cataloging-in-Publication Data

Thomas, Graham P., 1938–
Prime minister and cabinet today / Graham P. Thomas.
p. cm. – (Politics today)
Includes bibliographical references (p.) and index.
ISBN 0-7190-3950-9 (cl). – ISBN 0-7190-3951-7 (pb)
1. Prime ministers – Great Britain. 2. Cabinet Officers – Great Britain. 3. Great Britain – Politics and government – 1945–
I. Title. II. Series: Politics today (Manchester, England)
JN405.T66 1998
321.8'043'0941–dc21 97-18845

ISBN 0 7190 3950 9 *hardback*
0 7190 3951 7 *paperback*

First published 1998
01 00 99 98 10 9 8 7 6 5 4 3 2 1

Typeset in Great Britain
by Servis Filmsetting Ltd, Manchester
Printed in Great Britain
by Biddles Ltd, Guildford and King's Lynn

Contents

Tables and figures

Tables

Figures

Preface

The aim of this book is to analyse the roles played by the Prime Minister and the Cabinet and to provide Advanced Level GCE and undergraduate students with a comprehensive yet accessible account of this crucial aspect of the British system of government.

The book falls into three parts. First, the Introduction and Chapters 1 and 2 constitute a historical introduction. The Introduction outlines the way in which the Cabinet and the office of Prime Minister evolved and takes the story up to the Second World War. Chapter 1 examines the careers of Prime Ministers from Attlee to Wilson while Chapter 2 looks at those from Heath to Blair. (The book was completed in May 1997, so it is too soon to do other than record that Tony Blair has become the fifth Labour Prime Minister.) Second, Chapters 3 to 8 examine various aspects of the role and functions of the Prime Minister. Chapter 3 surveys the way in which post-war Premiers have gained and lost office. Chapter 4 looks at the debate about the power of the Prime Minister and Chapter 5 outlines the functions of the head of the government. Chapter 6 deals with the relationship between the Premier and the wider world and examines how he or she relates to Parliament, the party and the electorate. Chapter 7 is concerned with how the Prime Minister interacts with the media and Chapter 8 considers the sources of support and advice available to him or her. Finally, Chapter 9 is an account of the Cabinet and attempts to explain its role and significance.

In all sorts of ways this book would not have been written without the support and encouragement of my students at Reading College of Arts and Technology, and I thank them for their great kindness over the years. I owe a particular debt of gratitude to Bill Jones for his never-failing friendship and support and for inviting me once again to contribute to the Politics Today series. Richard Purslow, formerly of Manchester University Press, gave me gentle reminders that yet another deadline had been missed and his successor Nicky

Viinikka has proved to be of great help. Shen has been there when I needed him and my children Gemma and Gideon have been a great source of support during the writing of this book. My wife, Gillian, shared the agonies of writing, especially as she was completing her Ph.D. thesis at the same time. I dedicate this book to her with love and my deepest admiration.

Introduction: the evolution of the Cabinet and the emergence of the Prime Minister

Although in a number of respects the Cabinet originated in the late seventeenth century, its development and the emergence of the Prime Minister were the products of the growing significance of Parliament in the eighteenth century, the widening of the franchise in the nineteenth century and pressures caused by the expansion of the activities of government in the twentieth century. However, as political institutions and practices in Britain tend to develop in a gradual and piecemeal fashion, there was nothing inevitable about this process. Much was due to accidents of history, the pressure of events and the impact of personalities, rather than being the product of some plan or theory.

It was an accident of history which brought about the Hanoverian succession in 1714. The first two monarchs had little interest in or knowledge of British affairs and spent much of their time in Hanover. This meant that ministers such as Sir Robert Walpole played a much more significant part in government than had their predecessors. Though this hastened the transfer of power from the monarch to ministers, it was not inevitable. Of considerable significance was the failure of various attempts to exclude ministers and other office holders from the House of Commons, which had clearly emerged as the more important of the two Chambers, with the aim of reducing royal influence. Had they succeeded, some form of separation of powers would have occurred (as *did* result in the United States), and the relations between the executive and the legislature and British constitutional history in general would have been fundamentally different.

Sir Robert Walpole, in office between 1721 and 1742, has been called 'the first Prime Minister'. His domination was based on personality and political skills rather than the office he occupied, that of First Lord of the Treasury and Chancellor of the Exchequer. Yet the concept of a Chief or Prime Minister was slowly developing, as was the notion that the government was responsible to

Parliament and increasingly to the House of Commons. The Cabinet gradually took on a clearer form.

The accession of George III in 1760 marked an important stage in the transition to Cabinet government as royal influence continued to decline. The monarch's role as head of the government was being transferred to the Prime Minister. The Cabinet was ceasing to be a collection of departments, operating separately and each individually responsible to the King, and was becoming a collective body responsible to and dependent on Parliament, and confined to the ministerial heads of the principal departments of state.

The 1832 Reform Act inaugurated fundamental changes in the British political system. It became increasingly obvious that no government could long survive which did not have the support of a majority in the House of Commons. The parties, conscious of the need to widen their appeal in the country, began to emerge as national organisations, increasing the tendency of the Cabinet to operate in a coherent fashion, headed by a clearly designated Prime Minister.

By now the position of Prime Minister had become clearly established. Yet the extent to which he was the dominant figure varied as his position depended on the support he received from leading colleagues, his standing in Parliament, his hold on the public and his appointment by the crown. He did not have a free hand in choosing colleagues and policy was decided by the whole Cabinet. Although occupying a special place as chairman of the Cabinet, the role played by the Prime Minister varied greatly; some were dominant figures, whilst others were seen more as *primus inter pares* (first among equals). Thus a Prime Minister might be the driving force in a government, one of a group of equally influential men, or he might have been selected largely as a figurehead. The office itself had no distinctive powers other than that of recommending appointments and of being the main channel of communication with the monarch.

The 1867 and 1884 Reform Acts continued the process of forging the modern political system. The result of general elections became increasingly dominant in the formation and survival of administrations rather than the support of the crown or opinion in the House of Commons. The main function of Parliament came to be to sustain the government chosen by the electors and passing its legislation. Gradually the executive came to control the legislature, rather than the other way round, and by 1900 the Cabinet clearly was the dominant force in British politics. The changes were profound. Party organisation grew in significance with the need to appeal to and manage a mass electorate. In turn this had repercussions inside Parliament as party discipline became tighter and more effective.

There was a significant shift of power to the Prime Minister from the Cabinet as a whole. The primary reason was that voters regarded party leaders as the embodiment of their respective parties. The Prime Minister normally had the support of the party organisation, which gave him some influence in the constituencies and in Parliament, a position enhanced by patronage. Honours were given in return for electoral support or to bolster the party in the

Commons and Lords. This increase in the Prime Minister's authority affected his relations with the Cabinet, which increasingly looked to the Premier to provide the effective leadership which previously had been provided collectively. The Prime Minister gained a measure of control over the working of the Cabinet. It was now clearly accepted that only the Premier could call a meeting. Once the meeting was called, the Premier controlled the discussion and decided the order of items. The old equality of Cabinet ministers was declining, to be replaced by a stronger sense of hierarchy. The Prime Minister's summary of the sense of the meeting was increasingly significant; by Asquith's time the practice of voting had gone into decline and it was clearly the Prime Minister's role to collect and interpret the general sense of what had been decided. Although questions relating to the dissolution of Parliament or the resignation of the government were still discussed in Cabinet, it was increasingly the pattern for there to be preliminary discussions between the Prime Minister, a few chosen colleagues and the whips.

The Prime Minister's powers should not be overstated. He was still bound by the notion of collective responsibility and had to conciliate his powerful colleagues. In general Premiers had to remain within bounds set by the Cabinet and could be on the losing side in arguments. However, if a Prime Minister chose to resign over an issue, that would be the end of the government. By the early 1900s it was clearly recognised that the Prime Minister was not *primus inter pares* but *primus*. Although other senior figures remained important figures to be conciliated, the position of the Prime Minister was clearly central to the success of the government.

The pressures of the First World War brought about far-reaching changes to both the functions and the organisation of the Cabinet. Asquith, Liberal Prime Minister at the outbreak of war, soon proved inadequate to the task of leading the nation. He was replaced in December 1916 by David Lloyd George, whose energy and proven administrative skills, combined with a fierce determination to win, gained him the support of the opposition parties. Paradoxically, the fall of Asquith demonstrated the importance of the role of the Prime Minister, in that a vacuum in leadership from the top could not be tolerated; the Premier had to be clearly in effective charge of the administration.

The circumstances of Lloyd George's rise to power meant that his position became increasingly impregnable. Far-reaching changes were made to the machinery of government; in particular the Cabinet Secretariat was established to provide greater coherence and continuity to the work of the government. Armed with the weapons of a reorganised and strengthened central machinery of administration and a personal domination over his colleagues, Lloyd George's authority mounted as the war went on, allowing him to impose civilian control over its conduct, a lesson Churchill was to emulate after 1940.

The coalition between Lloyd George's wing of the Liberal Party and the Conservatives under Bonar Law continued after the war. Lloyd George still had to carry his colleagues and to work within political limits. But his success in leading Britain to victory and in the peace settlement that followed gave him increased strength within the coalition. For a while his domination was almost complete; the Cabinet was, to a considerable degree, *his*. All major business went through the Prime Minister before going to the Cabinet and he continued to direct major policies personally. When he considered the timing of the 1918 dissolution, there was no question of the Cabinet being consulted and the final decision was his. Yet despite his enormous prestige, disillusion and distrust quickly set in. He fell from power in October 1922, not as the result of a Cabinet coup but through a revolt by Tory backbenchers at the famous Carlton Club meeting.

Both at the time and later, some commentators have seen Lloyd George's period in office as the moment when prime ministerial government replaced Cabinet government. Contemporary critics accused him of having instituted a virtual dictatorship, and later Richard Crossman implied that there had been a fundamental shift in the balance of power between Prime Minister and Cabinet during this time. Yet the evidence is that it was a temporary phenomenon. The failure to perpetuate a personal domination reflects a fundamental difference between the positions of the British Prime Minister and the American President.

Yet it cannot be denied that some fundamental readjustments to the system occurred during this period. Essentially, Lloyd George set the pattern for the relations between Prime Minister, Cabinet and Parliament and, despite changes which have mainly related to the varying personalities of holders of the position, the picture has remained much the same ever since. Some attempts were made to revert to a more traditional pattern; under the brief Premiership of Bonar Law some of the changes to the organisation of the Cabinet were abolished, although the Cabinet Secretariat survived, contributing to the growth in the power and authority of the Premier. The decline in the ability of the Commons to criticise and check the executive was confirmed, and the Cabinet's authority declined while that of the Prime Minister increased.

The other inter-war Premiers made no fundamental alterations to the system. Andrew Bonar Law held office for the shortest time this century before retiring through ill-health. Perhaps the most important decision of the Cabinet was to prune but not abolish the Cabinet Secretariat. The so-called 'Garden Suburb', Lloyd George's personal organisation, was abolished, but Law took a pragmatic line and decided to retain the Secretariat itself while dismantling most of the rest of the machinery of government installed by his predecessor.

Law's successor, Stanley Baldwin, often left the initiative to powerful colleagues and was later accused of indolence and complacency. In many ways his perception of the job was quite different from that of any other modern holder of the office. Partly because of his temperament, partly as a reaction against everything Lloyd George stood for, and partly because of the sudden and unexpected way in which Baldwin became Premier, he had an unusually static conception of his task. He had few positive ambitions that could be formulated in legislation, in which he had little interest.

Labour's first Prime Minister was James Ramsay MacDonald. Though he formed three administrations, he never enjoyed a majority in the House of his own supporters. When he first formed a government, in January 1924, he did not depart from the existing pattern, despite some rumblings from the Labour left. After consultation with a few senior colleagues, he chose the Cabinet himself rather than submitting the matter to the Parliamentary Labour Party (PLP) as some had demanded. He was a firm leader in Cabinet and took special interest in foreign affairs; during the first Labour government (January–November 1924) he was also Foreign Secretary. But he also gave a great deal of authority to trusted colleagues. When the second Labour government collapsed in 1931 because of an economic crisis, MacDonald formed a coalition with the Conservatives and the Liberals. He and those colleagues who joined the National Government were expelled by the Labour Party. The National Government became increasingly Conservative-dominated and MacDonald was very much a figure-head leader.

On MacDonald's retirement in 1935 Baldwin again became Premier, to be succeeded in 1937 by Neville Chamberlain. A growing recognition of the inadequacies of Baldwin's leadership led Chamberlain to adopt a very different style. This revealed itself in his conduct of Cabinet. Chamberlain thought that Baldwin had been 'unbusinesslike' and believed that the Prime Minister had a primary responsibility to extract the maximum amount of effective work from his ministers. He was a strong Prime Minister; his domination of the Cabinet and his tendency to make policy in several areas, especially foreign affairs, was marked. Some critics of the Thatcher style later detected echoes of Chamberlain's approach to the job. However, this did not create prime ministerial domination; he realised he could not do the work of his colleagues. He seldom spoke first, but his summing up was lucid, ordered, and showed a grasp of essentials. He was little interested in reforming the Cabinet system, preferring to emphasise the need for harmonious relations and to bring out the personal qualities of his ministers. Unrest over his handling of the war led to Chamberlain's resignation and his replacement by Winston Churchill on 10 May 1940, 'Britain's darkest hour'.

Winston Churchill formed a coalition which lasted until the defeat of Germany in 1945. Churchill took over the Ministry of Defence and assumed responsibility for the direction of the war. He presided at Cabinet meetings in a relaxed yet authoritative manner. Meetings often were a monologue, highly entertaining, yet often time-consuming. This was a deliberate strategy. Churchill aimed to secure compliance with his wishes after reasonable discussion. Although he was a dominant figure, in many respects Churchill took an old-fashioned view of his role. He was careful to obtain the views of the Cabinet on policy issues and to keep the Commons as informed as was possible. He took pains to conciliate the Labour members of the government and Attlee was Deputy Prime Minister from 1942 to the end of the coalition. Yet Churchill was the dominant figure in that government and his control over the House of

Commons was virtually unchallenged. Churchill's support among the public was enormous. Opinion polls showed a percentage of support in the high 80s and as late as April 1945 91 per cent declared their approval of his leadership.

The end of the coalition came amidst exchanges of real regard between the parties; it had been one of the most successful and harmonious governments in British history. Shortly afterwards the electorate rejected the Conservative Party and Winston Churchill. Clearly, the mass support given to Churchill had been granted for the purpose of military victory; once achieved, he was rejected to be replaced by the man he dubbed as 'a sheep in sheep's clothing', Clement Attlee.

1

Prime Ministers and their Cabinets, 1945–1970: Attlee to Wilson

This chapter looks at the careers of post-war Prime Ministers from Attlee to Wilson and examines the way in which they approached the task of heading the government of Great Britain. Amongst other things, it looks at their relationships with their colleagues and how they conducted their Cabinets.

Clement Attlee, 1945–51

Attlee was a junior minister in the first two Labour governments and was elected leader of the party in 1935. He held several important posts in the wartime coalition goverment, including that of Deputy Prime Minister. Attlee led the Labour Party to a landslide victory in 1945. When Labour lost office in 1951 Attlee served as Leader of the Opposition until his retirement after the 1955 election. He was created Earl Attlee in 1955 and died in 1967.

Attlee as Prime Minister

Attlee was one of the most efficient Prime Ministers of the post-war period. His great strength was his ability to read official papers extremely quickly and to make decisions with equal dispatch. Attlee's efficiency is shown by the massive and unprecedented amount of legislation enacted between 1945 and 1951; every item in the 1945 manifesto was put on the statute book. Most of Labour's legislation remained virtually untouched by the incoming Conservatives in 1951.

Relations with colleagues

Attlee was the supreme Cabinet manager of the twentieth century. He controlled a highly talented administration, especially the informal 'inner' Cabinet, consisting of Bevin, Morrison, Dalton and Cripps. Prime Ministers need to be good butchers; they must be able to dispense with the services of even their closest colleagues when required. Some Premiers have found this easier than have others. Attlee is generally considered to have been a model for later Premiers to follow. Loyal to those ministers who were doing their job, he did not hesitate to get rid of those who displeased him, usually because they were ineffective or inefficient.

The conduct of Cabinet

Several commentators have seen Attlee's conduct of the Cabinet as a model for later Premiers. Meetings were efficiently organised, crisp and to the point. Attlee's object was to get through business as quickly as possible. On major issues he would ask Morrison's opinion first and then work round the table to end with Bevin. His views of the role of the Prime Minister have often been quoted:

> A Prime Minister has to know when to ask for an opinion. He can't always stop some Ministers offering theirs – you always have some people who'll talk on everything. But he can make sure to extract the opinions of those he wants when he needs them. The job of the Prime Minister is to get the general feeling – collect the voices. And then, when everything reasonable has been said, to get on with the job and say, 'Well, I think the decision of the Cabinet is this, that or the other. Any objections?' Usually there aren't. I didn't often find my Cabinet disagreeing with me . . . To go through the agenda you must stop people talking – unnecessary talk, unnecessary approval of things already agreed, pleasant byways that may be interesting but not strictly relevant. And you shouldn't talk too much yourself however good you are at it.[1]

Attlee disliked what he regarded as unnecessary discussion. He limited conversation in Cabinet by putting matters in the negative, asking not for comment but simply whether anyone had anything to add or whether anyone opposed the decision. While the Prime Minister was able to obtain the opinions of those he needed, others without something pertinent to say stayed silent. In this way the diverse tendencies in even such a united Labour Cabinet as Attlee's were kept facing in the same direction. Attlee maintained close control over the Cabinet agenda. If he desired he kept matters to himself or discussed them with one or two others. This was particularly the case concerning Britain's manufacture of nuclear weapons. Such was the secrecy involved that after it was revealed that Britain had successfully developed nuclear weapons several members of the former Labour Cabinet denied all knowledge of the programme.

Attlee was reflecting not only his own preferred style of government, something of which he was perhaps the supreme twentieth-century exponent, but also his impatience with Churchill's rambling, discursive style. Attlee believed that the job of the Prime Minister was to lead but within the context of a consensus, both party and national, not to try to reshape the ideas and attitudes of his followers. Unlike some of his successors, he was free of that certainty that he knew what was right for his party and his country and that he was entitled to impose his views on both.

The advantages of this style were several. It helped to bind together the disparate groups which made up the Labour Party. The broad agreement about the aims of the government in 1945 persisted largely unaltered throughout the first post-war term; this meant that business could be got through in an expeditious manner. Much of the claim to efficiency of Attlee's government rests on this fact.

Summary

In the years following Labour's fall from power, Attlee's reputation went into decline. However, the very different style of government personified by Margaret Thatcher led to a reassessment of Attlee's contribution to British government. He seemed to typify traditional values and to combine a sense of duty, vision (however understated), integrity and efficiency.

His rise to the leadership of the Labour Party was in a sense an accident. Yet his abilities quickly became apparent, both in opposition and in government, and most of his potential rivals gave him their ungrudging support. The legislation enacted by Attlee's government between 1945 and 1950 was far-reaching in its implications for the British people and its essential legacy dominated political thinking for a generation; elements of the post-war settlement, embodied in the term 'Butskellism', have survived the free-market assaults of Thatcherism. Attlee presided over a government and party which was united in pursuit of its goals, although that unity cracked after the 1950 election and Attlee contributed to the schisms which affected Labour after it left office in 1951. It would have been better for his reputation had he retired in 1950, although anxiety about the succession made this impossible.

Attitudes to Attlee depend on how commentators react to his political and personal style and method of governing. As a statesman he had successes; by general consent the independence of India was his greatest achievement, Palestine his greatest failure. His attitude to Europe was typical of his time: though welcoming greater integration, he refused to take positive steps to bring Britain into closer political ties with the war-ravaged continent. The Attlee government strove to keep the United States involved in Europe and Britain became a nuclear power. Yet it is on the domestic record of the post-war Labour government that Attlee will be remembered and judged. His biographer has no doubt of the verdict: 'Seen in the context of his time and events, he was a great prime minister'.[2]

Winston Churchill, 1951–55

Winston Churchill held ministerial office in Liberal, coalition and Conservative governments. He became Prime Minister on Chamberlain's resignation in 1940 and leader of the Conservative Party on his death a few months later. After serving as Leader of the Opposition from 1945 he returned as Prime

Minister in 1951, finally retiring in April 1955 at the age of eighty-one. He died in 1965.

Churchill as Prime Minister

Churchill was seventy-seven when the Conservatives regained office in 1951. Although the public knew little of the real situation, he had already suffered two strokes and had two more during his premiership. There are divided views about Churchill as Prime Minister. In many ways, his reputation would have been enhanced had he resigned as leader of the Conservative Party after the defeat of 1945; Eden's subsequent career might not have suffered its catastrophic end if he had inherited the leadership in 1945 rather than in 1955.

Churchill's method of running his government was similar to that of his wartime administration. He was not a great administrator. He did not shine as a chief executive, unlike Attlee or Macmillan. Nor did he have a desire to know everything that was going on in his government; in this respect he presented a sharp contrast with his catastrophic successor, Anthony Eden. Unlike Margaret Thatcher, Churchill did not have a burning desire to change the British people, to conduct a massive experiment in social engineering. In his final administration he gave little leadership in economic policy or in domestic matters generally. Although he wanted Eden to gain experience in areas other than those concerned with foreign policy, he did not insist; this meant that Eden came to office with limited experience of crucial matters such as the running of the economy.

Relations with colleagues

Churchill maintained a moderate and undoctrinaire look to his Cabinet throughout the period of his peacetime premiership. Right-wingers were either kept on the back benches or under tight control in office. Although Churchill made several highly successful appointments and brought younger, able men into his government, he also kept some whose performances were below standard. Anthony Eden, R. A. Butler and the Marquess of Salisbury were the most influential men in the Cabinet. Eden, who was Deputy Prime Minister, had unchallengeable authority regarding foreign affairs and dealt direct with Churchill on most matters. By the autumn of 1952 Butler was taking the chair at Cabinet when both Churchill and Eden were away. Salisbury was an important member of the government, but did not help himself by frequent threats of resignation; also his health was fragile. Although they stood out above their colleagues, Churchill seldom if ever tried to take key decisions with them, either as a group or individually. Thus, unlike many post-war Premiers, Churchill did not rely on an inner circle or inner Cabinet. A second tier of ministers owed their position to their personalities or positions while others rose rapidly because of the success they made of their responsibilities.

Churchill has been accused of 'government by cronies'. He enjoyed the company of a coterie of trusted friends and colleagues. However, this did not constitute a 'kitchen cabinet' and few had sustained influence on him, acting more as a foil and stimulus for his ideas; Churchill would often argue the opposite view later in Cabinet. On the whole, once he had appointed a minister he left him alone to get on with the job, and in general backed them regardless of his own ideas on policy. There were exceptions to this. He took a keen interest in foreign affairs and acted as Foreign Secretary during Eden's illness in April 1953. Macmillan, promoted to Defence in the 1954 reshuffle, also felt the weight of Churchill's keen interest in the subject.

The conduct of Cabinet

Churchill had an almost mystical belief in Cabinet government and held more meetings than his predecessor. He was rather old-fashioned in his relations with the Cabinet, allowing each member the chance to contribute. He tended to raise large issues of principle and to use much of the time in general discussions, thus restoring to the Cabinet some of its control over the formulation of government policy. On a number of occasions this led to the Cabinet successfully resisting Churchill's ideas. In July 1954 he argued fiercely for a summit with the Soviet leaders but was forced to back down by opposition, which included threats of resignation. At other times, Churchill would avoid argument by letting an item slip down the agenda until time ran out. This would give the Prime Minister another opportunity to try to get Cabinet agreement to his proposals.

Churchill began each Cabinet meeting by outlining the subject then asking the appropriate minister to open the discussion, which he had to do fairly briefly or run the risk of being cut short. The Prime Minister would then allow ministers to comment, with Churchill summing up on matters he felt to be of particular importance. Other matters were left to the Cabinet Secretariat to deal with. He often allowed discussions to run on, unlike his predecessor, a habit which annoyed some members of the Cabinet, who felt that he was too slack and indecisive. Only in his last six months did his preferred style of Cabinet government, of allowing ministerial colleagues a largely free hand to get on with their work, begin to break down. He became too tired to properly attend to his duties and the co-ordination of the government suffered. Contemporary observers paid tribute to his continuing mastery of the political scene up to the last six months of his premiership; there is little evidence to support those historians who argue that he was senile during his last few months in office.

When he did eventually decide to retire it was not related to his health or because of pressure from colleagues but because of the failure of his plans for a summit meeting. Churchill accused Eden of thwarting him and preventing his plans coming to fruition. By this time relations between Churchill and Eden had soured, Churchill accusing his deputy of seeking to force him out, while Eden became increasingly frustrated at being kept waiting.

Summary

In his final term as Prime Minister Churchill showed enormous durability. He survived two strokes and growing deafness, and was buoyed up in his determination not to retire partly by an almost obsessive belief that he could contribute to the maintenance of world peace by his ability to deal with the Russian leaders and partly by a growing feeling that Eden lacked the qualities necessary to become Prime Minister. He defied pressure from his colleagues to step down, demonstrating both his personal domination and the powers inherent in the office. Churchill retained the trust and affection of the bulk of the Conservative Party in the country and, critically, of most Tory MPs. It was only those close to him who realised the extent to which, by the end, he had become unfit for the duties of his office. Reluctantly, Churchill gave way to the crown prince, the 'golden boy' of British politics, Anthony Eden.

Anthony Eden, 1955–57

Anthony Eden held various ministerial offices from 1931. When the Conservatives regained power in 1951 Eden was appointed Foreign Secretary. He succeeded Churchill as Prime Minister and leader of the Conservative Party in April 1955 but resigned in January 1957. He died in 1977, having been created Earl of Avon in 1961.

Eden as Prime Minister

Apart from Bonar Law and Alec Douglas-Home, Eden's time as Prime Minister was the shortest in the twentieth century. It was also one of the most unsuccessful. Though some expected great things of Eden, whose experience in foreign affairs was considerable, he proved unsuited to the highest office. Very soon after he became Premier, the *Daily Telegraph* called for 'the smack of firm government'. He led Britain into the disastrous fiasco of the Suez adventure, in which Britain, isolated even from the United States and most members of the Commonwealth, was forced to accept a humiliating cease-fire and the loss of much of her international prestige. Eden's premiership has been overshadowed by Suez. According to some observers he broke down both physically and mentally and he left office under a cloud. It appears he was not asked to give advice to the Queen as to his successor, and when Macmillan 'emerged' he set about distancing himself and his government from the failures of Eden's time in office.

Eden's career was unusual in several respects. Although he had much ministerial experience, including being Foreign Secretary for over ten years, it was limited to foreign, imperial and defence matters. This was to be a significant handicap when Eden became Prime Minister. Also, he spent almost fifteen years as Churchill's heir apparent; this time as 'crown prince' was far longer than that spent by any other Prime Minister of the twentieth century. His increasing frustration at Churchill's reluctance to step down soured their private relationship and contributed to Eden's lack of confidence in his own fitness for the highest office.

However, on 5 April 1955 Eden was appointed Prime Minister. He decided on an immediate general election, in which the government's majority rose from seventeen to nearly sixty; most commentators predicted a long and successful Premiership. It was not to be.

Relations with colleagues

There is a consensus that Eden was a failure in dealing with his ministers. Nervous and tense, he was always poking into the departmental affairs of his colleagues and could not stand opposition. Lacking self-confidence outside his speciality of foreign affairs, Eden reacted against Churchill's method of conducting long and often inconclusive Cabinet meetings by choosing to see principal colleagues alone, leading to problems of communication and co-ordination. Eden's method caused maximum annoyance. His outbursts of temper led to an atmosphere of tension and his private staff were frightened of him.

The conduct of Cabinet

Eden made little impact on the machinery of government or the conduct of Cabinet. Butler as Chancellor of the Exchequer continued to chair the Economic Policy Committee, while the committees Eden chaired reflected his interest in foreign and defence matters as opposed to domestic policy issues. In Cabinet, Eden took the lead wherever possible. His colleagues thought him a good chairman of Cabinet, certainly much more businesslike than Churchill, and where he was clear in his own views he would lead the discussion. But in many areas of policy his lack of experience meant he did not give clear leadship. His colleagues tended to interpret his occasional displays of indecision and bouts of obstinacy as lack of confidence, while his tendency to worry his ministers with niggling matters of detail caused them to think he was interfering in their responsibilities.

Although Eden sought to save his Cabinet some of the stress of business, there is little evidence that he bypassed the Cabinet on anything that really mattered. The Cabinet was involved in all the key decisions concerning Suez. Although the Prime Minister chaired most of the meetings of the Egypt Committee, it was not usual for him to chair Cabinet committees, especially those concerning domestic or economic affairs.

The end of Eden's premiership

Eden was a sick man even before Suez. However, the strain of the invasion of Egypt made the situation worse. In the middle of the crisis Eden was advised by his doctors to take a long holiday in the West Indies, leaving Butler as acting Prime Minister with Macmillan taking an increasingly prominent role. When Eden returned from his vacation he appeared fit and to be continuing as Premier. However, there was growing realisation that Britain and France had colluded with Israel in the attack on Egypt, despite Eden's vehement denials. It was an ominous sign when Conservative backbenchers greeted his return to the Commons with something less than enthusiasm. As the scale of Britain's humiliation was perceived by the Conservative Party, pressure grew for Eden's resignation, and on 8 January 1957 he went. A number of factors were at work: Eden's health, pressure from colleagues (and rivals) and a realisation of the extent of failure.

As was then the practice when a Conservative government was left without a leader, a senior Cabinet minister was asked to take 'soundings'. The Marquess of Salisbury was chosen for this role, and he and the Lord Chancellor, Lord Kilmuir, saw Cabinet colleagues separately and asked them to express a preference for either Macmillan or Butler. Salisbury, who lisped, asked them: 'Well, which is it, Wab or Hawold?'. Most chose Macmillan, who was then asked by the Queen on 10 January 1957 to form a government.

Summary

The Suez affair is an example of British central government under stress. Efforts by some of Eden's ministers to assert that they had not been informed about the Suez affair seem to lack substance and none can deny their share of responsibility for what happened. Despite this, it was an intensely personal method of government. Although a Cabinet committee was established, the attack on Egypt was directed in the main by the Prime Minister and a small group of colleagues or by Eden himself.

Although there is much controversy about the extent to which Eden's health clouded his judgement during the Suez crisis, his miscalculations were not related to his health but stemmed from much wider causes, including the failure to understand the realities of Britain and France's changed position in the world, the attitude of the United States and the possible consequences of the invasion. These errors of judgement influenced the whole of the Conservative Party and a large proportion, perhaps a majority, of the electorate. However, his illness probably made his resignation inevitable; had it not been for the state of his health, he might have survived as Prime Minister.

Harold Macmillan, 1957–63

Harold Macmillan served throughout Churchill's wartime government before losing his seat in 1945. Macmillan re-entered Parliament later the same year, finally retiring in 1964. He held various offices under Churchill and Eden before 'emerging' to succeed Anthony Eden in January 1957, remaining Prime Minister and leader of the Conservative Party until his retirement in October 1963. In 1984 he became the Earl of Stockton and died in 1986.

Macmillan as Prime Minister

As Peter Hennessy has remarked, 'Harold Macmillan was not a reluctant prime minister. He savoured the office, its history and its place in the scheme of things.'[3] Suez provided Macmillan with his opportunity, which he seized with ruthless courage. His career as Prime Minister began with the Conservative

Party deeply divided and with the government expected to collapse within a matter of weeks. However, by a brilliant exercise in party management (and aided by the chronically divided state of the Labour opposition) Macmillan succeeded in reversing the tide. In his 'Supermac' phase he largely restored Britain's international position and was credited with the economic prosperity of the time; this was the 'you've never had it so good' period. Macmillan came to office with very considerable power. All members of the party realised the urgent necessity of loyalty and unity. He quickly achieved a mastery of the House of Commons which rallied his backbenchers and restored the credibility of the government. As Prime Minister he exercised a quite astonishing dominance over the Commons. Macmillan's reputation, carefully cultivated but only partly true, was one of 'unflappability', an image which needed to be worked on before it became a part of his public persona.

Macmillan was probably the last British Prime Minister to make a virtue of appearing not to work too hard. In fact, he was a very hard worker; he was a committed 'night owl', something he shared with Margaret Thatcher. Compared with Eden, there was a distinct change of 'style'; Macmillan was determined that being Prime Minister would be 'fun'. In fact, he was highly nervous and prone to deep depression, a feature of his personality accentuated by an unhappy and loveless marriage. He was physically sick before Prime Minister's Question Time in the Commons, an institution for which Macmillan was responsible.

Many commentators have remarked on the actor in Macmillan's complex and subtle personality. He clearly revelled in his ability to present himself in a variety of guises. At times he appeared an Edwardian fop, a light-weight survival from the past. But he also liked to appear as a man of the people, simple and full of common-sense, while at other times he seemed the international statesman, gently guiding Jack Kennedy in the ways of diplomacy or reproving the Russian leader Nikita Khrushchev for yet another outburst of temper at the United Nations. Later on in his premiership Macmillan was portrayed in an unflattering light in the media for his preference for plus-fours and shot-guns as he tramped around the grass moors of his aristocratic relatives, shooting pheasants in what seemed like a parody of Edwardian England.

Relations with colleagues

Unlike Eden, Macmillan did not spend time on the telephone, worrying his ministers with demands for information. Though accessible, Macmillan did not often send for colleagues, preferring to let them get on with their jobs. He used the network of Private Secretaries and the Cabinet Office to keep in touch with events. He was more interested in the broad sweep of policy than in the details of departmental work and interfered only if there was a clear and compelling reason. This had a very good effect on the Cabinet. Ministers acquired greater confidence and were more ready to take decisions without fearing they would be scrutinised and undermined.

Macmillan's skill in appointments meant that he was outstanding in the way he got people into the jobs he wanted. He was especially skilled in balancing the various factions within the party, especially in the wake of Suez, and he did not bear grudges. He showed considerable judgement in giving opportunities to younger men such as Heath, Macleod and Maudling. He was good at managing his ministers, mainly by securing affection and devotion. Generally he would back his colleagues; one mistake did not mean the end of a career, although his reputation has been tarnished by the panic sackings of the 'night of the long knives'.

He used a small group when he wanted to get to grips with an issue, calling together a few colleagues when an especially tricky matter had to be resolved, such as defence and economic policy. However, although he paid special attention to the views of ministers such as Home, Heath and Maudling, Macmillan had no special inner group, although as time passed Edward Heath became close.

The conduct of Cabinet

Until towards the end Macmillan presided over a largely united Cabinet. He tended not to show his hand until the end of a discussion; this allowed others to have their say while Macmillan gauged the strength of feeling. He did not take votes but would adjourn the meeting or set up a committee if he felt sentiment moving against him. Macmillan stressed that all important issues should be dealt with by the full Cabinet. He would often ask senior colleagues such as Butler and Kilmuir to bring a matter to the Cabinet. He tended not to make pronouncements or to use the arts of chairmanship to dominate or repress. Briefed by the Cabinet Secretary, Sir Norman Brook, he had the ability to gauge the distribution of views in the Cabinet, know whom to call to speak and how to steer the discussion. He knew how to use a variety of styles, from the sometimes maddeningly discursive to the brisk and laconic. Macmillan made particularly effective use of the Cabinet committee system, especially of standing as opposed to *ad hoc* committees. Though there was genuine discussion in Macmillan's Cabinet, it was unlikely that his policies were ever rejected, although at times he had to move slowly in order to win over doubters. One example is Europe. He watched over most crucial aspects of policy and was virtually his own Foreign Secretary until Lord Home took over from Selwyn Lloyd in 1960. Macmillan took a keen interest in industrial disputes (a growing problem during his premiership) and many disputes were settled over 'beer and sandwiches at No. 10'.

Occasionally he became bored during Cabinet meetings and would end the meeting as quickly as possible. Sometimes he would be affected by depression, so he would go away and read Jane Austen, leaving Butler to deputise. His successor Alec Douglas-Home agreed that Cabinets were fun, but thought that Macmillan was over-indulgent and allowed colleagues to talk too much. If necessary, he would postpone a discussion until the next Cabinet meeting, using the interval to seek to persuade colleagues to his standpoint. His skill at summing-up, at drawing together both those points on which there was agreement and those where differences still existed, showed Macmillan at his best.

Macmillan's retirement

There was a distinct downturn in the popularity of Macmillan and the Conservative Party by the end of 1961. Macmillan's preoccupation with summit meetings and with efforts to maintain world peace meant that he had less time and mental energy to devote to domestic problems. The Cabinet became less united as serious economic problems, known as 'stop–go', appeared. By-elections were going against the government, and the loss of the 'safe' Tory seat of Orpington to the Liberals was the last straw.

Macmillan came under pressure to take action to restore the government's fortunes. So on Friday 13 July 1962 he undertook a wholesale restructuring of the administration, the 'night of the long knives'. The Chancellor of the Exchequer, the Lord Chancellor and five other Cabinet ministers were sacked. Three days later nine junior ministers were also removed. This act of political carnage was unprecedented in British political history. The general feeling was that Macmillan had been too hasty and had acted in an ungrateful and unfeeling manner to his most loyal supporters. The Liberal MP Jeremy Thorpe damaged Macmillan with the jibe 'Greater love hath no man than this, that he lays down his friends for his life'. Macmillan's opinion poll rating plunged and he never regained his 'unflappable' reputation. He later admitted that the dismissals had been an error of judgement. 'Supermac' had become 'Mac the Knife'.

Then came the Profumo Affair, in which John Profumo, the War Minister, was eventually forced to admit an involvement with a prostitute, Christine Keeler. Macmillan came under intense criticism for failing to be aware of what was going on and for compromising national security; Keeler was also involved with the Russian Naval Attaché.

There was a debate in the Commons, at the end of which the government's majority fell to fifty-seven, the worst result Macmillan ever obtained in the Commons. He left the House bowed and dispirited. It was the low ebb of the administration. Macmillan was obliged to set up an inquiry under a judge, Lord Denning, which revealed sexual wrongdoings among a section of the upper class, which by extension further discredited Macmillan and his government. The Prime Minister never quite got over the affair.

Ill-health was the reason given for Macmillan's resignation, although the degree of illness was exaggerated. Whatever the reason, Macmillan decided to go. He handed over the running of the government to Butler and most members of the Cabinet left for the Conservative Party Conference due to begin in Blackpool. From his hospital bed Macmillan supervised the 'usual soundings', and finally decided that Douglas-Home should be the next leader of the Conservative Party and Prime Minister. When the Queen visited him on 18 October 1963, Macmillan said he could not continue in office. She asked him if he had any advice to give her and he recommended that the Foreign Secretary, the Earl of Home, would be the most likely choice to gain general support. Shortly after, Home, was called to Buckingham Palace.

Thus, at the end of this convoluted procedure Sir Alec Douglas-Home 'emerged' as the new leader of the Conservative Party and Prime Minister of Great Britain. Two Cabinet ministers, Iain Macleod and Enoch Powell, refused to serve in Home's administration. The damage done to the reputation of the Conservative Party by the manoeuvrings of the 'Magic Circle' led to the adoption in 1965 of a system of election for the leadership.

Summary

Historians have varied in their summing-up of Macmillan as Prime Minister. Some claim that he was one of the most successful of post-war Premiers. He can be compared to Attlee as an effective and businesslike manager of the Cabinet and the equal of Wilson as a parliamentarian and party manager. He had a creative imagination and provided leadership to his government and party, and until the end had a sense of timing and an almost theatrical feel for what the public wanted. As with all Prime Ministers there is much on the debit side. But overall he was a man of considerable achievements. The recovery of national morale after Suez and the restoration of close links with the United States, the recognition that Britain's position in the world had undergone a fundamental and irreversible change and must seek its future as a member of the European Community were some of the landmarks of Macmillan's time as Premier.

Alec Douglas-Home, 1963–64

Alexander Frederick Douglas-Home spent some years in the Commons before becoming the fourteenth Earl of Home in 1951. Given junior ministerial office by Churchill, he entered the Cabinet under Eden. He became Foreign Secretary in 1960 and succeeded Macmillan as Prime Minister and leader of the Conservative Party in October 1963, renouncing his title and being returned to the Commons in a by-election. He served as Prime Minister for just one year and resigned as Leader of the Opposition and leader of the Conservative Party in July 1965 after sustained criticism of his failings in those offices. He served in the Heath government as Foreign Secretary before returning to the Lords as a life peer, taking the title of Lord Home of the Hirsel. He died in October 1995.

Home as Prime Minister

Home faced several handicaps throughout his brief term of office. First, the party was to some extent divided over his accession. Second, it was clear that an election could not be long delayed, and with the Conservatives continuing to trail behind Labour Home's tenure of office was always likely to be short. Finally, his inability to come to grips with modern methods of political communication, particularly television, was a continuing handicap. The surprising thing about Home's premiership was not that he led his party to defeat but that he almost led it to victory in 1964. In forming his government, Douglas-Home had even less of a free hand than most other post-war Premiers. His ignorance of economics meant that he needed a strong Chancellor. The manner of his elevation meant that he desperately needed to have the support of Butler and so was obliged to give him the Foreign Office.

Most of his time in office was concerned with preparation for the forthcoming general election so his conduct of affairs differed little from that of his predecessors. Though he lacked experience in domestic matters and clearly felt more at home dealing with foreign policy, he allowed colleagues he trusted, such as Heath, considerable latitude.

In several respects, Home was an unusual Prime Minister. Because of his peerage he had no expectations of achieving the highest office, but when the opportunity came, a result of a change in the law allowing peers to renounce their titles, he seized it with both hands. Like Attlee, he disliked and distrusted media domination of the political agenda. He admitted to being bored by political presentation, feeling that television was bound to be superficial. However, he realised his mistake as he saw Wilson thrive politically through his ability to exploit the media, especially television.

In a newspaper interview given two years before he became Prime Minister, Home declared: 'Every Cabinet minister is in a sense the Prime Minister's agent – his assistant. There's no question about that . . . no minister could make a really important move without consulting the Prime Minister, and if the Prime Minister wanted to take a certain step, the Cabinet minister concerned would either have to agree, argue it out in Cabinet, or resign.'[4] He maintained this view after he ceased to be Premier, although there is a general consensus among his ministers that he did not run his government in an overbearing manner and that he did not interfere in the manner of an Eden.

In reality, Douglas-Home was a classic 'chairman of the board', who pushed as much out of No. 10 as he could for action elsewhere by other people. His ministers had to compensate for his reluctance to take a lead. In Cabinet, Home was sparing of his energy and time. He disliked unnecessary talk, believing that Macmillan, like Churchill, had been given to discursive and even rambling discussion. He believed in devolving responsibility to his ministers, partly because of his lack of experience in domestic affairs. He was publicly candid about his lack of knowledge of economics and did not take the chair of the Economic Policy Committee, leaving it to the Chancellor, Reginald Maudling. Douglas-Home's failure to give a clear lead was a weakness.

Summary

Douglas-Home added little to the office of Prime Minister, although whether this was due entirely to a lack of time to make a mark or the absence of a personal agenda is a matter of conjecture. It is possible that had the Conservatives won the 1964 election Douglas-Home, whose self-deprecating and somewhat self-mocking air was deemed old-fashioned and out of touch with the times, might have made a more lasting impact. Although the result of the 1964 election was close, Home was replaced by the 'moderniser' Harold Wilson, who was determined to make his mark as quickly as possible.

Harold Wilson, 1964–70, 1974–76

Harold Wilson entered Parliament in 1945. After two years as a junior minister he entered the Cabinet, at thirty-one the youngest Cabinet minister since 1806. He resigned in 1951 along with Aneurin Bevan and John Freeman. After serving on the Opposition front bench he was elected leader of the Labour Party in 1963, becoming Prime Minister in 1964 and again in February 1974. He retired in April 1976. He left the Commons at the 1983 general election, taking a life peerage as Lord Wilson of Rievaulx. He died in May 1995.

Wilson as Prime Minister

Harold Wilson holds a unique place in post-war British political history, being the only Prime Minister to have come back to office after having been defeated in a general election. In addition, he led his party to victory in four general elections. When he resigned in April 1976 there were many rumours that the cause was a looming scandal, although time has shown that he went because he had had enough. Thus Wilson's retirement was unforced by electoral, party or popular pressure; Wilson had planned to go around his sixtieth birthday. His last years were clouded by illness and it is likely that early intimations of its long-term effect played a part in his decision, which came like a bombshell to all but his closest family and friends.

Wilson's reputation has fluctuated over the years. A brilliant Leader of the Opposition, he was held in high respect by Harold Macmillan and he outmatched the rather ineffectual Alec Douglas-Home, whom he ridiculed as the product of a bygone age and dubbed 'the fourteenth Earl'. Wilson brought his party out of thirteen years of opposition, even though the eventual majority was much smaller than had been expected.

From 1964 to 1966 Wilson dominated the scene in a way only matched by Margaret Thatcher in post-war politics. He understood the demand for change, for an end to the outmoded social conventions which the Conservatives under Douglas-Home seemed to personify, and for the opportunity for personal advancement within the security provided by a 'cradle-to-grave' welfare system. In the early years he struck a chord with the bulk of the press, even that section normally sympathetic to the Tories. His ability to communicate with the public, to convince them that he was one of them, a man of the people, owed little to image-makers and spin doctors. In addition, Wilson was an outstanding party manager who kept together the disparate coalition which was the Labour Party, despite the growing divisions which occurred over an array of policy issues. Despite rumours of coups, his leadership never came under serious threats, partly because of his skill in balancing left and right. He had little recreation, and work took up almost all his waking hours. Labour's small majority kept the Parliamentary Labour Party together and only Wilson and two other ministers had Cabinet experience. This meant that for the first two or three years he enjoyed supremecy in the Cabinet. It was in this period that Wilson played what he later termed the centre-forward role, as compared to that of the centre-half role of his second administration.

This triumphant phase did not last long. Soon after the triumph of the 1966 general election there was an economic crisis and a humiliating devaluation of the pound, something Wilson had fought to avoid. Relations with the press soured and then broke down almost completely. Wilson was transformed from the 'cheeky chappie' into a figure of duplicity, lacking any purpose save that of staying in office. Public disillusion with Wilson and the Labour Party meant the loss of by-elections even in the party's safest seats, and defeats in local elections which saw councils which had been Labour for generations falling to their opponents. Morale within the Labour Party plummeted and many members left. Yet, despite the growing troubles of the government, Wilson found the job fulfilling and absorbing. He, rather than Macmillan, was unflappable; he had an emotional immunity which was the secret of his success, putting troubles behind him.

Driven from office in 1970, Wilson and his Shadow Cabinet seemed 'Yesterday's Men'. Before 1966 Wilson was over-praised; after 1966 he was over-criticised. Though he was easy to like, he was hard to love. He did not attract generosity. Thus when he fell from power in 1970 he received more than his fair share of blame.

When Wilson somewhat unexpectedly returned to power in 1974 he was less dominant, and there was a distinct change of tempo. He wanted a less frenetic and personalised style. Ministers would run their own departments and he would be a 'sweeper' rather than a 'striker', a 'deep-lying centre-half'. Wilson was slowing up psychologically and even physically. In addition, his aspirations for his government were much more modest than they had been in 1964.

Wilson's last period in office was not a happy one. Labour's 'victory' in February 1974 was more a rejection of the failed Heath government than an embracing of Labour, and the wafer-thin majority achieved in October 1974 was soon eroded by by-election defeats. Wilson was tiring, exhausted by the constant economic difficulties and by disputes within the government and the wider Labour movement. He had seen it all before; the problems seemed to reappear like a circus merry-go-round and he had no answers.

Relations with colleagues

In 1964 Wilson aimed to build a government which would keep the party united. His Cabinet contained a majority of those who had supported the previous Labour leader, Hugh Gaitskell, whose death early in 1963 opened the way for Wilson. This disappointed his friends, but they had nowhere else to go.

Wilson tended to make ministerial appointments for various reasons besides ability and fitness for the job. These included simple patronage, that is to ensure loyalty and support in Parliament and on Labour's National Executive Committee (NEC), to keep the unions happy and to balance the various factions in the party. Wilson promoted talent and was willing to tolerate people who disagreed with him provided they kept their hostility within bounds. In the period after 1964 Wilson worked closely with George Brown and James Callaghan, both former Gaitskellites. After Callaghan and Jenkins switched places following the 1967 devaluation, the latter was admitted to the inner circle, while Callaghan was excluded when he opposed the trade union reforms envisaged by the White Paper, 'In Place of Strife'. After 1974 there were several experienced and powerful figures who were influential in the government.

In the early days many decisions were taken by Wilson, Brown and Callaghan. This was not, however, an inner Cabinet on the Attlee model as it was not based on the same relationship of trust. As time went on, Wilson increasingly dealt directly with individual ministers or took decisions himself. He took over responsibility for dealing with the Rhodesian problem and often intervened in industrial disputes. In August 1967 he took over direction of economic policy. These forays into departmental responsibilities caused increasing tension within the administration. Though Wilson considered setting up a smaller Cabinet, perhaps half the size of the existing one, he contented himself with an inner Cabinet (officially termed the Parliamentary Committee) with the aim not of replacing the full Cabinet but of giving a more coherent political direction to the government and increasing the awareness of parliamentary reactions.

Although meetings of the inner Cabinet continued, increasing divisions at the top led to decisions being taken in small groups. When questions came up in the normal way in Cabinet, Wilson introduced the discussion and often commented on the contributions of each minister, rather than waiting for senior figures to speak and then simply summing up. Over especially difficult issues, he tended to go round the table counting up those for and against, so that something very like a vote took place. There was an indecisiveness in Wilson's personality and a desire to keep options open for as long as possible. Wilson was a reluctant 'butcher'. He preferred to neutralise his opponents by keeping them inside the government; hence his repeated Cabinet reshuffles. Ministers who were sacked were usually found other posts, either inside or outside Parliament; the latter then led to some difficult by-elections.

Wilson was never isolated in Cabinet. He kept the support of most of the leading left-wingers such as Barbara Castle, Crossman, Shore and Benn, although he had firm support from less prominent colleagues. However, there were few ministers who could be counted as unqualified admirers of Wilson as Prime Minister. Some found him too autocratic, others too pliable. Some criticised his style of government, especially accusing him of making decisions in secret with his coterie, and then trying to bounce colleagues into accepting them. Others said he was too tolerant in Cabinet and allowed ministers to talk too much. Some found him shifty and feared that he was holding something back, while others said he was deeply uninspiring. Wilson was a past-master at the art of isolating his more troublesome opponents, as instanced by his handling of Tony Benn.

The conduct of Cabinet

Wilson in 1964 headed an extremely inexperienced Cabinet and for this reason took many decisions himself. Because his main aim was to keep Labour in power he had no clear-cut strategy; he ran the Cabinet on an easy rein. He improvised a formula to meet unexpected troubles, placate supporters with reshuffles and plan election campaigns. Wilson allowed full discussion in Cabinet of most issues. However, a number of policy matters were decided by the Wilson–Brown–Callaghan triumvirate before the Cabinet was formed and it was hard for other members to challenge what they had decided. One such was the decision to defend the value of sterling and thus to avoid devaluation at all costs. Wilson refused to allow this policy, known in Whitehall as 'the unmentionable', to be discussed in Cabinet.

In general, Wilson was a good manager and usually got his way, using the Cabinet to establish priorities and reconcile conflicts between spending departments. Wilson sought consensus by going round the table and listening to the views of those who had something to say. This was criticised by some on the grounds that it encouraged ministers to be too aware of the needs and interests of their own departments and too little aware of the overall position. Sometimes if faced with a divided Cabinet Wilson could vacillate and fail to decide on a course of action. On the other hand he could also be most decisive. In December 1967 the Defence and Overseas Policy Committee, of which Wilson was chairman, agreed in principle to support a relaxation of the ban on the sale of certain arms to South Africa. However, once the news reached Labour backbenchers there was a great row and Wilson instructed the Chief Whip to orchestrate the protest against the decision. Wilson switched sides and the full Cabinet agreed to back his stance. However, on occasions Wilson was defeated. One such was over the proposals contained in 'In Place of Strife' for trade union reform which Wilson and his Minister of Labour, Barbara Castle, brought to Cabinet.

In Cabinet Wilson was a stickler for procedure; if a Cabinet view was required he went through the members one by one, gathering opinions. Some ministers felt that the aim was rather to stifle than to encourage debate. He tended to let ministers talk themselves to a standstill. He was also criticised for trying to fix Cabinets beforehand. Some saw this as prudence, others as highly manipulative; which view was taken somewhat depended on whether the minister concerned agreed with Wilson's line or not. When the going got tough in Cabinet, one of Wilson's tactics was to set up a Cabinet committee, often with himself as chairman. This ploy was also used to settle disputes between ministers. Wilson decided that matters could only be brought from Cabinet committees with the permission of the chairperson of that committee and that only issues of principle not of fact could come before the Cabinet.

Summary

Wilson was initially the subject of admiration by most commentators. However, as time went on what had been seen as a virtue – his ability as a conciliator, as the reconciler of differences both in the country and in the party – came to be seen as a defect. Wilson in opposition had kept the Labour Party together, especially over nuclear weapons. But in office it was different. The government was seen not to have delivered on the promises made in 1964, and increasingly Wilson's skills were devoted to getting over the next problem, usually by pretending that all was well. Wilson was accused of a policy of short-term expediency, shifting ground and facing both ways simultaneously, all with the aim of staying in power at all costs. His constant shifts over membership of the European Community, while designed to avoid a split in the party, seemed to be cynical opportunism. The acceptance of a referendum after having argued against it as incompatible with the British system of government, his attacks on Heath's industrial relations legislation, which had been modelled on Labour's failed 'In Place of Strife', and other examples of seeming inconsistency and lack of political honesty were all held to have contributed to an atmosphere of cynicism which led to a marked decline among the public of trust in politicians and respect for the political system.

More recently Wilson's legacy has been re-examined in a biography by Ben Pimlott. He argues that far from lacking principles, on many issues Wilson appears to have had too many beliefs which were too consistently held, as over the value of sterling and trade union reform. 'On these two issues, in particular, he was much more open to the charge of reckless or stubborn courage, than that of cowardice and amorality.'[5] There was much that Wilson could boast of. In 1970 Heath took over the strongest economic position within living memory. Some very important decisions were taken, although some were by default. The change in the value of the pound, the ending of the 'East of Suez' policy, the crucial steps to prepare for EC entry, the isolating of Rhodesia and the preservation of the Commonwealth were all examples of crucial changes made during the first Wilson government. There was no committment of British troops to Vietnam, despite ferocious American pressure. Higher education was expanded, the gap between rich and poor narrowed and there was extensive social reform, which led to an increase in social mobility. Though much of the credit goes to Wilson's colleagues, he shares the success. 'But outcome is only one kind of measure. In politics, judgements are made swiftly, as on a battlefield: much of political success or failure is tied up with the instinctive reactions of press, public and fellow politicians at a particular historical moment. Here Wilson fares much less well.'[6] His initial success lay partly in his optimism and his ability to generate it among his audience. Wilson promised much; thus the betrayal of promise affected the government for the rest of its term and arguably contributed to Labour's decline as an electoral force in the 1980s.

Notes

1 Quoted in Kenneth Harris, *Attlee*, Weidenfeld and Nicholson, 1984, p. 403.
2 Ibid., p. 569.
3 Peter Hennessy, *Cabinet*, Blackwell, 1986, p. 58.
4 *Observer*, 16 September 1962.
5 Ben Pimlott, *Harold Wilson*, Harper Collins, 1992, p. 563.
6 Ibid., pp. 564–5.

2

Prime Ministers and their Cabinets, 1970–1997: Heath to Blair

This chapter continues the examination of the careers of post-war Prime Ministers from 1970 to the present. Edward Heath, Jim Callaghan, Margaret Thatcher and John Major are examined in an analysis of how they conducted their governments, and there is a brief look ahead to the premiership of Tony Blair.

Edward Heath, 1970–74

Edward Heath entered Parliament in 1950, serving first as a whip and then as Chief Whip. He entered the Cabinet in 1959 and held several posts under Macmillan and Home. He succeeded Home as leader of the Conservative Party in 1965, becoming the first to be elected by his fellow Conservative MPs. He was Prime Minister from 1970 to 1974 but in 1975 became the first Conservative leader to be voted out of office by his parliamentary colleagues. Heath remained a backbencher throughout the Thatcher years, constantly criticising many aspects of her policies and leadership style.

Heath as Prime Minister

Heath served only four years as Prime Minister and, apart from membership of the European Union, little of his legislation remains on the statute books. Ironically, his legacy has been most comprehensively disavowed by Conservative governments since 1979. Heath has been attacked by the Thatcherites, first for failing to carry out the 'silent revolution' promised by the 1970 manifesto, and second for attacking Margaret Thatcher for successfully implementing the sort of policies on which Heath, according to this interpretation of history, was originally elected. Heath has denied that he was animated by the sort of ideological presuppositions of Margaret Thatcher; his aim was to modernise Britain rather than to attempt the wholescale social engineering of the neo-liberal experiment of the 1980s. However, Heath has remained a rather isolated figure since his defeat in 1975, as indeed he was during his premiership.

Heath clearly enjoyed being Prime Minister. He was more interested in the processes of government than in its politics, a factor which led him into deep trouble with the electorate and with his own party. His neglect of communication and presentation, his tendency to rely on the advice of officials rather than party colleagues, were grave faults.

In a technical sense, Heath ran a highly efficient government. There was an absence of leaks and of dissent, even over the 'U-turn'. Heath is often portrayed as an autocratic Prime Minister, although most of his colleagues have spoken of the harmony and unity of the government. There were no resignations because of policy disagreements during his time at the head of the government. More serious was the growing feeling on the back benches that Heath was aloof, unfriendly and even contemptuous of most ordinary Conservative MPs. Thus to a very large extent when he was defeated by Margaret Thatcher in 1975 it was more a vote *against* Heath than a vote *for* his challenger.

Heath set out to be a Prime Minister above party who would lead Britain to modernisation and national pride. But he was attacked by his opponents as the most reactionary Tory leader since Neville Chamberlain. Even after the 'U-turn' he was still seen as stubborn and inflexible. Though he wanted to unite the country, it ended up more divided than for many years. A man of wide interests, Heath came across as a robot, unable to convey his enthusiasms to anyone outside a close circle.

In many ways Heath was an unlucky Prime Minister, especially in the context of the outbreak of war in the Middle East in 1973 which resulted in the Arab oil boycott of the West and the quadrupling of oil prices, and which coincided with the highly damaging miners' strike at home. To an international energy crisis was added domestic chaos. Yet in many ways he was the author of his own misfortunes. His government fell because he was unable to persuade the country to support what he was trying to do. His pride and stubborness in refusing to step down allowed Thatcher to seize the leadership, and by refusing to accept defeat and by appearing sour he allowed her to sideline him and prevent him softening the harshness of the revolution she inaugurated.

There was a fatal ambiguity in Heath's policies which crippled his attempt to modernise Britain. Conservative policy aims in the 1970 election marked a break with the Butskellite consensus. Most of these policies were abandoned during the famous 'U-turn' of 1971–72. This led Thatcherites to deride Heath for a lack of 'intestinal fortitude'. There is some truth in the allegation that the 1970 agenda was broadly the same as that of 1979. But in reality, Heath went along with a set of right-wing, free market ideas in which he did not believe. He aimed to change attitudes and remove obstacles to growth, not to threaten the post-war settlement. Heath allowed himself to be thought more radical than he was. He fell between two stools, unable to convince either his more right-wing supporters or his critics about what he stood for.

Relations with colleagues

Heath was without doubt the dominant figure in his administration, more so than Wilson after 1967 and much more than Home or even Macmillan in his last phase. However, although Heath appeared to have a free hand in the construction of his Cabinet, in reality he was much constrained. The Cabinet was rather like-minded, contained few people of stature and gradually became detached from the mood of many Conservative backbenchers. Initially Heath wanted a Cabinet of only sixteen people, which he thought would add to efficiency and speed of decision-making. But in order to avoid giving offence to powerful figures in the party he was unable to go below eighteen, three less than that of his predecessor. Though Macleod, Maudling, Home and Hailsham gave the government an apparent weight of experience, the reality was different. Macleod died one month after the election, thus depriving the administration of possibly its greatest asset and delivering a blow from which the government never recovered. Heath replaced him with Anthony Barber, a political lightweight and an unimpressive speaker, who could never stand up to Heath and who allowed himself to be pushed into the 'dash for growth' which disfigured the end of Heath's administration. Although Maudling was nominally Deputy Prime Minister he was never in Heath's confidence. The Foreign Secretary Lord Home and the Lord Chancellor Lord Hailsham were both somewhat remote figures because of the nature of their jobs. Heath was also close to Lord Carrington, the Chairman of the party. There was a recognisable inner Cabinet; its regular members were Carrington, Jim Prior, William Whitelaw, Robert Carr, Francis Pym and Peter Walker. The other leading ministers were mostly middle-class 'Heathmen', widely seen as his creations.

As Prime Minister, Heath was dominant, even autocratic, in some policy areas. But in others he was happy to delegate. Unlike Eden and Thatcher, he did not feel it necessary to interfere across the whole range of government business but allowed ministers to get on with their jobs. Heath concentrated on Europe, Northern Ireland and prices and incomes policy, believing that only the Prime Minister had the necessary authority to deal with the various groups and interests involved. In addition, he was intimately concerned with economic policy, completely dominating Anthony Barber, and was largely responsible for the Industry Act, which conferred sweeping powers on the government. However, in general he limited his direct involvement to certain key areas and left his ministers far more autonomy than Margaret Thatcher ever did.

There was a mutual dislike between Heath and his Minister of Education, Margaret Thatcher. Though obliged to have her in his government, her harsh voice and tendency to talk too much aroused his intense dislike. He kept her out of sight at Cabinet meetings and often shut her up. The dislike was mutual. She knew Heath saw her as the statutory woman, there to keep colleagues informed about what 'women' felt about things. Her judgement on Heath as Prime Minister is harsh; in her view, after the 'U-turn' he 'proposed and almost implemented the most radical form of socialism ever contemplated by an elected British government'.[1]

The conduct of Cabinet

Heath usually held two Cabinets a week. The agenda was dealt with in an efficient manner. In practice, however, there were limited opportunities for wide-ranging strategic discussion, a gap which Heath vainly hoped would be filled by the Central Policy Review Staff (CPRS), known as the 'Think Tank'. Heath's domination of his Cabinet derived partly from the absence of heavyweight ministers and partly from his mastery of detail. He was exceptionally well briefed and would subject ministers to a barrage of questions about their proposals. Yet, unlike Margaret Thatcher, he did not pre-empt the decision by stating at the outset what his views were and daring his colleagues to differ, preferring to hear all sides of the case before revealing his hand. He argued fiercely and could be brutal with ministers who failed to sustain their arguments, although if convinced he would throw all his weight behind the minister concerned. Heath believed that his job in Cabinet was to analyse what had happened, what the problems were and what were the options for dealing with the issue. At his best he was superb at leading discussions along these lines. But he could be fiercely uncommunicative, especially when tired.

Heath used Cabinet committees as much as possible to take decisions, leaving the full Cabinet to take strategic decisions and to give directions to the government as a whole. He reduced the number from around 140 to about 70. In addition, he adopted a system of committees which mixed ministers and civil servants, although it was generally unsuccessful; civil servants found it difficult to contradict their ministers or to pursue a line different from that being followed by their political masters.

Heath's downfall

By the autumn of 1973 the government was in deep trouble. Inflation had soared and there was an energy crisis caused by the miners' strike and by the oil crisis following the Yom Kippur War. Heath's plans for an expanding economy were abandoned. In the growing crisis Heath failed to give a clear lead; he was undecided whether to call for resolute action against the miners or to stress the need for compromise. This failure of political leadership came to haunt him later. By this time Heath was ill; he was suffering from a thyroid deficiency not diagnosed until 1975. His health was a contributory factor to what amounted to a paralysis of will which afflicted him at this time. Plainly, Heath and his colleagues were exhausted.

He was uncharacteristically indecisive about whether to call an early general election. Events then moved swiftly as the miners' dispute worsened and the energy crisis tightened its grip. After one last attempt by the government to get agreement failed, Heath reluctantly decided on an election for 28 February. This was the 'Who Governs' election. In a television broadcast Heath said 'The issue before you is a simple one . . . Do you want a strong government which has clear authority for the future to take the decisions which will be needed? Do you want Parliament and the elected government to continue to fight strenuously against inflation? Or do you want them to abandon the struggle against rising prices under pressure from one particular group of workers?'

The February 1974 election produced a hung Parliament in which Labour, despite winning *less* votes than the Conservatives, had more seats, but without an overall majority. After attempting to form a coalition with the Liberals, Heath resigned and Wilson formed his second administration. It was the end for Heath. In October the Conservatives lost another election and in February 1975 he was challenged for the leadership by Margaret Thatcher. Although she did not win on the first ballot, Heath withdrew and has remained on the back benches ever since.

In 1975 the Tory Party replaced Heath with Thatcher partly because he had lost three out of four elections and because it did not appear that he would be able to reverse the trend. Also, Heath had made almost a virtue of ignoring most of his parliamentary colleagues; many Tory MPs had been outraged by his rudeness.

Summary

Despite winning the 1970 general election Heath failed to achieve, even for a short period, widespread affection or even respect from the electorate. At the heart of this failure was an inability to communicate. Heath was perceived as remote, technocratic and lacking in emotion. He lacked interest in the presentation of policy and thus disliked the Wilson approach.

Heath had wide interests outside politics including sailing and music; he had been an organ scholar at Oxford and was a talented pianist and a conductor of considerable ability. This gave him a wider perspective than was usual with leading politicians, but tended to mean that he found his deepest friendships outside politics.

He became over-reliant on advisers, particulary from the Civil Service.

> All prime ministers are inclined to get cut off from reality, overwhelmened by the ceaseless demands of the job and increasingly blinkered by a narrow view of the world as seen from Whitehall. But Heath by temperament was particularly prone to this danger, and in the end he paid for it . . . Heath's downfall is a lesson to prime ministers of the consequences of an over-administrative approach to government which paid too little attention to the political dimension of national leadership.[2]

In the end, the Heath government became overloaded, it tried to do too much. It depended on the co-operation of many other groups and when it was not forthcoming lacked the political skill to find a way round the problem.

Jim Callaghan, 1976–79

James Callaghan became a Member of Parliament in 1945 and held junior office under Attlee. In 1964 he became Chancellor of the Exchequer and then Home Secretary. In February 1974 he was appointed Foreign Secretary before succeeding Wilson in April 1976. Thus Callaghan holds the unique distinction of having been Prime Minister, Foreign Secretary, Chancellor of the Exchequer and Home Secretary. He served from 1979 to 1980 as Leader of the Opposition and retired from the Commons at the 1987 election, being made a life peer later that year.

Jim Callagahan as Prime Minister

Jim Callaghan was Prime Minister for just over three years. For practically the whole time, Callaghan had to contend with being in a minority in the Commons, and to sustain his government in office he was forced into the 'Lib–Lab Pact'. His government was defeated by a single vote on a motion of no confidence on 28 March 1979, losing the subsequent general election.

Several commentators thought that he was better at being Prime Minister than he had been in the other jobs he had held. Despite the problems he faced, especially the lack of a parliamentary majority, 'he never lost his sense of direction, until at the end the overconfidence created by his very success combined with physical exhaustion to cloud his judgement'.[3] Healey rated Callaghan highly, especially as compared to Wilson. He 'was totally different in style. He was a very good prime minister because he always had a clear view about what he wanted to get out of a cabinet discussion, and he guided the discussion in his direction. If it was going off the rails he would intervene and make it quite clear what his own intention was.'[4]

Callaghan took a comparatively relaxed view of his role. The Prime Minister need not be the hardest working member of the government. He must delegate and ensure that he has a politically sensitive network about him. Several ministers noted the more relaxed, less conspiracy-laden atmosphere which led to a more confident atmosphere in Cabinet. Callaghan was much less obsessed by the media than was his predecessor. He built up close relationships with his two chief lieutenants, Denis Healey and Michael Foot, and was able to ward off the constant criticisms coming from Tony Benn. Until the last few months, his position as a minority Prime Minister was remarkably secure.

The need to seek a loan from the International Monetary Fund (IMF) in the autumn of 1976 threatened to split the government and the Labour Party. During the crisis twenty-six separate Cabinet meetings were needed to resolve the crisis, something accomplished without a single resignation. Callaghan put aside the normal system of consulting only those ministers particularly concerned with an issue in favour of carrying all twenty-two members of the Cabinet; Hennessy called this 'the high-water mark of collective Cabinet government of the traditional type in recent years'.[5] Callaghan had great success with the international financial markets and with Parliament, which he managed so as to secure the survival of his minority government. His failure came with the group he knew best and with which he felt he was on good terms, the unions.

Relations with colleagues

Generally, Callaghan had good relations with the members of his Cabinet. Friendship or enmity played a significant part in his choice of ministers; on the other hand, both stopped short at the point where they might affect the unity of the party. Beneath the kindly 'Sunny Jim' exterior there was a tough politician who did not hesitate to pay back old scores and reward faithful friends. He restored Benn to some of the Cabinet committees from which he had been excluded by Wilson, but with the proviso that he would be dismissed if he failed to observe collective responsibility. He brought into the No. 10 private staff two people he had known and worked with for years, his press officer Tom McCaffrey and his secretary Ruth Sharpe, but there was no question of creating a 'kitchen cabinet' which would compete with Whitehall and become a centre of gossip and intrigue.

The conduct of Cabinet

After a somewhat nervous start, Callaghan soon became an efficient manager of the Cabinet. He allowed discussion to run on, but he was an active chairman who initiated matters as well as responding to points raised by others. He offered support to his ministers when they needed it, and in return was given greater support and loyalty than had been offered to his predecessor.

During the discussions leading up to the IMF loan Callaghan allowed the Cabinet members to have their say. He wanted the Cabinet to reach what he regarded as the right conclusion and to remain united. This provides an instructive comparison between Callaghan and both his predecessor and successor. Wilson had been nervous of Cabinet discussion of economic matters, fearing that leaks would lead to damaging party splits, and so tended to try to slip things through without anyone noticing. Callaghan, on the other hand, was more open with colleagues and would outline economic problems in a stark fashion. He wanted to leave no one feeling that their point of view had been ignored and with no alternative to resignation, in contrast to the way Mrs Thatcher dealt with Heseltine and other critics such as Nigel Lawson and Geoffrey Howe. Callaghan sought to include everybody in the discussion while at the same time giving a clear lead. Thatcher treated those who were not 'one of us' at any particular time as an enemy, while Wilson preferred to blur the differences and hope no one would object.

On some other policy matters Callaghan did not use the full Cabinet. Sensitive issues of economic policy, such as interest rates, open discussion of which would have affected market confidence, were not raised in Cabinet. Instead they were made the exclusive province of a highly secret 'economic seminar'.

Members included the Prime Minister, the Chancellor of the Exchequer and the Chancellor of the Duchy of Lancaster; the others were mainly officials, who outnumbered ministers by three or four to one. The Cabinet was not informed of the existence of the 'seminar' nor of its conclusions.

The end of Callaghan's administration

In the autumn of 1978 Callaghan's skill as a political manager and fixer deserted him. As expectations grew of an autumn dissolution, Callaghan announced at the Trades Union Congress (TUC) annual conference that there would be no election. An attempt was made to limit pay increases to 5 per cent, which met fierce union resistance. A wave of strikes broke out, mainly in the public sector, and was dubbed 'the winter of discontent' by the newspapers. As industrial unrest grew, Callaghan failed to face up to the magnitude of the growing crisis, shrinking from declaring a state of emergency and using troops to move essential supplies. Callaghan's personal popularity fell dramatically, especially as on his return from an economic summit in Guadeloupe he was misquoted by the *Sun* as saying 'Crisis, what crisis?'.

Then came the referendums about Scottish and Welsh devolution which failed to obtain the required 40 per cent 'yes' vote. Callaghan had by this time lost the support of the Liberals, and the Nationalists now had no reason to sustain the government. So the vote of no confidence was lost and the government fell.

There has been much speculation about why Callaghan failed to hold a general election in the autumn of 1978, when there was a chance of a Labour victory. Callaghan himself felt that not enough time had elapsed following the traumas of 1976 and believed that a hung Parliament would have been the likeliest outcome of an autumn election. He did not relish the prospect of continuing to head a minority administration. In the event, an avalanche of public disapproval swept away his government.

Summary

Until the last period of his short premiership, Jim Callaghan displayed considerable political skill in leading a minority government through appalling economic problems. He managed to keep a chronically divided party together, retaining the services of ministers both from the right and left, and weathering the worst of the political storms through which his government passed. However, at the end his touch deserted him. The failure to hold a general election in the autumn of 1978 was probably a mistake, although opinion was divided at the time and several of his leading colleagues agreed with the decision. The policy of imposing a pay limit of 5 per cent was a brave attempt to deal with the threat of inflation without resorting to mass unemployment, but in the circumstances of the time it was too restrictive and led to industrial dislocation unprecedented since the 1926 General Strike. Callaghan's prescient remark to Bernard Donoughue, head of the No. 10 Policy Unit, that there was a sea-change in British politics in 1979 was to be proved correct. The era of Margaret Thatcher was about to begin.

Margaret Thatcher, 1979–90

Margaret Thatcher entered Parliament in 1959 and held junior office under Macmillan and Home. As Secretary of State for Education and Science, she was the only woman in the Heath Cabinet. In February 1975 she displaced Edward Heath as leader of the Conservative Party, serving as Leader of the Opposition until the Conservative victory in May 1979, when she became Prime Minister. She resigned from both posts in November 1990 and became a life peeress in 1992.

Margaret Thatcher as Prime Minister

Attitudes to Margaret Thatcher have run the whole gamut of emotions from adoration to a hostility bordering on hatred. Few if any have been indifferent or neutral. Several historians have drawn comparisons between the Labour government elected in 1945 and the Conservative governments of the 1980s, seeing them as the 'book-ends' of post-war British politics. She established a number of records. Not only the first woman Prime Minister, she was the longest-serving Premier this century and the first to win three successive general elections since Lord Liverpool at the beginning of the nineteenth century. By any standards she dominated British politics during the 1980s, to such an extent that her style of government was, by common consent, referred to as 'Thatcherism'. Her supporters credited her with turning Britain around, reversing the national decline which had been accelerating since the end of the Second World War, challenging and defeating the 'Butskellite' consensus which had been at the root of that decline, and producing an economic 'miracle' which had revitalised the British economy. She had ended the defeatism which had marked Britain's relations with the rest of the world and had made Britain great once again, admired by allies such as the United States and a force to be feared by enemies. The retaking of the Falkland Islands in 1982 from Argentina was a mark of her determination to reassert Britain's place in the world, adroitly used for the benefit of the Conservative Party in the 1983 election. Indeed, her supporters go further; they assert that 'Thatcherism' was one of this country's most successful exports. Her attitudes to the role of the market, her support for economic liberalism and hostility to state economic planning and a constantly reiterated belief in individual freedom were said to have been factors in the collapse of Communism throughout Eastern Europe.

Critics have painted a very different picture. The economic 'miracle' lost its lustre as the economy slid into the deepest recession since the 1930s and mass unemployment reappeared. The legacy of Thatcher was a deeply divided society; the gulf between the haves and have-nots widened, crime increased and the public services, starved of the necessary investment because of the need to control public expenditure so as to make room for tax cuts, failed to provide the support people needed. The system of 'cradle-to-grave security' was gradually eroded, leaving people at the mercy of a market system which produced some winners but many losers. Under her successor, John Major, Britain's role in the world again contracted. Relations with Europe continued to be difficult and the 'special relationship' with the United States went into sharp decline. Those hostile to Thatcher claimed that the boasted 'turn round' in Britain's fortunes had been more the product of the image she and her public relations advisers had managed to project rather than of reality.

Even before she became Prime Minister Margaret Thatcher proclaimed her intention to run her administration in a manner quite different from that of her predecessors of both parties. In a newspaper interview she set out how she would run her government. She stated: 'I'm not a consensus politician or a pragmatic politician: I'm a conviction politician. And I believe in the politics of persuasion: it's my job to put forward what I believe and try to get people to agree with me.' She made clear how she expected her Cabinet to operate. 'When the time comes to form a real Cabinet, I do think I've got to have a Cabinet with equal unity of purpose and a sense of dedication to it. It must be a Cabinet that works on something much more than pragmatism or consensus. It must be a *conviction* Cabinet.' According to Thatcher, there were two types of Cabinet. One consisted of representatives of the various factions and groups in the party. The other consisted of those who believed in the same things, who were united in knowing which way to go. She favoured the latter, and in a phrase which was to typify her style in government, she said: 'As Prime Minister I couldn't waste time having any internal arguments'.[6]

Anthony King pointed out that Thatcher was a very unusual Prime Minister for two reasons. First, she was in a minority within her government and her party. Most Prime Ministers represent a broad consensus of opinion within their party; Thatcher, on the other hand, was a more isolated figure. Second, though most Premiers have a few major policy aims, most simply want to stay in power. 'Margaret Thatcher is different. She is probably unique among 20th-century British prime ministers in having a policy agenda – a set of views and a set of priorities – that is peculiarly her own and is in no way merely an emanation of her government or party.'[7] Thatcher's aims were *her* aims, not necessarily those of the Conservative Party. It was this growing realisation that the interests of Margaret Thatcher and those of the Conservative Party were not necessarily synonymous which led, in part, to her eventual demise. It was also a factor in her curious habit of seeming to distance herself from her own government, of saying 'they' should do something about matters of which she disapproved. She was also more than a 'conviction' politician; she was a 'substance' politician, more concerned with arriving at the right outcome than with how that outcome was reached.

Margaret Thatcher's physical stamina was remarkable. She worked long hours and needed very little sleep. Her health was excellent; she had very little illness during her long period as Premier and took few holidays. Her physical courage was never in doubt; her fortitude after the Brighton bombing aroused the admiration of many who were normally critical. To her admirers she exhibited political courage of the highest order. As recession deepened at the start of the 1980s there came demands for a change of course similar to that of the Heath government. However, she told the 1980 Conservative Party conference: 'You turn if you like. The Lady's not for turning . . . I will not change just to court popularity . . . if ever a Conservative government starts to do what it knows is wrong because it is afraid to do what is right, that is the time for the Tories to cry "Stop". But you will never need to do that while I am Prime Minister.'[8] To her critics, however, this was not courage but a stubborn insensitivity to the consequences of her policies.

There was a shifting balance during her time in office between the presidential and the collective, depending on the nature of the issue and the willingness of colleagues to stand up to her. Peter Hennessy examined the way the balance shifted towards a more personal style of government. But in the end, his conclusion was that: 'At worst she has put Cabinet government on ice. In a political and administrative system as riddled with tradition as the British, the old model could, and probably will, be restored in the few minutes it takes a new prime minister to travel from Buckingham Palace to Downing Street.'[9]

Relations with colleagues

Several commentators have referred to Margaret Thatcher's kindness and consideration towards intimates. Two of her of her closest allies were murdered by the IRA. One was Airey Neave who masterminded her challenge to Ted Heath. It was said that she grieved greatly at his loss and perhaps never quite got over it. The other was Ian Gow, her former Parliamentary Private Secretary (PPS). When Cecil Parkinson was obliged to resign as the result of publicity about his affair with his secretary, Margaret Thatcher was kindness and understanding personified. On the other hand a number of her former supporters, including some who certainly at one time would have counted themselves among the elect, tell another story. Ian Gilmour, never an admirer of Margaret Thatcher, pointed to her unpopularity among the British people: 'Taking the whole of her three terms into account, she was, apart from Ted Heath, the least well-regarded of all post-war prime ministers'.[10] Nigel Lawson, another early admirer of Margaret Thatcher, provides a vivid picture of her style in Cabinet.

> Her conduct of meetings also became increasingly authoritarian. Some of her predecesssors, including Harold Macmillan, would allow other colleagues to have their say before summing up and stating a conclusion. Margaret on the other hand, when there was an issue on which she already held a firm view, would start with an unashamedly tendentious introduction of her own, before inviting the responsible and sometimes cowed Minister to have his say. Thus what began as a method for the most expedient conduct of business ended as a means of getting her own way irrespective of the merits or political costs.[11]

An example of how Thatcher dealt with colleagues with whom she fell out came in the Westland affair. As Heseltine became increasingly at odds with the Prime Minister and with Leon Brittan, the Secretary of State for Trade and Industry, both sides began a bitter propaganda war and sought to win over support on the Tory back benches, as well as in the City. Eventually a letter from the Solicitor-General which contained material critical of Heseltine was leaked to the press in circumstances which have led most critics to conclude that the leak was orchestrated by Bernard Ingham and Charles Powell, advisers to Margaret Thatcher at No. 10. This leak led indirectly to the resignation of Brittan, who was made the scapegoat for the whole affair. Thatcher then tried to prevent Heseltine making any further comments on the matter unless they had been cleared with her office. This led the Defence Secretary to resign and set in train the sequence of events which was eventually to lead to Thatcher's downfall.

This episode illustrates the difficulty of describing the Prime Minister's relations with her colleagues in any but political terms.

> For despite the grand constitutional language in which much of the Westland debate has been couched inside Parliament and out, it was raw politics and not matters of convention or probity that prevailed throughout. Managing a difficult colleague . . . determined Mrs Thatcher's initial decision to let Michael Heseltine go rogue and prepare a European alternative to Sikorsky. Damage limitation and not the imperatives of collective responsibility lay behind her efforts to rein him in in mid-December 1985. Assertion of her political supremecy explains her determination to foreclose discussion in the Economic Strategy Committee of the Cabinet. The need to turn the tide in the battle for public opinion led (by whatever route history may eventually uncover) to the leaking of the Solicitor-General's letter on 6 January 1986.[12]

Most of the Cabinet owed their place to her patronage rather than to any independent standing within the Conservative Party. Margaret Thatcher did not leave ministers secure in their posts. By the end of her term in office she was the only remaining member of the original 1979 Cabinet. The changes she made were not primarily on the grounds of competence but in order to shift the ideological balance within the government. Her stamp upon every area of government policy was immense. No minister, perhaps until the last period in office, was able to protect his department from her interference.

The conduct of Cabinet

Margaret Thatcher not only wanted a conviction Cabinet, she also wanted a complaisant Cabinet. She rarely had more than one Cabinet meeting a week. The number of Cabinet papers also fell to around sixty to seventy a year, well down on previous figures, as was the number of Cabinet committees. She rarely used the Cabinet to discuss major issues but treated it as a reporting session on decisions already taken, either by herself in conjunction with the minister concerned (and sometimes by herself, perhaps with a few advisers), by Cabinet committees (invariably dominated by her supporters) or by small groups of ministers and advisers. The difficulty of getting a majority in the Cabinet was the principal reason for what in effect became its treatment as a 'dignified' rather than 'efficient' part of the constitution. Between 1979 and 1981 the 'wets' predominated and there was much resistance to some Thatcherite policies, especially concerning the running of the economy. By almost universal consent this was probably the most divided and unhappy Conservative Cabinet ever. There were bitter rows and a spate of leaks in which ministers attempted to establish their positions in the various disputes which were such a feature of the period. Gradually Thatcher purged her most bitter opponents, either sacking them or sidelining them into areas where they could, from her point of view, do no harm. Then came the Falklands War which fed Thatcher's certainty that she had an almost mystical union with the British people; from then on a more 'conviction' style marked her approach to the Cabinet and indeed to much else.

Her method of conducting her Cabinets was unusual. She spoke first and outlined what the policy of the government was going to be and what **she** proposed to do to make the policy work. Those opposing this line would come next, but they did not always get a chance to complete their argument. The Prime Minister would often interrupt them, telling them in simple and sometimes brutal language that they were wrong. Then she would sum up, restating the action she had proposed at the beginning of the meeting. When Jim Prior resigned he reminded Thatcher about the need for frankness in Cabinet. Thatcher's reply aroused much mirth in Whitehall. 'I take your point about frankness! That's what Cabinets are for, and lively discussions usually lead to good decisions.'[13]

Margaret Thatcher's usual practice was to require the Cabinet minister responsible for a certain matter to prepare a paper for her alone, rather than for Cabinet discussion. The minister would then defend the paper with his departmental team in No. 10, facing interrogators from the Private Office, the Policy Unit and the Cabinet Office. If it survived this ordeal she would support the proposal in Cabinet, which was usually enough to ensure its success.

Under Margaret Thatcher much government business was conducted in small groups. The most important was her version of Callaghan's 'economic seminar', known as the 'E Committee'. It handled similar subjects: monetary policy, highly sensitive issues which affected the money markets. It constantly changed according to circumstances, consisting mainly of key supporters of the Prime Minister, most notably Geoffrey Howe, Keith Joseph and John Biffen. Those immediately affected by a particular problem would be called together and figures such as Whitelaw might join if problems with the Cabinet were foreseen. The membership was an example of the 'one of us' principle, defined as 'Are they hardworking, do they believe in personal responsibility, do they believe in endeavour, do they believe in the voluntary spirit? Do they believe fundamentally in the same philosophy I believe in?'[14] Another example was the group called to consider Michael Heseltine's plans for dealing with inner-city problems, based on his paper 'It Took A Riot' in September 1981. It contained a majority who were hostile to Heseltine's plan, and included the Chancellor, Geoffrey Howe, Keith Joseph and Whitelaw (put there to pour oil on troubled waters). Heseltine was left isolated and backed down, unlike the later occasion which led to his resignation.

An important innovation was the establishment of a Cabinet committee known as Misc 62, nicknamed the 'Star Chamber'. This was the body set up to control public expenditure. It consisted of a group of senior, mainly non-departmental ministers, whose job was to adjudicate between the Treasury and spending ministers. It was headed for some years by Lord Whitelaw in what was probably his most important contribution to the Thatcher government. It effectively neutralised the 'wets'. Margaret Thatcher put Jim Prior, her most powerful critic, on the E Committee. This was a very astute move. He was tied down by departmental responsibilities and so was distracted from paying too close attention to economic problems. Also, it kept the discussion of economic policy away from Gilmour and St John Stevas, who, being free of departmental responsibilities, might have had time to gather counter-arguments. The Star Chamber system led to bitter arguments which led Thatcher to operate in even smaller groups to avoid hostile leaks.

The extent to which Thatcher practised collective government varied according to the circumstances. During the Falklands War she was most careful to keep the full Cabinet informed about events and consulted before major decisions were made, even though day-do-day control was removed to the War Cabinet, consisting of herself, her deputy William Whitelaw, the Foreign Secretary Francis Pym, the Defence Secretary John Nott, and, in a politically shrewd move, Cecil Parkinson, the Chairman of the Conservative Party. Later, it was expected that in the aftermath of Westland a more collective style would be adopted. For a while it looked as if this would be the case. The planned sale of Land Rover and BL Trucks to the American firm General Motors was abandoned early in 1986 in face of backbench hostility and doubts among members of the Cabinet. However, in April Thatcher, without consulting those ministers most closely involved, gave permission to the American government to bomb Libya from British bases. No one resigned, illustrating the point that the Prime Minister is in a very powerful position as long as the Cabinet go along with it.

Clearly, Margaret Thatcher was, on most occasions, anything but a chairperson-figure in Cabinet. A number of accounts of life in the Cabinet room written by those who, for a variety of reasons, left her government, speak of the excitement and sense of challenge, and, at least for a while, of being engaged on a great mission. But there is much evidence of the disagreeable nature of life under a Prime Minister variously dubbed the 'Iron Lady' and TINA (There Is No Alternative). However, although Hennessy portrays Thatcher 'as Queen Boadicia driving a chariot of conviction politics through the conventions of Cabinet government',[15] he warns that critics have gone too far in speculating about Thatcher's dominance in Cabinet. 'She may have siphoned much of the collective spirit from the Cabinet Room in the way meetings are conducted, but more than a shadow remains. Her style is not collegiate. But to call it "presidential" is both to go too far and to dignify it.'[16] It was the failure of the bulk of the Cabinet to support her which in the end was a vital factor in her decision to resign.

Margaret Thatcher's downfall

The 1987 general election was another triumph for the Conservative Party under Margaret Thatcher. However, the economic situation quickly worsened, the poll tax proved to be a disaster, Thatcher's attitude to Europe divided the party and added to her reputation for shrill hectoring. It was clear that the electorate was tiring of a Prime Minister who, though perhaps respected, was never much liked. The political signals were unmistakable. By-elections went against the government, which lost seats both to the Liberal Democrats and to Labour. The governing party did disastrously badly in local elections and the 1989 European election was a significant setback for the Tories. Opinion polls showed Labour well ahead and Thatcher's personal popularity slumped. Increasingly commentators were writing off the chances of the government at the next election, especially if Thatcher remained leader. The Prime Minister's most loyal supporter in the Cabinet, Nicholas Ridley, was forced to resign in July 1989 following the publication of an interview in the right-wing journal the *Spectator* in which he was reported to have made offensive remarks about Britain's European allies. Then came an even more politically damaging departure. In October of the same year the Chancellor Nigel Lawson resigned following a well-publicised row with Thatcher over economic policy and over the influence wielded by her unofficial adviser, Sir Alan Walters.

As pressure grew for a change of leader, Sir Anthony Meyer emerged as a 'stalking horse' candidate in 1989. A significant number of Conservative MPs failed to vote for the Prime Minister: 33 voted for Meyer, 24 spoiled their ballots and 3 abstained, against 314 who voted for Mrs Thatcher.

The pressure seemed to ease as the need for unity was constantly proclaimed. However, the resignation in November 1990 of Sir Geoffrey Howe, the Deputy Prime Minister, proved to be mortal. The Commons speech setting out his reasons for going was devastating. As with the resignation of Nigel Lawson, Thatcher professed herself unable to understand why Howe felt the need to leave the government; a difference of style seemed the most likely explanation. Howe rejected this explanation and drew attention to wide differences over policy, especially regarding Europe. Commenting on the difficulties caused to British ministers in negotiating with their European counterparts, Howe used a cricketing analogy: 'It is rather like sending your opening batsmen to the crease only for them to find, the moment the first balls are bowled, that their bats have been broken before the game by the team captain'.[17] His conclusion was devastating: 'The time has come for others to consider their own response to the tragic conflict of loyalties with which I have myself wrestled for perhaps too long'.[18]

This dramatic event forced Michael Heseltine into the open. Although after his resignation he had proclaimed his loyalty to the Conservative Party and denied leadership ambitions, it was clear he was biding his time. A bitter struggle ensued, in which Thatcher accused Heseltine of being a crypto-socialist, while he warned that the party was unelectable under her leadership. As the campaign drew to a close Thatcher went to Paris for a conference on European security, leaving her campaign in the hands of a team which included her PPS Peter Morrison and former Cabinet ministers George Younger and Norman Tebbit. The choice was less than inspired. The first-round voting was 204 for Thatcher, 152 for Heseltine, with 16 spoilt ballots. Although she had gained an overall majority she was two votes short of the 15 per cent margin required for an outright victory.

Although in an impromptu press conference on the steps of the British Embassy in Paris Thatcher declared she would let her name go forward to the second ballot, her cause was hopeless. Instead of uniting the party behind her leadership she had demonstrated that she was now a divisive force; Conservative MPs increasingly felt that the party's chance of success at the next election (and hence their own survival) would be increased under another leader. Support drained away. Most members of the Cabinet had backed her in the first round; Douglas Hurd had proposed her and John Major had seconded the nomination. However, her failure in the first round left them free to advise her to go with dignity. Some members of the Cabinet threatened to resign if she did not go. Reluctantly she went, though with little grace. According to her, 'It was treachery with a smile on its face. Perhaps that was the worst thing of all.'[19] Although she endorsed John Major as her successor, almost immediately she began to criticise him. He was to be in for a bumpy ride.

Summary

Historians will argue about the place of Margaret Thatcher in the long list of British Prime Ministers. Supporters continue to sing her praises; to them, she restored what one admirer referred to as the 'vigorous virtues', and was 'upright, self-sufficient, energetic, adventurous, independent-minded, loyal to friends and robust against enemies'.[20] Her achievements were heroic and almost earth-shattering. Her critics accuse her of hubris, of a sin of pride verging on megalomania, believing that towards the end of her time as Prime Minister the certainty she felt about her policies and actions became monumental. She made no real distinction between herself, her government, the Conservative Party and Britain itself. Her interests, particularly concerning her own hold on power, became those of the British people. The accumulation of policy errors such as the poll tax, the rapidly worsening economic situation, her attitude to Europe and, perhaps above all, the fact that Thatcher stayed too long all contributed to her fall from power.

Hugo Young put Thatcher in a historical context. As he pointed out, 'How much leaders count, as compared to the shifting tides and structures over which they temporarily preside, is a matter of perennial discussion'.[21] Among post-war Premiers the record is variable. Eden, Home and Callaghan had little impact on the life of their country, though Eden's obsessions had a major impact on Britain's world reputation. Churchill, in his second administration, can be added to this category. Rather more significant were Macmillan, Heath and Wilson. For a while Macmillan exerted considerable dominance over the public mind and seemed to personify his country. Heath, dominated by Europe, was largely a victim of events and his domestic programme was a failure. Wilson adopted a tactical approach characterised by deviousness and short-termism. Clement Attlee comes into a different category. His administration established the post-war consensus and set the parameters of government action for a generation.

> As for Attlee himself, he was the crucial artificer of the engine, the leader of the team. But he was dominated by brevity rather than grandiloquence, in firm obscurity more than brilliant limelight. Although Mrs Thatcher's apologists correctly likened the social and economic consequences of her programme to that of the Attlee Government, his personal role compared with hers only in the starkest contrast.[22]

Clearly, Margaret Thatcher dominated her government to a degree perhaps unique in the twentieth century. She was convinced of her own rightness and brooked no opposition, either from her political enemies or from those who were, at least in theory, on her side. Her populism gave her a direct line to a substantial section of the electorate, including many won over from other parties. She realised the need to create images, of which there were several: beside the Iron Lady there were Britannia, Boadicea, Florence Nightingale and even Mother Teresa. Though some deny she was a visionary, stressing instead the pragmatic, problem-solving politician,

> it would be a mistake to say she had no large picture of what she wanted to achieve . . . her politics were informed more than any other post-war prime minister's by guiding beliefs to which she referred in almost all situations. She saw a smaller state, a more market-oriented economy, a citizenry required to make more choices of its own. She wanted weaker unions and stronger businessmen, an enfeeblement of collective provision and greater opportunities for self-help.[23]

Yet in the end all was in vain. The scene was set for the very different premiership of John Major.

John Major, 1990–97

John Major entered the Commons in 1979. He held several junior posts before entering the Cabinet in 1987 as Chief Secretary to the Treasury. He was briefly Foreign Secretary for a few months in 1989 and then succeeded Nigel Lawson as Chancellor, a post he held from 1989 until he became Prime Minister and leader of the Conservative Party following the resignation of Margaret Thatcher in November 1990.

John Major as Prime Minister

Major's rise was rapid. Thatcher's resignation opened the way for John Major and Douglas Hurd to seek to head off Heseltine's bid for the leadership, both men projecting themselves as candidates who could unite a deeply divided party. Major, who was backed by Thatcher as the 'one of us' candidate, gained support from across the spectrum of party opinion. In the second ballot he gained 185 votes to 131 for Heseltine and 56 for Hurd. Although Major was two votes short of an overall majority, the other two candidates withdrew in the interests of party unity. Major had climbed to the top of the 'greasy pole'. His election as leader of the Conservative Party followed by his appointment as Prime Minister on 28 November 1990 came after only eleven and a half years in the Commons. Although he was very much the outsider in terms of succeeding Thatcher, his strength lay in his working-class, self-made image. This appealed to many of the newer Conservative MPs, who were dedicated to ending the upper-class, paternalistic Toryism of the past. On the other hand, he had little experience of high office.

John Major had quickly come to the attention of government business managers in the Commons. In 1981 he became Parliamentary Private Secretary to Sir Patrick Mayhew, then a minister of state at the Home Office. Major was appointed an assistant whip in January 1983, where he quickly made a mark with his feel for the Commons. He gained a reputation for sound judgement and for his ability to understand what motivates politicians. He was particularly effective as a Treasury whip, where his assessment of the backbench mood and his handling of the Finance Bill during the summer was noted by senior ministers. He had a heated exchange with Margaret Thatcher in July 1985 during a dinner for the whips; the issue was party worries over the economy. But this did not prevent him being given a ministerial post as Under Secretary for Social Security in September 1985, where his capacity for hard work and his ability to master the details of the job impressed senior figures in the government.

Major was a candidate for promotion after the 1987 election, having won much praise for the way he had handled several difficult matters. His sights were set on becoming Chief Whip but Nigel Lawson was looking for a new Chief Secretary. His first choice, John Wakeham, was not interested, so Lawson turned to Major, feeling that his unusual combination of mastery of detail and likeable manner would fit him for the post. Thatcher wanted Major as Chief Whip but Lawson suggested David Waddington. After Whitelaw, who had originally supported Major as Chief Whip, came round, Thatcher agreed. He was the first of the 1979 intake to reach the Cabinet.

Once he joined the Cabinet he gained rapid promotion. His success at the Treasury attracted Thatcher, who liked good housekeeping and a mastery of detail. His shock promotion to Foreign Secretary did not last long, which was fortunate for Major as he almost certainly would have fallen out with Thatcher over her attitude to Europe. 'Just as good generals need luck, so do political leaders. Major's great stroke of good fortune occurred when Lawson resigned as Chancellor in October 1989 and Major took command of the familiar terrain of the Treasury in the ensuing reshuffle.'[24] When he became Prime Minister Major was able to cultivate the myth that he headed a new government, one untainted by the errors of his predecessors, both as Prime Minister and as Chancellor. His succession to the premiership also demonstrates the importance of timing, of being in the right place at the right time.

Major's use of his powers was less authoritarian than that of his predecessor. The Cabinet had a more prominent role in policy-making and ministers had more significance. The handover from Thatcher to Major saw a marked transformation in the role of the Cabinet. More matters were dealt with in Cabinet committees. There were fewer bilateral meetings and *ad hoc* groups, a reflection of the differences in style and approach. There was a permanent ministerial committee to deal with the public expenditure question; the *ad hoc* Star Chamber method was ended. The advantage of this style was that Major was able to take controversial policy decisions, such as the abandonment of the poll tax and the ratification of the Maastricht Treaty, without any Cabinet resignations. The disadvantage was slowness of decision-making and the appearance of drift, indecisiveness and weakness.

John Major was conscious of the criticisms of Thatcher's style of government. This, plus his more collegiate approach to the premiership, inevitably meant a less strident type of leadership. However, even after Major's unexpected victory in the 1992 general election, he remained in a weaker position than his predecessor. There are several reasons for this.

(1) Major was elected by a party which had just ousted its leader as much for the defects of her personality as for her policy errors. Tory MPs wanted someone who could listen, and Major showed he was just such a person, but who was a follower of Thatcher who could be trusted to follow along basically the same line. As Hugo Young has pointed out, the party 'rejected the opportunity to make an ideological break with the past. It wanted Thatcherism pursued by non-thatcherite means, neglecting to consider the possibility that this might be an unattainable ambition. Mr Major personifies a dilemma that four years have failed to resolve. The faultline between these two objectives has reached into most of the areas that mattered.'[25]

(2) Initially he was dependent on Cabinet heavyweights such as Michael Heseltine (especially following his promotion to Deputy Prime Minister in July 1995) and Kenneth Clarke, significant political figures in their own right who did not owe their position to Major in the way that most members of Thatcher's Cabinet had been her creatures. Subsequently, in an effort to prevent the party splitting over Europe, Major tilted to the right and his relations with Clark cooled.

(3) By temperament he sought consensus and made a virtue of reasserting the Cabinet's pre-eminence. This was demonstrated in episodes such as Major's handling of the Maastricht negotiations, the withdrawal from the Exchange Rate Mechanism (ERM) and the debate over pit closures. Unlike his predecessor, Major appeared to act more as a chairman of the Cabinet, to allow debate, to permit ministers to question other colleagues and to sum up the discussion at the end rather than at the beginning. However, this led to accusations of incoherence in policy-making; on several occasions, most notably over the pit closures, ministers were caught off-guard by policy initiatives of which they had no advance warning. The 'back to basics' policy also showed signs of incoherence, with various ministers giving it markedly divergent interpretations.

(4) Major had less control over the Conservative Party than did his predecessor, especially in Parliament, where the reduced majority limited the government's room for manoeuvre. The presence of a large and fairly cohesive Eurosceptic group on the back benches made the task of managing both Parliament and the party much more difficult than it was for Margaret Thatcher. At times, Lady Thatcher seemed like a member of the opposition, criticising Major's leadership on several grounds, most notably on policy towards Europe. The real opposition, particularly the Labour Party, was much more effective than it was during the 1980s and Tony Blair a more formidable Leader of the Opposition than was Neil Kinnock.

(5) Major had little of the ideological certainty of his predecessor. Major's problems must be seen in the context of the economic recession, the legacy of the boom of the late 1980s, which prevented the government seizing the initiative. The failure of the 'feel good factor' to make its reappearance, despite the improved economic position, baffled ministers, who failed to translate better economic indicators into an improved political situation.

There was a widespread impression of Major that he was a Prime Minister 'on trial', that he was somehow temporary. This was rather extraordinary. He was in power longer than post-war Prime Ministers such as Eden, Home and Callaghan. It was probably related to the image of Major conveyed by programmes such as *Spitting Image* as a grey, boring nonentity. It was also due to the unprecedented press campaign in papers such as *The Times*, the *Sunday Times* and the *Sun*, normally loyal to the Conservative Party and almost fanatically devoted to Margaret Thatcher when she was Premier.

These factors meant that Major was forced to consolidate many of the Thatcherite initiatives, such as privatisation and Civil Service reform, while seeking to establish his own agenda through the emphasis on improving the quality of public services (by further extension of market forces) and by issuing numerous Citizen's Charters. These were designed to increase the quality of public services and to make 'clients' aware of their legal rights. More recently, the renewed emphasis on 'law and order' and 'family values' coupled the concerns of the New Right with Major's projection of his 'down to earth', 'commonsense' approach to his job. His task was made harder by the constant criticisms, sometimes veiled, sometimes open, of Lady Thatcher and her supporters.

Another feature of the Major premiership was the proclamation of a belief in 'open government'. In May 1992 the Prime Minister followed up his manifesto commitment of greater access to official information by imposing on his ministers a general obligation to be as open as possible with Parliament and the public. William Waldegrave, then the Cabinet minister responsible for the Citizen's Charter, published for the first time a list of twenty-six standing Cabinet committees with membership and terms of reference. The Cabinet rulebook, *Questions of Procedure for Ministers*, previously classified as 'confidential', was also published. Although critics of government secrecy generally welcomed the greater openness, there was some scepticism that much of substance would be revealed.

There were several criticisms of John Major.

(1) He was accused of not being a good butcher, of being unable to sack ministers when necessary. This was the case when Norman Lamont stayed on after the fiasco of Britain's forced withdrawal from the ERM. Equally, when eventually Lamont was sacked, Major was attacked for having made a scapegoat of someone who was, after all, merely carrying out the Prime Minister's own policy. Lamont was incensed by his dismissal. Instead of sending the usual letter full of pious words about 'being grateful for having had the opportunity to serve', Lamont faxed a letter of resignation and has since been a constant and vociferous critic of Major's leadership. Major was accused of letting personal friendship get in the way of doing the correct thing when he tried to hang on to David Mellor. Major was loath to sack colleagues except when unavoidable.

(2) It was suggested that Major's nerve went in a crisis, especially on 'Black Wednesday', when he was said to have had a virtual nervous breakdown. On the other hand, he showed great poise and real qualities of leadership during the Gulf War, which he inherited on becoming Prime Minister. He was said to be too sensitive to criticism. He read the press obsessively, in contrast with his predecessor whose Press Secretary made a carefully filleted summary for her.

(3) Mainly from the Thatcherite right came the jibe that Major lacked vision. He was attacked for embracing the consensus, especially over Europe. It was clear that Major was not a 'vision' person, and his calls for a 'classless society' and an appeal to 'back to basics' fell flat. He was a poor speaker, although he was better with small groups of supporters than with a large and perhaps sceptical audience.

(4) A significant criticism was that he dithered and could not make up his mind. The result was an impression of drift, uncertainty and indecision, especially over Europe. Supporters pointed out that he swiftly disposed of the poll tax, which was converted into a 'council tax' and disappeared from view as a political issue. In addition, he largely managed to avoid Europe causing a split similar to that which divided the Tories over the Corn Laws in 1846.

By the end of 1992 the government appeared to be drifting helplessly, battered by a series of policy reverses such as the forced withdrawal from the ERM. Critics from a variety of perspectives were united in finding John Major's government the least competent for many years. The Prime Minister's popularity also slumped. The dismissal of Norman Lamont in May 1993 was seen as another example of Major's weakness in the face of public anger at the handling of the economy and party anxiety about electoral prospects. Lamont's resignation speech in the Commons added to Major's woes; the sacked Chancellor said 'We give the impression of being in office, but not in power'.

Criticism of Major's leadership grew. In an unguarded off-camera talk to a television journalist, he referred to three right-wing Eurosceptic Cabinet ministers (thought to be Peter Lilley, Michael Portillo and John Redwood) as 'bastards'. He accused them of threatening resignation over the Social Chapter. Later another leak had Major referring to some of the rebel backbenchers as 'barmy' and as several 'apples short of a picnic'. In the autumn of 1994 a group of eight Eurosceptic MPs were deprived of the Tory whip. However, Major was obliged by the weakness of his parliamentary position to quickly restore it without having secured promises of good behaviour. As criticisms grew, Major surprised most political commentators and the bulk of his own party in June 1995 by resigning the leadership of the Conservative Party (but not as Premier) and offering himself for re-election. His decision was triggered by continuing press and party unrest about his leadership. There was much speculation about which if any of his Cabinet would pick up the gauntlet; there was a general view that if Major failed to win on the first ballot he would resign, leading Cabinet heavyweights such as Heseltine, Clarke and Portillo to enter the fray. However, in the event Major was challenged for the leadership by the Eurosceptic Welsh Secretary, John Redwood, who resigned from the Cabinet.

The rest of the Cabinet rallied to Major, although with varying degrees of zeal, and at least one, Michael Portillo, set up a campaign machine to be ready in case of an inconclusive first ballot. Most of the 1922 Committee signed his nomination papers and Major received the lukewarm support of Lady Thatcher. She stated he was her preferred candidate but praised Redwood as a 'very articulate and able politician'. During the campaign Major and his campaign team made sure they did not repeat Thatcher's complacency. They made strenuous efforts to win over wavering Tory MPs and mobilised support among constituency chairmen. In the event their work paid off and on 4 July Major was re-elected leader by 218 votes to 89 for Redwood, with the surprisingly low number of 20 abstentions.

The end of Major's government

Although Major's position was somewhat strengthened by his re-election, he was unable to restore public confidence in his administration. Electoral opinion remained hostile to the Conservatives, who suffered damaging defeats in parliamentary by-elections and local elections, while public opinion polls showed large and consistent leads for the Labour Party. Major clung to power until almost the last moment despite losing his Commons majority. In April 1997 he announced that a general election would be held on 1 May, after what would be the longest election campaign since 1918. Major hoped that this would give his party the opportunity to erode the Labour lead, but the poll ratings of the various parties stayed largely unchanged. The result of the 1997 general election was a triumph for the Labour Party under Tony Blair, winning 418 seats with 43.2 per cent of the vote. For the Conservatives it was one of the worst defeats ever. They won only 165 seats, the lowest since the Liberal landslide of 1906, and their share of the vote (38.7 per cent) was the smallest since 1832. On the day following his defeat John Major accounced that he was resigning both as Prime Minister and as leader of the Conservative Party.

Summary

John Major was Prime Minister for six and a half years, longer than post-war Premiers such as Churchill, Eden, Home, Heath and Callaghan. Yet he remained little known to the public and aroused little affection outside his circle of intimates. His party seemed to cling to him as leader because of an inability to decide on anyone else. His image was one of 'greyness'; his grey hair and pale complexion seeming to reflect a personality devoid of excitement and verve. He was unable to rid himself of the legacy, some would say of the incubus, of Thatcher. Although the main lines of policy followed those of his predecessor, he wanted to carve out a reputation which would be one of radicalism combined with greater humanity and pragmatism. In the end he failed. Although he showed great gifts of party management in avoiding an open split over relations with Europe and managing to stave off defeat in the Commons, he could not prevent a landslide sweeping his party into opposition. Although the prevailing view was that Major was an essentially decent man, there was a widespread feeling that his government and party had become arrogant, complacent and out of touch with the mass of the electorate. The electoral coalition so skilfully built up by Thatcher and her advisers fell apart and the Conservatives massively lost support among all sections of the population and in all regions.

Commentators put forward a variety of explanations for this massive defeat. There was a general agreement that there was a desire for change after eighteen years of Tory rule. The absence of the 'feel-good' factor despite an improved economic position, a refusal to accept ministerial assurances that Britain had one of the strongest economies in the developed world, meant that the 1997 election was a rare, possibly unique, example of a 'vote-less recovery'. Britain's ignominious departure from the ERM in the autumn of 1992 meant that the myth that the Conservatives were the party of economic competence finally disappeared. What were widely seen as the broken promises, especially on tax, of the 1992 election were another potent factor. Policy errors abounded and during the campaign Labour skilfully (and according to the Tories, unscrupulously) exploited fears over the future of the welfare state and especially the state pension in the event of another term of Conservative rule. The atmosphere of 'sleaze', both sexual and financial, which pervaded the government and the Conservative Party added to Major's difficulties, and intensified the general perception of Major as a weak and indecisive leader. But perhaps above all it was the divisions in the government and the Conservative Party about Europe which most clearly sealed the fate of Major's government. As in 1846 and 1906, the failure of the Conservative Party to decide how Britain should relate to the outside world, and the inability of the leader of the party to impose some kind of unity, led the party into the electoral wilderness.

Tony Blair as Prime Minister, 1997–

Tony Blair swept into Downing Street on 2 May 1997 at the head of the largest parliamentary majority since the 1930s. He joined Ramsay MacDonald in having had no previous ministerial experience before reaching the top. Despite his efforts and those of his colleagues to deny that there would be significant departures from many of the policies of the outgoing government, especially concerning the management of the economy, taxation and the welfare state, the sheer scale of the victory has aroused expectations which will be difficult to fulfil. Only the future will show how he and his government carry out their responsibilities. The experience of most post-war Premiers is that the triumphs are short-lived and the 'great adventure' ends in anti-climax and sometimes in near farce. Whether Blair will break the mould remains to be seen.

Notes

1 Margaret Thatcher, *The Downing Street Years*, Harper Collins, 1993, p. 7.
2 John Campbell, *Edward Heath. A Biography*, Cape, 1993, p. 492.
3 Denis Healey, *The Time of My Life*, Michael Joseph, 1989, p. 448.
4 Denis Healey, quoted in Peter Hennessy and Anthony Seldon (eds), *Ruling Performance. British Governments from Attlee to Thatcher*, Blackwell, 1989, p. 255.
5 Peter Hennessy, *Cabinet*, Blackwell, 1986, p. 91.
6 *Observer*, 25 February 1979.
7 Anthony King (ed.), *The British Prime Minister*, Macmillan, 1985, 2nd edn, p. 98.
8 Quoted in Kenneth Harris, *Thatcher*, Weidenfeld and Nicholson, 1988, p. 107.
9 Hennessy, *Cabinet*, p. 122.
10 Ian Gilmour, *Dancing with Dogma. Britain under Thatcherism*, Simon and Schuster, 1992, p. 7.
11 Nigel Lawson, *The View From No. 11. Memoirs of a Tory Radical*, Bantam Press, 1992, p. 128.
12 Peter Hennessy, *Whitehall*, Fontana, 1990, pp. 306–7.
13 *The Times* 1 September 1984, reporting Thatcher's reply to Prior's letter of resignation.
14 Harris, *Thatcher*, p. 94.
15 Hennessy, *Cabinet*, p. 89.
16 Ibid., p. 111.

17 Geoffrey Howe, *Conflict of Loyalty*, Macmillan, 1994, p. 702.
18 Ibid., p. 703.
19 'Thatcher: The Downing Street Years', Woman at War, BBC1, 20 October 1993.
20 Shirley Robin Letwin, *The Anatomy of Thatcherism*, Fontana, 1992, p. 33.
21 Hugo Young, *One of Us*, Macmillan, 1991, p. 598.
22 Ibid., p. 599.
23 Ibid., p. 604.
24 Robert Shepherd, *The Power Brokers. The Tory Party and its Leaders*, Hutchinson, 1991, p. 57.
25 Dennis Kavanagh and Anthony Seldon (eds), *The Major Effect*, Macmillan, 1994, p. 18.

3

Post-war Prime Ministers: gaining and losing office

This chapter examines the process of becoming Prime Minister. The role of the crown, the three routes to the top, factors in the rise of the Prime Minister and the internal party rules for leadership selection are all considered in this section. Loss of office is the next aspect to be discussed. The characteristics of Prime Ministers and their backgrounds are then examined before an attempt is made to drawn up a prime ministerial typology.

Introduction

Since the 1867 Reform Act most Prime Ministers have been leaders of the majority party in the Commons. Thus the Prime Minister usually gets his or her authority from being head of the government *and* from being leader of the majority party, which in turn normally means being able to dominate the Commons. The position is somewhat more complicated during coalition or minority governments, although the power of the Prime Minister differs according to the precise circumstances of each administration. This fusion of executive and legislative power is a feature of British government, and is a significant contrast to the situation in the United States, where the President is commonly faced with a hostile Congress.

The process of becoming Prime Minister

The role of the crown

In formal constitutional terms, appointment as Prime Minister is in the hands of the monarch. However, the person appointed is the one most likely to command a majority in the Commons, usually the leader of the majority or the largest party in the House. Thus the Prime Minister is the person summoned to Buckingham Palace after being previously chosen as the leader of the governing party. There have been a handful of exceptions this century and these will be discussed later.

Usually the choice is automatic, although in other cases the apparent exercise of discretion by the monarch may be involved. If an election result is not clear-cut, if the leadership of the majority party is in dispute, or if the distribution of support in the Commons is uncertain, the monarch's role may be more than purely formal.

Twice this century the choice of Prime Minister has been, at least nominally, in the hands of the monarch. In 1923 Andrew Bonar Law, the Conservative Prime Minister, resigned because of ill-health. There were two possible successors: Lord Curzon and Stanley Baldwin. After the usual soundings had been taken among prominent Conservative politicians, Baldwin 'emerged' and was asked by George V to form a government. In 1931 the collapse of the Labour government under MacDonald led to another exercise of the prerogative power. George V, after consultations with the leaders of the Conservative and Liberal parties, asked MacDonald to head a National government.

Since 1945 the role of the monarch has declined. However, twice before 1965 the lack of a formal method of choosing the leader of the Conservative Party did involve some element of apparent royal discretion. In January 1957 the abrupt resignation of Sir Anthony Eden meant that the Queen had to initiate the choice of a successor. After soundings were taken with prominent Conservatives, Harold Macmillan 'emerged' as the new Premier. The outcome of the 'customary processes' of consultation when Macmillan resigned in October 1963 was less satisfactory. There were several possible successors and after behind-the-scenes negotiations the Queen sent for the Foreign Secretary, the Earl of Home, who renounced his peerage to become Sir Alec Douglas-Home. Home was able to form a government, although some senior figures refused to serve in his Cabinet. Following the inconclusive election of February 1974, Edward Heath tried to negotiate a pact with the Liberals. When that failed, in accordance with constitutional precedents the Queen sent for the Leader of the Opposition, and Wilson was able to form a minority government, the first since 1929.

However, the role of the monarch in these various episodes was in reality limited to giving formal sanction to the political manoeuvrings of leading figures in the Conservative Party. The major parties now have procedures for electing their leaders which reduce the role of the monarch to a formality; these will be discussed later.

Ways of becoming Prime Minister

Under normal circumstances there are three ways in which a person can become Prime Minister:

1 Winning a general election and ousting the previous administration.
2 Succeeding the outgoing Prime Minister of his or her own party.
3 By emerging as the head of a coalition.

Ten men and one woman have headed administrations in Britain since the

Table 3.1 *Becoming Prime Minister*

Winning a general election	*Succeeding outgoing PM of same party*
Attlee 1945	Eden 1955
Churchill 1951	Macmillan 1957
Wilson 1964	Home 1963
Heath 1970	Callaghan 1976
Wilson Feb. 1974	Major 1990
Thatcher 1979	
Blair 1997	

end of the Second World War, although one, Harold Wilson, formed two separate governments. On seven occasions a person became Prime Minister through leading his or her party to victory in a general election, and on five occasions the premiership was achieved through succeeding to the leadership of the governing party during the lifetime of a Parliament, as shown in Table 3.1.

Since 1945 all governments have been either Conservative or Labour single-party administrations. Thus coalition Premiers, sometimes not even leaders of the majority party, a marked feature of pre-war governments, have been absent. However, the greater ability of the Conservative Party to win elections has meant that all seven of its post-war leaders (up to and including Major) have reached the top of the 'greasy pole', while only four of Labour's eight have attained this position.

Factors in the rise of Prime Ministers

Many factors determine who will get to the top in British politics: 'the key characteristics of the career politician are commitment and energy, as well as good luck and timing'.[1] Several recent British Prime Ministers have shown an overwhelming interest in politics from a very early age. Harold Wilson's obsessive concern for the realities of power was not just a feature of his mature years:

> In 1923, at the age of seven, I had an operation for appendicitis . . . It took place on the day of the general election, called by Stanley Baldwin, who was seeking a mandate to introduce tariff reform protection for Britain's industries. That evening my parents came to see me in hospital as I came round from the anasthetic. As they lingered, I kept urging them to leave so that they would be in time to vote for Philip – my hero Philip Snowden.[2]

A later Premier, remembering his first visit to the Commons at the age of thirteen, also shared the fascination of political life:

> John [Major] sat in the Strangers' Gallery and watched a debate. The whole experience hit him with the force of the cannon ball. 'I was pretty clear that I wanted to go back to the House of Commons. Indeed, so clear was I that I wouldn't actually go back very often and listen to the debates because it was frustrating to go there and not be a part of it. I feared I might never get there.' '[3]

Many politicians have been born into political families, ones where politics was discussed and where political activity was part of life. Margaret Thatcher was one such. Her father, Alderman Alfred Roberts, passed on his commitment to politics which inspired and sustained her throughout her career. For an earlier generation of Conservative leaders such as Churchill, Eden, Macmillan and Douglas-Home, political involvement was a family affair, a part of the tradition of the Tory upper class. Many others become politically active for broadly ideological reasons, a reaction to external events or as a result of being converted, or a mixture of the two. Clement Attlee, who was from a prosperous middle-class background, was converted to socialism and joined the Fabian Society in 1907 and the Independent Labour Party in 1908 as the result of his experience of managing a settlement which provided welfare and recreational facilities for the poor of the East End of London. Jim Callaghan's socialism was rooted in his early experiences of poverty and deprivation. Involvement in Labour politics was taken for granted in those circumstances.

There are many ways into active politics. On the Labour side the trade unions were the nearest equivalent to the route provided by land and family in the Conservative Party of an earlier era. However, the only Labour Prime Minister to base his early career on the unions has been Jim Callaghan, who was a union official before entering Parliament in 1945. Labour's first Premier, James Ramsey MacDonald, was illegitimate and suffered grinding poverty as a boy. He later made a precarious living from journalism and from paid political work before being elected to Parliament in 1906. Attlee qualified as a solicitor, worked as a volunteer in various charitable organisations in London and then taught at the London School of Economics before becoming an MP. Harold Wilson, from a lower-middle-class background, became a don at Oxford and then a wartime civil servant before being swept into Parliament in 1945. Tony Blair was a barrister before entering the Commons in 1983.

For several Conservative Prime Ministers of the earlier part of the century, going into politics was part of family tradition. Balfour was the nephew of the Marquess of Salisbury, four times Prime Minister. Winston Churchill was the grandson of a duke and the son of Lord Randolph Churchill, who served for a short time as Chancellor of the Exchequer. After service in the army, Churchill entered Parliament in 1900, where he remained, although with several gaps, until 1964. Eden served with distinction in the First World War before entering Parliament in his mid-twenties. Like Alec Douglas-Home he came from a landed background. Harold Macmillan's ancestors were less illustrious; his grandfather was a Scottish crofter. However, Macmillan's father was a viscount and money derived from the family publishing firm meant that he was educated at Eton and Oxford before entering Parliament.

Inter-war Conservative Prime Ministers were of a different social background. Bonar Law ran a family iron business in Glasgow before entering Parliament at the comparatively late age of forty-two. Stanley Baldwin, also an iron-master, was in his early forties when he became an MP. Neville

Chamberlain was a rarity in British politics, a Prime Minister who had been prominent in local government. He was the son of Joseph Chamberlain, leader of the Liberal Unionists and a Cabinet minister in both Liberal and Conservative governments. Neville followed his father as Lord Mayor of Birmingham and worked in the family business before entering the Commons at the advanced age of forty-nine.

Since the war the social changes associated with the expansion of state education have shaped the careers of a generation of politicians. University education has provided a springboard for many politicians. Both Edward Heath and Margaret Thatcher came from comparatively humble backgrounds but were educated at Oxford. Their political interests were shaped by that experience. Heath was active in the Conservative Association and after war service he worked at Conservative Central Office before entering Parliament in 1950. Mrs Thatcher (then Margaret Roberts) was President of the Oxford University Conservative Association in 1946–47. After graduation she became an industrial chemist and then a barrister before she married and had twins. She entered Parliament in 1959, representing Finchley for thirty-three years. John Major enjoyed none of the advantages of his predecessors. He left school at sixteen after his father's business failed, and after a spell of unemployment he entered banking. A period as a councillor in the London borough of Lambeth was the prelude to a parliamentary career, when he became MP for Huntingdon in 1979.

The next step is getting into Parliament. In earlier days the family name or position as a significant local employer helped in being chosen as a candidate. Balfour was a Cecil and found little difficulty in being adopted for a borough dominated by his family, while Baldwin succeeded his father as MP for Bewdley. Churchill, as the younger son of a younger son, had to rely more on his own vivid journalistic accounts of his army exploits in order to secure the nomination in Oldham in 1900. He represented in all five constituencies in his long career, moving from the Conservative Party to the Liberals and back again. Bonar Law and Chamberlain both represented seats in the cities in which the family businesses were large employers.

More recently such advantages have been less useful. The process of selecting parliamentary candidates is both uncertain and even haphazard. Local selection committees, especially in the Conservative Party, have considerable autonomy and tend to look for evidence of previous success in a career or in business as the main criterion of selection. The days when Conservative Central Office (or even the Labour Party headquarters) could pressurise a constituency party to adopt a favoured candidate seem to have gone, although the National Executive Committee of the Labour Party has power to override local choice. Luck, persistence and local support are among the factors which bring success. Before 1939 most Tory MPs entered Parliament at the first attempt, but since the war it has become customary to expect candidates to prove themselves by fighting hopeless seats. Mrs Thatcher unsuccessfully stood for Dartford, then a

Labour stronghold, in 1950 and 1951. Marriage and twins followed, but she was soon on the hunt for a constituency. After having been rejected by some of the safest Tory seats, generally on the grounds of sex, she sought the nomination for Finchley in 1958. By now an experienced seeker after seats, she beat three more traditional Conservative candidates, public school ex-officers, to gain the nomination for a safe seat which re-elected her with large majorities until her retirement in 1992. John Major fought two hopeless contests before being selected for one of the safest Tory constituencies in the country. Tony Blair was the hapless Labour candidate in a by-election in a safe Tory seat in 1982.

The next stage in reaching the top of the 'greasy pole' is gaining ministerial office. To become leader it is not just necessary to be an MP; it is also vital to be a member of the Cabinet or Shadow Cabinet. Virtually every Prime Minister this century had extensive experience of government before becoming leader. Most Prime Ministers have progressed from junior ministerial posts into the Cabinet and thence to the top. Occupation of one of the three great offices of state (the Foreign Office, the Treasury and the Home Office) is a common feature of a career leading to No.10. Seven Foreign Secretaries have reached the post of Prime Minister; Balfour became Foreign Secretary after he ceased to be Premier and Alec Douglas-Home held the post both before and after. Nine Chancellors of the Exchequer went on to become Premier. Only three Home Secretaries reached the top. Callaghan held all three offices prior to succeeding Wilson in 1976; this remains a record. Edward Heath and John Major share a rare distinction: they are the only whips to have reached No. 10 this century.

In the twentieth century there have been some exceptions to the pattern. Bonar Law had resigned as Tory leader in March 1921 because of ill-health. As a backbencher he took part in the Carlton Club revolt against the Lloyd George coalition and his successor as party leader, Austen Chamberlain, and was re-elected Conservative leader before becoming Prime Minister. MacDonald had never served as a minister before forming his first government, and Blair also never held office. Lloyd George was not leader of his party when he became Prime Minister in December 1916. Churchill did not become leader of the Conservative Party until five months after he became Prime Minister.

Prime Ministers vary greatly in terms of the age at which they have entered the Commons, the Cabinet and then No.10, as shown in Table 3.2.

The importance of luck and timing can be illustrated in a number of cases. It is vital to be in the right place at the right time. Perhaps no one illustrates the importance of timing in politics more clearly than John Major. It was also true of Prime Ministers such as Attlee. He managed to hold on to his seat in 1931, when most leading Labour figures were swept away. He then became deputy leader of the tiny handful of Labour MPs who survived. This put him in a good position to succeed George Lansbury after the 1935 election, even though a number of former stars had returned to the Commons. He remained leader for twenty years, the longest period in office of any party leader this century.

However, it is also true that the ability to seize the opportunity is at least as

Table 3.2 *Prime Ministers: Salisbury to Blair*

	Age on entering Commons	*Age on entering Cabinet*	*Age on entering No. 10*	*Age at end of Premiership*
Salisbury	23	36	55	72
Balfour	26	38	54	57
Campbell-Bannerman	32	50	69	72
Asquith	34	40	56	64
Lloyd George	27	42	53	59
Bonar Law	42	57	64	65
Baldwin	41	54	56	70
MacDonald	40	58	58	69
Chamberlain	49	54	68	71
Churchill	26	34	66	81
Attlee	39	57	62	68
Eden	26	38	58	60
Macmillan	28	51	63	69
Douglas-Home	28	52	60	61
Wilson	29	31	48	60
Heath	34	43	54	58
Callaghan	33	52	64	67
Thatcher	34	45	54	65
Major	36	44	47	54
Blair	30	44	44	

important as luck. Mrs Thatcher look advantage of the reluctance of Heath's lieutenants to run against him in 1975 and so was able to capitalise on the widespread desire for change among Tory MPs. Macmillan was ideally placed to succeed Eden following his resignation in the aftermath of the Suez affair; his ambiguous stance over the invasion of Egypt convinced right-wingers that he had favoured intervention, while left-wingers thought he had opposed the action.

It is difficult to predict who will reach the top, especially when the previous leader has been forced out. Only when the Prime Minister steps down more or less voluntarily does the obvious heir-apparent take over. Churchill, despite reservations about Eden's suitability, had little option but to 'recommend' him to the Queen, especially as the outgoing Prime Minister was determined to prevent Butler becoming Prime Minister. Wilson timed his retirement to give Callaghan the best chance of gaining the support of the majority of the Parliamentary Labour Party. However, when there is a fierce contest the winner is often not the person initially favoured by the public in opinion polls. In October 1963 Lord Home was the least favoured of the eight candidates in a

Gallup poll. Macmillan's eventual support plus tactical errors made by the other contenders swung it for the Foreign Secretary, 'everybody's second choice'. In 1965 Maudling was ahead of Heath in the opinion polls but failed to win over enough Tory MPs to ensure election. Just before the first ballot in November 1990 opinion polls showed that Major was fifth out of six possible successors to Thatcher. Thus Major beat those who had initially been much more favoured.

The possession of the 'right' temperament is vital. Though no guarantee of success, its absence is virtually a guarantee of failure. Temperament is not easy to define. 'Courage, tenacity, determination, firm nerves, and clarity of mind are some of the qualities. So, too, are a certain toughness of the skin and a certain insensitivity, or at least a lack of great sensitivity. Nor should a Prime Minister be worried too much by scruples and doubts. And if tact and the power to manage men are there too, so much the better.'[4]

Chance plays an important part. Death or fatal illness allowed Asquith to replace Campbell-Bannerman, Baldwin to take over from Bonar Law, and Wilson to follow Gaitskell as leader of the Labour Party. The death of the highly regarded Oliver Stanley in 1950 opened the way for Butler and Macmillan to contend for the leadership when the time came. Tony Blair, who joins MacDonald in being without previous ministerial experience, owes his election as Prime Minister to the death of John Smith in 1994.

To a marked degree, waiting for the succession as heir apparent seems to lead to failure in office. Balfour, Chamberlain and Eden were in this category. On the other hand, Prime Ministers who triumph after a bitter battle often remain in office for a long time; this was true of Baldwin, Macmillan, Wilson and Thatcher. However, there are exceptions to these general rules. Asquith succeeded the dying Campbell-Bannerman to general acclaim and lasted eight years.

In any Cabinet there is likely to be a number of past, future or possible contenders for the leadership. Fashions change rapidly. During Mrs Thatcher's long period in office commentators picked on a series of 'successors'. Reputations rise and fall rapidly in politics and how ministers stand at the time of the contest is vital. Denis Healey had a well-publicised row with a group of left-wing Labour MPs just before Wilson stepped down; this probably destroyed whatever chance he had had of becoming Prime Minister and allowed Jim Callaghan, who had avoided alienating any section of the party, to take over.

An important factor is the strength of opposition to the other candidates. Macmillan's desire to prevent Butler succeeding him was a significant factor in the eventual choice of Home. In 1990 Margaret Thatcher's passionate resolve to stop Heseltine led her to phone Tory MPs to rally support for Major. Determination to succeed, the 'killer instinct', is also a factor. A lack of single-minded ruthlessness helps account for the failure of Austen Chamberlain, Lord Halifax and, perhaps above all, Rab Butler to reach the highest office.

Internal party machinery
Success in a general election is only part of the story. The choice of Prime Minister is also related to the internal machinery of the party in question.

The Conservative Party Conservative MPs do not hesitate to remove leaders who prove to be an electoral liability or who in some way offend major sections of the party. Of the twelve leaders since 1902, six have been removed by pressure from within (Balfour 1911, Austen Chamberlain 1922, Neville Chamberlain 1940, Douglas-Home 1965, Heath 1975, Thatcher 1990). Two resigned on the grounds of ill-health, but were under considerable pressure to go (Eden 1957, Macmillan 1963). Bonar Law resigned because of ill-health in 1923, Baldwin retired of his own volition in 1937. Even Churchill was subject to discreet pressure prior to his resignation in 1955. The immediate resignation of John Major following his party's shattering defeat in the 1997 general election was a continuation of Conservative tradition.

Since 1965 the leader has been elected by Conservative MPs. Before that there was no clear procedure. When the party was in opposition the former Prime Minister would be regarded as leader; when no one filled this role, it was customary to elect separate leaders in the Commons and the Lords. In these circumstances, it was not always clear who the leader was.

When the party was in government a new leader (and therefore Prime Minister) would be chosen *either* by the outgoing leader nominating his or her successor, as when Churchill chose Eden in 1955, *or* by a complex series of consultations between leading Tories who were not themselves candidates, with the monarch's private secretary acting as go-between. The aim was to allow the monarch to 'choose' someone who would be able to unite the party and thus form a stable government. It was said that the leader thus 'emerged'.

In general the procedure worked smoothly and new leaders were generally able to assert their authority and to form a government without great difficulty. The 'choice' by George V of Baldwin in 1922 and by Elizabeth II of Macmillan in 1957 were in this category. However, the choice of Home in 1963 divided the party and seemed to involve the Queen in its internal affairs. This had a number of consequences. There were criticisms that the process had been managed by a 'magic circle' who stood in the way of democratic practices in the party. The bad publicity resulted in important changes in the selection procedures in 1965, when the party adopted a process of election by Conservative MPs, a procedure modified on several subsequent occasions. There was provision for annual election at the request of only two MPs. To be elected on the first ballot a candidate had to receive an overall majority of those *qualified to vote*, a figure which had to be 15 per cent more than that received by the runner-up. If this was not achieved, a second ballot had to be held for which new candidates could be nominated (and first-round ones could withdraw). Only an overall majority was required. If this was still not achieved, a third ballot was held, restricted to the three leading candidates on the second ballot, with voters indicating first and second preferences. The third candidate was eliminated and his or her vote re-distributed according to second preferences. The winner was then presented to a party meeting of Conservative MPs, peers, candidates and members of the National Union Executive Committee. Elections took place at the beginning of each parliamentary session, if the incumbent was challenged.

In practice, however, the process has been less complex. In 1965, although Heath failed to win a clear majority his opponents withdrew, so there was no second ballot. In 1975 Thatcher won an overall majority in the second round after Heath withdrew. In 1989 she won easily at the first stage, even though around sixty Tory MPs failed to support her. In 1990 she failed by four votes to beat Heseltine on the first ballot. Following her withdrawal, Major was elected on the second ballot. Although he failed by just two votes to gain an overall majority, Heseltine and Hurd withdrew in the interests of party unity.

Almost immediately after the fall of Mrs Thatcher, the 1922 Committee began a review of the procedure. Under the new procedure, should the leadership become vacant (as when Major resigned and stood for re-election in June 1995), an election should be held as soon as possible. Otherwise an election will be held within twenty-eight days of the start of each new session of Parliament (except when there is a new Parliament, when the election will take place not earlier than three months nor later than six months from the start of that Parliament) *provided that* the Chairman of the 1922 Committee receives a written request from not less than 10 per cent of Conservative MPs. The names of the signatories will not be disclosed, although the names of the proposer and seconder of each candidate will continue to be made public.

Throughout the process voting is secret. The rules for the first ballot remained unchanged. To win outright, a candidate needs *both* an overall majority of those entitled to vote *and* 15 per cent more votes than his or her nearest rival. This enables the successful candidate to demonstrate the support of a convincing majority of parliamentary colleagues. There were substantial changes to the rules for the second and subsequent ballots. The rule requiring only an overall majority of those entitled to vote for victory on the second ballot remained. However, if no candidate receives an overall majority, there is now a formal procedure allowing any candidate to withdraw his or her name. The two remaining candidates with the largest number of votes go through to a third ballot, with the candidate receiving a majority of votes winning, thus eliminating the transferable vote formerly used at this stage. Should this ballot result in a tie (and unless the two candidates can resolve the matter between themselves, presumably in 'smoke-filled rooms') a fourth ballot will be held. Formal adoption as leader then follows.

The Labour Party Until the constitutional changes of the early 1980s, the leader was elected solely by Labour MPs, the last being Michael Foot in 1980.

Although both leader and deputy could be challenged annually when in opposition, the rules did not allow a challenge when in government. Thus Labour's four Prime Ministers were all elected by their fellow-Labour MPs. However, this is no longer the position, and Labour Premiers will now reach the leadership of the party by a very different route.

In 1981 a new method was adopted, something widely seen as marking the dominance of the left. The monopoly of the PLP was broken and an electoral college was established for the election of the leader and deputy leader which extended the franchise to the mass party. At the special conference in early 1981 it was decided that 40 per cent of the votes should go to the affiliated unions, 30 per cent to the constituency parties and 30 per cent to Labour MPs. As under the old system, a successful candidate would need a majority of votes on the first ballot. If this was not achieved the bottom candidate was eliminated and his or her second preferences redistributed. Candidates had to be Labour MPs and to be supported by 5 per cent of the parliamentary party.

The new procedure was first used at the 1981 conference when Tony Benn challenged Denis Healey for the deputy leadership. Benn almost won, polling 49.6 per cent to Healey's 50.4 per cent on the second ballot. However, from then on the influence of the left waned, and when Foot resigned following Labour's humiliation in 1983, Neil Kinnock won the leadership with 71.3 per cent of the vote while Hattersley won the deputy's post with 67.3 per cent.

Opinion in the party again changed as it came increasingly to believe this cumbersome and lengthy process was itself in need of fundamental change; a leadership challenge meant not a swift overthrow of an unpopular leader but a prolonged struggle, in which the Tories would get six months' free publicity at Labour's expense. The present system differs according to whether or not Labour is in government. When there is a vacancy (such as that following John Smith's death in May 1994) contestants need the backing of 121/2 per cent of the PLP. However, when an incumbent faces a challenge there is a complex prodedure. In opposition a challenger requires support from 20 per cent of the PLP. The electoral college system comes into use at the next annual conference. If no candidate receives 50 per cent of the vote a second ballot is held in which the second preference votes of the bottom candidate are redistributed. When there is a vacancy for leader or deputy leader (as in 1992 and 1994) the NEC can shorten the length of the contest and the electoral college meets in a special conference. For a contest to take place while Labour is in government, challengers require 20 per cent backing from the PLP. The next annual conference must approve the contest by a two-thirds majority and the electoral college system is used at a special conference. This is coming under increasing criticism and pressures for fundamental changes, which may involve leaving the decision to MPs, although Labour's method, which gives a vote to over 4 million party

Table 3.3 *Losing office*

Defeat in a general election	*Resignation/retirement during a Parliament*
Attlee 1951	Churchill 1955
Home 1964	Eden 1957
Wilson 1970	Macmillan 1963
Heath Feb. 1974	Wilson 1976
Callaghan 1979	Thatcher 1990
Major 1997	

members, allows the party to point a contrast with the elitism of the Conservative Party.

Losing office: how Prime Ministers fall from power

Since 1945 Prime Ministers have lost office in one of three ways:

1 Defeat in a general election.
2 Retirement from a mixture of choice, ill-health and party pressure.
3 Loss of support from the parliamentary party.

Only five Premiers this century have retired 'voluntarily', largely on the grounds of health and age. These were Salisbury, MacDonald, Baldwin, Churchill and Wilson. Four went because of terminal illness or ill-health: Campbell-Bannerman, Bonar Law, Eden and Macmillan. Attlee, Home, Heath, Callaghan and Major went because their party lost power in a general election and Balfour resigned just ahead of certain defeat. Asquith, Lloyd George, Neville Chamberlain and Thatcher were all removed following internal party revolts. The tendency is for the incumbent Prime Minister to lose his or her touch, as in the case of Asquith and Thatcher.

The precise cause of the end of the Prime Minister's term of office is often the culmination of a loss of confidence by the electorate or by the party in the Premier and/or the government. Governments differ in the conditions in which they operate; some have been dominated by events largely outside their control, such as the oil crisis which overwhelmed the administrations led by Heath, Wilson and Callaghan. Sometimes the crisis is sudden and the end of the Prime Minister unexpected, as in the case of Eden. Sometimes it comes as the result of an accumulation of problems and grievances, as it did with the downfall of Mrs Thatcher.

The loss of power, the feeling of not being a national figure whose doings dominate the headlines, deprivation of the trappings of office such as the right to live in Downing Street and Chequers, are all traumas faced by former Prime Ministers, especially those who have been in one way or another forced out of office.

Characteristics of post-1945 Prime Ministers

There are some common factors in the appointment of Prime Ministers:

1 They are bound to be a member of the House of Commons.
2 They are likely to have been a Member of Parliament for some time.
3 They are likely to have been a leading figure in the party prior to appointment.
4 They are likely to have had considerable ministerial experience, with appointment as Prime Minister coming as the culminating point in a series of promotions. Alternatively, they are likely to have served as Leader of the Opposition.
5 To some extent, most Prime Ministers owe their position to their predecessor who first appointed them to the Cabinet or Shadow Cabinet.

British Prime Ministers largely learn how to do the job by doing it or by having worked under other Prime Ministers and thus having learned from their experience. Service in the House of Commons means that, at the very least, they will have observed their predecessors at the dispatch box. Up to 1997, all post-war Premiers had served in Cabinets under other Prime Ministers. Whether consciously or unconsciously all will have absorbed much from their predecessors.

Both parties look for a number of characteristics when choosing a new leader, including the ability to rally, inspire and unite the party faithful, to provide a clear sense of direction, to attract the broadest possible electoral support, and (increasingly important) to be able to handle the media. Yet parties are also limited by the availability of candidates. The choice of Margaret Thatcher in 1975 was only in part related to the vigour with which she projected a new direction for the Conservative Party; there was no credible alternative once the decision had been made to topple Heath. Had senior figures such as William Whitelaw entered the first ballot it is at least possible that she would not have been elected. Similarly, a party may decide to skip a generation in the search for a new leader, as when Neil Kinnock was elected to succeed Michael Foot in 1983. If a party has been out of power long enough it may be forced to choose someone without experience. When Tony Blair was elected leader of the Labour Party in 1994 no one with Cabinet experience was available.

When the governing party needs to choose a new leader it may be tempted to select a candidate who can unite the party rather than one who will inspire but possibly divide. Labour's choice of Callaghan in 1976 is a case in point. Widely known as 'Sunny Jim' or 'Uncle Jim', he had built his career largely on seeking to unite the Labour Party. He avoided the factional fights which had divided Labour under Wilson and was well placed to project himself as a reconciler, in contrast with men such as Foot and Healey. Similarly in 1990 Major and his backers skilfully projected him as the person who could bind up the wounds the Conservative Party had inflicted upon itself in the last period of Mrs Thatcher's

Table 3.4 *Classifying Prime Ministers*

Chairperson	*Chief Executive*
consensus building	decisive leadership
reactive	pro-active
'hands-off'	interventionist
looking to survival	specific objectives
gradualist	purposive
keeping convoy together	racing ahead

leadership. The better-known candidates, Heseltine and Hurd, were unacceptable to significant sections of the parliamentary party; Major, perhaps because he was less well known, was able simultaneously to reassure the Thatcherites that he would continue the broad thrust of her policies while giving hope to the anti-Thatcherites that there would be a significant shift in priorities.

In opposition the party will have different criteria for selection. It may be that the preferred candidate will be the one who, it is hoped, can heal the party after a period of division, as when the PLP chose Foot rather than Healey. Alternatively the party may deliberately take the risk of choosing a candidate clearly associated with one wing or the other, perhaps out of a wish to put the past firmly behind it. In 1975 the Conservatives elected Mrs Thatcher *despite* her firmly stated right-wing views because of the general desire to oust the unpopular and unsuccessful Edward Heath. A willingness to take a risk may pay off; Mrs Thatcher, though lagging behind her party in 1979, did not look incredible as a Prime Minister in the way that Foot did in 1983 and as Kinnock did in the two elections Labour fought under his leadership.

A prime ministerial typology

There are various ways of classifying prime ministerial style and power. Peter Madgwick pointed out that within rough guidelines set by structure and custom and the political circumstances of the time, Prime Ministers are free to decide how to do the job. The role of national leader is only a small part of the role and 'In the day-to-day work of the Prime Minister in governing, the choice lies between the role of Chairman and Chief Executive.'[5] He analyses the two roles in terms shown in Table 3.4.

However, the two models are not mutually exclusive. Under modern conditions the chairmanship role is inappropriate, as Alec Douglas-Home discovered. Prime ministers must lead but within a collective context. The balance is hard to achieve. Wilson's Cabinet colleagues complained about a lack of leadership, an obsession with getting agreement and avoiding hard choices, especially in his second administration of 1974–76. Madgwick drew a contrast between Wilson and Thatcher. 'Wilson was concerned to conjure agreement, dominating the process, though not always choosing the policy outcome. Thatcher started with a desired policy, did not want to know about alternatives, and did not much care about agreement.'[6] This meant that Cabinet critics (after they left office) referred, often in harsh and bitter tones, to her domineering style and to an unwillingness to consult or to listen to the views of others. Her dislike of consensus and hostility to the collegiate style, which at first was a source of strength as she claimed to be the 'only man in the Cabinet', came over time to grate with many of her colleagues and (even worse from the point of view of Conservative MPs) with the electors. Geoffrey Howe in his resignation speech summed up the growing mood of disenchantment.

> In my letter of resignation, which I tendered with the utmost sadness and dismay, I said: 'Cabinet government is all about trying to persuade one another from within.' That was my commitment to government by persuasion – persuading my colleagues and the nation. I have tried to do that as Foreign Secretary and since, but I realize now that the task has become futile: trying to stretch the words beyond what was credible, and trying to pretend that there was a common policy when every step forward risked being subverted by some casual comment or impulsive answer.[7]

Prime Ministers display many traits, usually to try to create an image which the media will fix on and magnify and which will strike a responsive chord with the voters. Macmillan tried to show himself as 'unflappable'; 'quiet, calm deliberation disentangles every knot' from *The Gondoliers* may have been the motto displayed in his office but the reality was very different. Like Churchill, Macmillan suffered from periods of deep depression and almost crippling self-doubt. Wilson

> wore his roots like a badge, continuing to speak in a Yorkshire accent which made some people feel, by a contorted logic, that the experience of Oxford and Whitehall *ought* to have ironed out the regional element, and the fact that it had not done so reflected a kind of phoniness. The truth was that, for all his other conceits, Wilson was the least seducable of politicians in social terms, remaining imperturbably close in his tastes and his values – as in his marriage – to the world in which he grew up.[8]

Yet even he could learn the black arts of presentation. His love of pipe-smoking came in very useful. When faced with a tricky question in a television interview he could gain valuable thinking time by repacking and relighting his pipe without appearing to dissemble or prevaricate. John Major's enthusiasm for football and cricket was obviously genuine, but was also part of the image-building which characterises modern politics. Yet no amount of presentation can disguise the underlying reality. 'The "image", no matter how contrived, has a basis in the person, and acquires a truth of its own.'[9]

Philip Norton sought to provide a framework for studying Prime Ministers. He dismissed the argument about prime ministerial versus Cabinet government as limited and overly institutional; personality, circumstances and historical

Table 3.5 *Framework of analysis*

Innovators	*Reformers*	
Churchill (wartime)	Campbell-Bannerman	
Heath	Asquith	
Thatcher	Chamberlain	
	Attlee	
Egoists	*Balancers*	
	Power-seeking	*Conscripts*
Lloyd-George ?	Salisbury	Bonar Law
MacDonald ?	Balfour ?	Douglas-Home
Eden	Baldwin	
Wilson	Churchill (peacetime)	
	Macmillan	
	Callaghan	
	[Major]	
	[Blair?]	

perspective are also significant and must be taken into account. Prime Ministers have power; but that is no guarantee that they will be able to *use* their power. Several variables determine the extent to which Prime Ministers use their power.

The first is *purpose.* This refers to the purpose of being in office and takes into account the differing reasons why a few individuals seek and achieve the highest office. Some have specific political or personal goals, while others seem simply to enjoy being Prime Minister. Mrs Thatcher's aims, though of a monumental nature, were clear and constantly articulated; they were to produce a revolution (or perhaps counter-revolution) in British attitudes and assumptions. In the view of many critics, Wilson's main aim seemed to be to get to the top of the 'greasy pole' and stay there, at least until he had had enough. His colleagues complained of a lack of leadership. Some reach No. 10 almost by accident, perhaps as a compromise choice; Alec Douglas-Home is an example of this category.

In terms of purpose, Norton draws up a typology of Prime Ministers, based on a four-fold classification (see Table 3.5):

1 *Innovators* seek power to achieve goals and are prepared to drag their party behind them if necessary.
2 *Reformers* seek power to achieve a particular programme, but one drawn up by the party rather than the leader.
3 *Egoists* seek power for the sake of power. They are concerned with the present rather than future goals.
4 *Balancers*, of which there are two categories:

a those who seek power to achieve balance within society and within party;
b those who have the same aim but do not seek power but have it thrust upon them. Usually they are a compromise choice for party leader.

These are not mutually exclusive categories: 'Prime Ministers cannot be rigorously "boxed" into one neat, confined category – in some cases one tendency may be preponderant, in others there may be a mixture.'[10] Also, Prime Ministers display different tendencies at different stages of their career and over different issues. In Norton's typology, Churchill was an innovator in wartime and a balancer in peacetime. However, the typology does identify preponderant tendencies.

Norton's article was written before John Major took over in 1990, but it can be suggested that he should be placed in the power-seeking balancer category. He was not an innovator; he did not have an agenda of his own which he wished to see brought to fruition almost at any cost. Nor was he a reformer. Most commentators have interpreted the Major government as 'Thatcherism with a human face'. By temperament he clearly was not an egoist, nor was he a compromise choice as Conservative Party leader. He appeared to be a power-seeking balancer, struggling to keep the party as united as possible and to stay in office as long as possible.

The second variable Norton identifies is *skill.* Purpose gives some idea of the 'why' of prime ministerial power, but does not indicate how or why Prime Ministers can achieve success. A variety of skills are required to determine outcomes. Broadly, there are two levels of skill.

There are *general* skills, such as looking the part, appearing to be prime ministerial. Mrs Thatcher increasingly appeared almost regal, certainly presidential, as her confidence grew. Prime Ministers have to have a feel for the office and to know how and when to use the skills they have. From 1964 to 1966 Wilson displayed the full range of prime ministerial skills but in his final period from 1974 to 1976 confessed that he had lost the taste for government. He had seen it all before; the same problems kept coming round and he was bored.

The second level consists of those *specific* skills which a Prime Minister needs in order to achieve what he or she wants. These include being able to select, to lead, to anticipate, to react. Prime Ministers vary considerably in the possession of these skills. Some lead by creating a united team who agree on the basic goals. Attlee did it by a combination of integrity, efficiency and determination. Heath led a united Cabinet, although he inspired little personal affection and was, according to some commentators, feared by many of his colleagues. His increasing remoteness from party was a factor in his fall from power. Thatcher sought, ultimately unsuccessfully, to create a 'one of us' Cabinet. Others have been indecisive and divisive; Eden is the most notable post-war example of this tendency. Prime Ministers must be able to persuade, to use a variety of methods to get their own way. These range from intellectual argument to appeals to personal friendship or party loyalty. The ability to listen is an essential tool; the

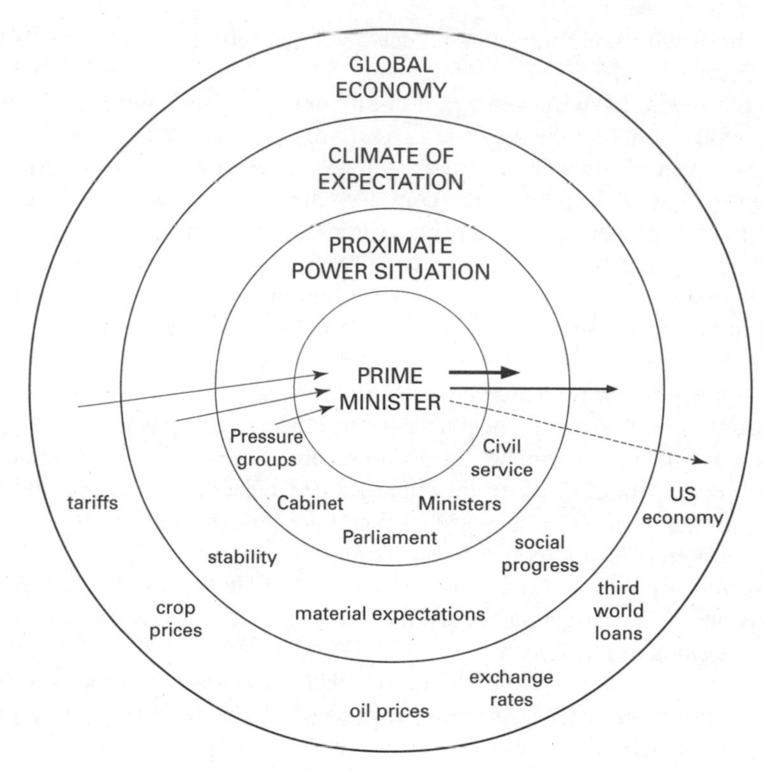

Figure 3.1 The Prime Minister's global environment (from Philip Norton, 'Prime Ministerial Power', *Social Studies Review*. Vol. 3, No. 3, January 1988, p. 113)

downfall of both Heath and Thatcher was attributed in part to their inability or refusal to listen to criticism even from friends. Persuasion may degenerate into manipulation; Wilson lost credibility by the increasingly blatant way he used people in order to get his way. Other desirable skills include the ability to decide when to leave ministers and others to get on with the job, and sensitive political antennae, the ability to judge a situation accurately.

However, whatever the purposes and skills of Prime Ministers might be, they also need favourable *circumstances* and more than a modicum of luck. Norton groups circumstances under three headings, three concentric circles around the Premier. These are shown in Figure 3.1

The outer circle is the global economy and is the variable likely to be least affected by what the Prime Minister does. The 1950s was a time of a tremendous growth in the world economy and the Conservatives reaped the domestic benefits, winning three successive general elections. Wilson, Heath and Callaghan faced the consequences of the oil price rise following the Yom Kippur War and faced electoral problems as a consequence. Part at least of the explanation for Mrs Thatcher's long spell in office is the 'cushion' provided by the abundant revenues from North Sea oil. Major tried to explain his problems by reference to the world recession of the early 1990s, although critics point instead to the consequences of the 'stop–go' policies of Nigel Lawson around the time of the 1987 election.

The middle circle is what Norton calls the climate of expectations, what the public expect of the government and what they are prepared to allow it to achieve its goals. The policy aims of the post-war Labour government and a sea-change in public expectations of government helped to lay the foundations of the Butskellite consensus that dominated British politics for a generation after 1945. Mrs Thatcher clearly changed the climate about the role of government in the management of the economy and other aspects of the post-war settlement, forcing Labour into a far-reaching and painful policy re-evaluation. However, she failed to erode public support for the welfare state, however hard she and her supporters tried.

The inner circle, the one which has the most impact on prime ministerial power and the one on which he or she has the most leverage, is the immediate political environment surrounding the Premier. It consists of a complex and shifting web of bodies, relationships and attitudes. It provides the greatest opportunities for the Prime Minister to use his or her skills of persuasion, leadership and (at times) inspiration. Alec Douglas-Home did not have the time or the opportunities to overcome the disadvantages of his elevation by the 'magic circle'. For most of her time as Prime Minister Mrs Thatcher dominated the political scene, displaying virtually every skill discussed by Norton. Sometimes luck runs out as it did for Eden in 1956 and Heath in 1973. But on occasions, hubris, the sin of pride, intervenes, as happened to Mrs Thatcher in 1990.

Norton concluded:

> Prime ministers come and go. Some stay in office longer than others. Purpose and skill may differ not only from one premier to another but during the incumbency of a particular premier. The political evironment can and does change dramatically. The individual in the office interacts with that environment. Prime ministerial power, then, has to be seen within the context of a dynamic political framework. Falling back on broad generalisations about powers is no explanation of power.[11]

Notes

1 Peter Riddell, *Honest Opportunism. The Rise of the Career Politician*, Hamish Hamilton, 1993, p. 7.
2 Harold Wilson, *Memoirs*, 1986, quoted in ibid., p. 29.
3 Nesta Wyn Ellis, *John Major: A Personal Biography*, 1991, quoted in ibid.
4 Lord Blake, *The Office of Prime Minister*, Oxford University Press, 1975, p. 19.
5 Peter Madgwick, *British Government: The Central Executive Territory*, Philip Allan, 1991, p. 119.
6 Ibid., p. 141.

7 Geoffrey Howe, *Conflict of Loyalty*, Macmillan, 1994, p. 702.
8 Ben Pimlott, *Harold Wilson*, Harper Collins, 1992, p. 33.
9 Madgwick, *British Government*, p. 145.
10 Philip Norton, 'Prime Ministerial Power', *Social Studies Review*, Vol. 3, No. 3, January 1988, p. 110.
11 Ibid., p. 115.

4

The power of the Prime Minister

This chapter examines the controversy about prime ministerial versus Cabinet government and concludes that both perspectives are defective and do not account for the complexity of what has been called 'The Central Executive Territory'. It analyses the view that the precise relationship depends on a variety of factors, such as personality and circumstances. The premiership of Margaret Thatcher is analysed in order to throw light on the question.

Prime ministerial power: the debate

There is general agreement that the Prime Minister is the key figure in the British political system, possessing a formidable range of powers and to a large extent determining the policy of the government. Yet there is no consensus on the precise nature of the Prime Minister's powers. Some have suggested, especially in the light of Mrs Thatcher's tenure of office, that Britain has *prime ministerial government*, that he or she totally dominates British government and Parliament alike. Whatever checks there are come from outside forces, such as pressure groups and international events. According to some proponents, Britain has developed a virtually presidential style of government, supposedly akin to that of the United States. Others argue that there are effective constraints on the Premier's power and that *Cabinet government*, the essence of which is collective decision-making, survives.

However, it will be argued that both theories are deficient. Both tend to portray the relationship as a 'zero-sum' one; if the Prime Minister gains power the Cabinet loses, and vice versa. In reality, the Prime Minister leads a team but is reliant on them for support. The premiership is a highly dynamic office; time and circumstances will alter the extent to which the incumbent can and will use his or her powers. As Asquith stated, 'The office of Prime Minister is what the holder chooses and is able to make of it'.[1]

The debate about the nature of prime ministerial power which concerned political scientists and politicians in the 1960s has been revived by the Thatcher phenomenon. There is general agreement about the development of British politics in the twentieth century. The functions of the government have grown dramatically; the Prime Minister, as head of the executive, has shared in this increase in power. However, the controversy is about the internal distribution of power within the executive. Some commentators, pointing to the formidable array of powers possessed by the Premier, feel that the balance has swung decisively away from the Cabinet to a more personal style of government. Others feel that this tendency has been over-stated and that significant restraints on the power of the Prime Minister continue to exist.

In the 1960s the dispute was between the prime ministerial and Cabinet models. However, the debate is sterile as it discusses the Prime Minister and Cabinet as institutions, ignoring factors such as the personality of each Prime Minister (and of their Cabinet colleagues) and the political and historical circumstances in which they work. Thus, no single approach will suffice, and there are three broad positions in the debate:

1 The prime ministerial or presidential model.
2 The 'chairmanship' model.
3 The personality/circumstances view.

The prime ministerial or presidential model

Prime ministerial government means that he or she is predominant in decision-making. The test is the extent to which the Prime Minister dominates the everyday running of the government as well as the major issues which preoccupy it. Thus the Prime Minister may possess a general power to decide policy in those areas in which he or she takes an interest. In this context, Mrs Thatcher's policy agenda was unusually wide, encompassing virtually every area of government action. Alternatively, he or she may concentrate only on key issues which then set the tone for other areas of government policy. The Prime Minister will seek to determine what are the 'key' issues, although a host of pressures will help to determine this crucial point. The Prime Minister may seek to define the ideology of his or her government; the other ministers may simply be agents of the Premier's will.

This model was most clearly expressed by Richard Crossman, a senior figure in the Wilson government from 1964 to 1970. In his 1963 Introduction to Walter Bagehot's *The English Constitution*, first published in 1867, he wrote that the powers of the Prime Minister have steadily increased and that 'The post-war epoch has seen the final transformation of Cabinet Government into Prime Ministerial Government'.[2] Crossman's view was that even in Bagehot's time it was probably misleading to describe the Prime Minister as *primus inter pares* (first among equals) or chairman of the Cabinet. The right to select the Cabinet and to dismiss members at will, to decide the agenda, to announce decisions without taking a vote and the control of patronage had already before 1867 given the Prime Ministers virtually presidential powers. Since then a number of factors have added to prime ministerial dominance: the power to select, shuffle and dismiss ministers, to control the business of the Cabinet, to appoint key civil servants and to control the machinery of the ruling party. The vast increase in the work of government and the centralisation at the top, means that the Cabinet no longer acts and takes decisions as a body. Instead, decisions are taken by departmental ministers and by Cabinet committees with the Prime Minister exercising a dominant role in all major areas of policy: 'the Cabinet becomes the place where busy executives seek formal sanction for their action from colleagues usually too busy – even if they do disagree – to do more than protest'.[3] In Crossman's view, this development had so far advanced as to make the British Cabinet resemble the American Cabinet, where collective responsibility does not exist: each Cabinet member is solely and directly responsible to the President.

Thus collective responsibility, which in Bagehot's day meant that members of the Cabinet were equally responsible for decisions taken collectively, has become 'collective obedience by the whole administration . . . to the will of the man at the apex of power'.[4] The Cabinet, in Crossman's view, has joined the other 'dignified' parts of the constitution such as the monarchy and the House of Lords, although it retains reserve powers which can sometimes be used to dramatic effect. Allied to the declining power of Parliament to check the executive, a consequence of the rise of disciplined parties, the power of the Prime Minister is awesome in the extreme. Crossman did say, however, that 'the use made of the Cabinet depends on the ideas of the premier, and the personnel and situation with which he has to deal'.[5] This casual comment rather undermines the strength of his general argument.

Crossman reasserted his thesis about prime ministerial government in *Inside View*, published after he left office in 1970. He accepted that any Prime Minister could by mismanagement undermine his or her own position and that the Cabinet had a reserve power which could reduce the Premier to *primus inter pares*. However, this power is rarely used, and a Prime Minister who chooses a chairmanship role consciously refrains from making use of the powers which constitutionally belong to the office.

The Prime Minister has a unique role in integrating the whole government and controls the three areas of central authority: the Cabinet with its base in Parliament, the Civil Service and the party machine. Crossman believed that it is because only the Prime Minister can exert central authority in *all* these fields that the system can be correctly described as prime ministerial.

Support from the thesis came from both sides of politics. Lord Hailsham called the British system of government 'an elective dictatorship'. He argued that 'the sovereignty of Parliament has increasingly become, in practice, the sovereignty of the Commons, and the sovereignty of the Commons has increasingly become the sovereignty of the government, which, in addition to its influence in Parliament, controls the party whips, the party machine, and the civil service'.[6] Within the government power has become more concentrated in the hands of the Prime Minister, who sits at the centre of the web. This is based on the power of dissolution, which can be used to the maximum advantage of the Prime Minister, who is able to manage the economy and thus to manipulate public opinion. Hailsham's remedies, a written constitution and a bill of rights, were designed to limit the power of government generally, not specifically that of the Premier.

A more thorough-going analysis was offered by Tony Benn in a chapter entitled 'The Case for a Constitutional Premiership'. In the case of Labour Prime Ministers, Benn's view was that the powers exercised within the government and the party

> are now so great as to encroach upon the legitimate right of the electorate, undermine the essential role of parliament, usurp some of the functions of collective cabinet decision making and neutralise much of the influence deriving from the internal democracy of the Labour party. In short, the present centralisation of power in the hands of one person has gone too far and amounts to a system of personal rule in the very heart of our parliamentary democracy.[7]

Benn drew up a list of the powers of the Prime Minister.

1. Most significant is the power to appoint and dismiss ministers without parliamentary or party approval, because it allows all other powers to fall into the Prime Minister's hands.
2. The Prime Minister has patronage powers. Beside the right to create peers, the Premier is involved in numerous other honours, decoration and appointments to a wide variety of posts in the public services. Its extent is breathtaking and far exceeds, both in numbers and importance, the patronage available even to medieval monarchs.
3. The Prime Minister has complete personal control of the work of ministers and of civil servants. This has several aspects, including:
   a. which items of business will be discussed by Cabinet and which will be excluded;
   b. setting up Cabinet committees: the Premier can appoint their members and keep their existence secret, even from other members of the Cabinet;
   c. wide powers over the operations of the Civil Service;
   d. control of the flow of government information: the Premier can directly communicate with Parliament and the public or can use the 'lobby' system to get his or her views across, a power used to the utmost by Mrs Thatcher;
   e. personal responsibility for the security services, a power which entitles the Premier to have any person put under surveillance.
4. The Prime Minister can use prerogative powers to ensure the ratification of treaties without the need for parliamentary approval. The same applies to agreements with the European Community which have legal force in the

United Kingdom. He or she has wide powers to control the operation of the armed forces.

5 The Prime Minister can request a dissolution of Parliament from the Queen and can end the government's life by tendering his or her resignation. In Benn's view these powers are significant: a Prime Minister's power is based on the ability to threaten to resign or to dissolve Parliament if the Cabinet will not give its support.

Hailsham's theme of 'elective dictatorship' was taken up by Rodney Brazier. He pointed out that although Mrs Thatcher's 'imperious premiership' has been blamed for upsetting the balance of the British constitution, many of the undesirable features of the system pre-dated her and will continue under other Premiers. The basic reason is the willingness of the legislature to accept successive extensions of executive power: the common factor is the cowardly way in which Members of Parliament have allowed successive Prime Ministers to act as an elected dictator. In addition, the Cabinet and the governing party have abdicated their responsibilities to act as a check on the head of the government. 'Nowadays few would dispute that the powers of the Prime Minister have increased, are increasing and ought to be diminished.'[8]

Thus the 'presidential' theory has a number of basic propositions.

(1) The first is the changed nature of general elections since the Second Reform Act of 1867. The extension of the franchise, the development of mass parties and of the mass media have contributed to a gladiatorial combat between party leaders. Because most electors are not very politically conscious, the personalisation of politics is vital to electoral success. As most people vote for a party rather than for a person, individual candidates count for little. Almost all MPs are elected because of the party they stand for rather than for any personal merit they may have. This means that the Prime Minister can be sure of party backing in the Commons; electoral pressure on MPs is reinforced by the strength of party discipline and pressure from constituency organisations. Prime Ministers claim a 'mandate' to govern and to implement their policies; collective responsibility of ministers has become a demand for collective obedience of the whole parliamentary party to the leader.

(2) The Prime Minister also dominates the party outside Parliament. Members see him or her as the embodiment of the party's 'image' and as the main vehicle of electoral success. Despite the formal dissimilarities between the Labour and the Conservative parties, there is little real difference in the actual position. A Prime Minister effectively controls his or her party and not vice versa. The restraints on leaders imposed by the Labour Party constitution disappear when that person becomes Prime Minister, and the powers of Labour Premiers are identical to those of their Conservative counterparts. Backbench MPs are restrained from criticism of their leaders by the desire for office or for honours; the Prime Minister's powers of patronage are crucial in ensuring loyalty and obedience. Party policy is the *Prime Minister's* policy, rather than a collective effort in which members are involved.

Thus the sovereignty of Parliament becomes in effect the will of the Prime Minister. The Premier can be sure of party backing for legislation in the Commons, the Lords is subordinate to the Lower House and the Royal Assent a mere formality. The Cabinet is no obstacle to the Prime Minister's will.

(3) The Prime Minister is master of the Cabinet. The ability to hire and fire, to promote and demote, means that the political future of colleagues is in the Prime Minister's hands. The way to advancement is to serve loyally. Ministers are unwilling to resign, both because of the damage which would be done to their careers and because of the repercussions on party standing and cohesion. A Prime Minister can sack a large part of the Cabinet, as Macmillan did in the 'night of the long knives' episode' or as Mrs Thatcher did in successive purges, and remain strong and secure. Prime Ministers create and destroy Cabinets at will.

In addition, the Prime Minister controls the operation of the Cabinet, deciding on the agenda and preventing discussion of things he or she doesn't want discussed. The Premier can guide debate along particular lines, summarise proceedings and give an assessment of the sense of the meeting (embodied in the Cabinet Conclusion) which is taken as the decision of the Cabinet on that particular issue. Though he or she may listen to the Cabinet's advice, the last word belongs to the Premier. As formal votes are rarely taken it is hard for those opposing this position to make their voice heard and it is rare for the Prime Minister's decisions to be challenged.

The Premier's power is most clearly seen in relations with individual Cabinet members. Through informal talks with individual ministers (who would find it even harder than in the comparative solidarity of a Cabinet meeting to oppose the person to whom they owe all the good things of life) the Premier can influence and perhaps dominate what the minister has in mind. Policy will be decided before it reaches Cabinet, with Cabinet committees or other avenues being used to determine a policy. Cabinet approval thus becomes a virtual formality. Some accounts speak of an 'inner Cabinet', consisting of a clique of personal advisers who take important decisions. Churchill, in the running of the Second World War, Attlee over the A Bomb, Eden over Suez and Mrs Thatcher over a host of policy decisions are cited as examples of Premiers who have ruled in this way. The Cabinet as a whole is kept largely in ignorance of major policy decisions, and individual ministers may even find decisions being taken regarding their own departments without their knowledge. Thus collective responsibility no longer applies; ministers have a choice of either blind obedience to the Prime Minister or resignation. This also applies to individual responsibility; departmental ministers are now said to be errand boys for the head of the government.

(4) The Prime Minister's use of the royal prerogative gives an enormous range of powers, most of which are not subject to parliamentary scrutiny let alone authority.

(5) The Civil Service is the servant of the Prime Minister, who, free from

departmental responsibilities, can take an overview of the whole range of government responsibilities and can intervene when and how he or she likes. The Cabinet Office and No. 10 Downing Street act as the eyes and ears of the Premier. The power to appoint all senior civil servants means that the Premier's will prevails throughout Whitehall.

The Prime Minister thus controls his or her party, Parliament, the Cabinet and the Civil Service. To a large extent the Prime Minister chooses a successor, decides the date of a general election and has a leading role in election campaigns. The Premier is in a position of unrivalled predominance, as shown by the decision to delay the start of a new parliamentary session in 1963 so that Lord Home could renounce his peerage and enter the Commons through a by-election.

The Prime Minister as President

A variant on the prime ministerial government theme is that of Michael Foley. He believed that the traditionally collegiate British political system has changed, especially in the 1980s with 'the emergence of a peacetime prime minister whose preeminence in government was comparable only to Winston Churchill in World War Two. In her attempt to change the face of Britain, Margaret Thatcher became in effect the face of Britain.'[9] This intensely personal style of government renewed interest in the nature of individual leadership and in the relationship between personality, government and history.

Foley argued that many commentators have sought to deny the prime ministerial thesis by emphasising the distinctions between the British and American systems. They point to formal differences, such as the separation of powers in the United States, the fixed-term nature of the presidency and the fact that the President is a directly elected head of state as well as head of government. None of this is true of the British Prime Minister, who is both dependent on Parliament for survival and simultaneously is in a position to control the legislature through the operation of party discipline, a concept of much less relevance in the American context. British general elections are about electing a party to govern rather than being focused on the individuals who head those parties. The differing cultural and intellectual traditions make it difficult to compare the two systems; this was used to explicitly deny that Britain had acquired a 'presidential system' and to argue that the collegiate nature of government in Britain still existed. Especially during the Thatcher era attempts to draw comparisons were seen as politically motivated; her supporters wished to demonstrate how she towered head and shoulders above the pygmies both in the opposition parties and in her own Conservative Party, while critics sought to show how she had subverted a system and introduced a deeply unhealthy 'cult of personality' into British politics. It was so personal that Thatcher's removal would lead to the system reverting to 'normal' under *any* successor. Thus Foley believed that both supporters and opponents had misunderstood the nature of the American system.

> Contrary to the impression prevalent in this country, the American presidency, like the British premiership, is noted for the elasticity of its power, for its numerous constraints, for its dependence upon social conditions and political issues, for its transformation with different incumbents and for the contingent nature of its authority. Those seeking to use the presidency to rebut the charges of prime ministerial power, therefore, come perilously close to refuting their own arguments.[10]

Foley argued that where the presidential analogy is correctly used it can provide significant insights into the development of British government. Prime ministerial leadership has undergone profound shifts from the 1970s onwards, changes brought to the surface during Thatcher's time, but not simply a product of her style or the circumstances of the 1980s. These changes represent the emergence of a British presidency.

In order to make a valid comparison it is necessary to look behind the institutional features which are usually held to make such analysis meaningless. Deeper political developments not only throw light on the presidency, they also illuminate the direction being taken by the premiership in Britain. Some of the most significant developments include the following:

(1) The phenomenon of 'spatial leadership', in which political authority is acquired by cultivating a sense of detachment from the government of which the incumbent is the head. Successive American Presidents have asserted their determination to combat the growth of the Federal government and to stand up for the ordinary people, the 'silent majority', against the vested interests of Washington. One of the most marked features of Mrs Thatcher's premiership was the way in which she distanced herself from her own government, acting almost as Leader of the Opposition as well as Prime Minister; she often expressed anger and sometimes bewilderment that 'they' were failing to do something about it (whatever 'it' was at the particular time). This was allied to a generalised desire to get government off the back of the people, to reduce the role of the state and to allow people to 'stand on their own two feet', although critics from several political perspectives pointed to the growth in the power and size of the state during the Thatcher era.

(2) Part of this image, at the same time genuine *and* carefully cultivated, is 'the leader as outsider'. Recent Presidents – Carter, Reagan, Clinton, even Nixon – projected themselves as being not part of the Washington establishment and therefore untainted by the moral corruption of the capital. Mrs Thatcher also saw herself as the outsider, a person with little ministerial experience and a marked distaste for the 'wheeler-dealing' and compromises of the past. John Major emphasised the ordinariness of his background and his lack of a public school education.

(3) The rise of a 'designer populism', 'in which leaders encourage and engage in self-inflicted forms of populist insurgency upon the structure, behaviour and policies of their own organisations'.[11] Prime Ministers intervene in government departments in order to enhance their own position rather than to strengthen

the government as a whole; leaders such as Thatcher seemed to see no difference between the two.

(4) The increased personalisation of politics, the manner in which elections become contests between party leaders rather than parties as such. Polls indicated that in 1992 Major was significantly more popular than Kinnock and that this was a factor in the surprise win of the Conservatives. Leaders are of crucial importance in determining how people view parties and the question of leadership is itself a political issue. One of the reasons for the lack of success of Major as Prime Minister was the extent to which many commentators, especially on the Tory right, criticised his leadership qualities in comparison with those of his predecessor. The importance of leadership as a quality, almost regardless of policy content, is a factor in Tony Blair's attempt to project an image of strength and decisiveness; he has even expressed some admiration for Mrs Thatcher's abilities in this area.

(5) Leaders tend increasingly to be separated from their party organisations and traditions. Prime Ministers such as Mrs Thatcher come increasingly to believe, often when the evidence is quite to the contrary, that they have a special, unique, almost mystical link with the British people, that they are in tune with the basic aspirations of their compatriots. This can lead to a weakening of the connection with the party, an impatience when the party seems to be not a link with the people but an obstacle to that sacred communion between leader and led.

(6) Prime Ministers seek to project themselves as the embodiment of the nation and of the national interest. This is given added significance by the vastly increased media attention which is paid to politics and to political leadership. This can be seen in the manner in which Mrs Thatcher projected herself as Brittania, especially in the wake of the Falklands War, to the extent that she virtually displaced the Queen as the symbol of the nation. Membership of the European Union, international summitry and even meetings of Commonwealth heads of government provide opportunities for Prime Ministers to seek to make their mark on posterity, perhaps when domestic triumphs become less and less easy to achieve. These developments mean that British leaders now occupy a world of their own, which Foley called 'leaderland', in which the battle for power is increasingly a contest about political leadership.

Foley emphasised that although there are sufficient parallels in the development of the American presidency and the British premiership which support his argument that a British presidency has arrived (or at least is in the process of formation), the two things are not the same. There will continue to be institutional differences, such as the separation of powers, and historical and cultural dissimilarities. However, the British Prime Minister is more similar to the presidency than to the old conception of the premiership. They are less representatives of their party than embodiments of it; the party takes its character from them, rather than the other way round. Instead of Prime Ministers taking their policies from the party, the party's policies are those of the Prime Minister (or Leader of the Opposition).

Foley ended by warning that in Britain, change is slow and therefore difficult to discern and to analyse. The changes he outlined are cumulative and move the office of Prime Minister inevitably down a presidential path. Most commentators have argued that after the 'excesses' of Mrs Thatcher, her successor reverted to a more traditional form of rule. Foley argued that this view is mistaken; evolution, even political evolution, cannot go backwards. Major was forced into replacing one form of high-profile leadership with another; 'he revealed the underlying evolutionary progression of the office. He showed that behind the surface fluctuations of individual incumbents, the position of chief executive is developing in accordance with the compulsive inheritance of the past and with the present imperatives of the changing political environment.'[12]

Foley's book has come in for a number of criticisms. Vernon Bogdanor believed that Foley exaggerated his thesis. Personalised leadership is not a guarantee of political success; Major defeated the more charismatic Heseltine for the leadership of the Conservative Party. The history of British politics shows that personalised leadership divorced from a strong party base swiftly leads to political oblivion; recent examples include Enoch Powell and David Owen. 'So, although personalized leadership has undoubtedly increased in importance in recent years, political circumstances still remain at least as crucial as leadership qualities in the winning and holding of power.'[13] Andrew Adonis,[14] while seeing much merit in Foley's book, criticised the unhistorical nature of the analysis, pointing out that in their day Gladstone, Disraeli and Pitt the Younger could be set against Thatcher. The importance of the individual holder of the office has long been recognised, pre-dating Asquith's statement of the position. Other criticisms concentrate on the differences between the British and American systems and the extent to which institutions as well as individuals are significant in the political process.

Yet although Foley's book has been criticised for overstatement, it acts as a valuable corrective to the second perspective, that of Cabinet government.

The 'chairmanship' model

The most notable critic of Crossman's thesis has been George Jones of the London School of Economics. He did not seek to deny that Prime Ministers have a formidable range of powers. However, they are surrounded by major constraints and are not figures set apart but the leaders of groups without whose support they are ineffective. This point is reinforced by Bernard Donoughue who in 1974 became head of Wilson's Policy Unit, a post he retained under Jim Callaghan. '[F]or much of the five and a half years during which I served in Downing Street, I was more aware of the constraints on, than the massive impact of, prime ministerial power.'[15] This is true both of the government and of the party; the Prime Minister is only as strong as Cabinet colleagues and the party will allow. In choosing a Cabinet the Premier does not have a free hand, and often has to choose those for whom he or she has little personal or political sympathy. Collective responsibility still exists, and does not mean simple obedience to the will of the Premier but reaching agreed views which all have to accept. The policy-making powers of the Prime Minister are limited partly because it is only possible to be involved in a small proportion of government business and partly because colleagues will protect their own departmental and political interests. Similarly, the party organisation (particularly in the case of Labour governments) does not simply do the Prime Minister's will. As party leader he or she can seek to guide and point the way, but the power to dominate is limited.

The 'chairmanship' view rests on a number of propositions.

Constraints from electorate and party

The idea that general elections are about electing a leader is an over-simplification. While it is clear that some elections, such as 1983, are influenced by the personalities of party leaders, voting for most people is a complex phenomenon.

The idea that MPs are 'mandated' to support their party's leader is not borne out by the facts. Their loyalty is to the party or to a particular version of party ideology, not to a particular person. Thus party loyalty can be over-stressed. Though the Prime Minister can usually rely on the loyalty of the party it cannot be taken for granted, as the fate of Mrs Thatcher demonstrated. Labour leaders have had to work to hold together their party. However, in recent years the Conservative Party has proved harder to manage; loyalty to the leader is not as automatic as in the past, as John Major found. Prime Ministers must woo their parties, not batter them into submission. Mrs Thatcher's downfall was in part related to the distance which had developed between herself and her backbenchers; in this she repeated the error often attributed to Heath. The party outside Parliament also requires caressing by frequent rousing and confident speeches by the Prime Minister and other senior party figures.

Constraints from Cabinet

The Prime Minister's control over the Cabinet can be exaggerated. The senior figures in the Cabinet have their own supporters in the party. Churchill, Attlee, Eden and Macmillan all faced manoeuvrings from those who thought they could do better, and Wilson became paranoid about threats of a takeover from George Brown and others during the 1964–70 administrations. Prime Ministers are only as strong as their colleagues will allow and without their support tenure of the premiership is extremely insecure. To become and remain Prime Minister the support of powerful colleagues is necessary; they must not be presented with the necessity and opportunity of removing the leader.

In terms of organisation, there are limits to the extent to which the Prime Minister can control what is discussed in Cabinet. Although the Premier may be able temporarily to keep items off the agenda, he or she is unable in the long run to prevent senior colleagues from bringing to the Cabinet a matter they think significant. Although Wilson was able to prevent the Cabinet considering devaluation between 1964 and 1967, eventually he had to agree to its being discussed and implemented. Mrs Thatcher's desperate attempts to prevent discussion of Westland in Cabinet led to Heseltine's resignation, setting in train her own eventual downfall. Nor is the agenda merely a matter for the Prime Minister's own whim or inclination. Outside pressures to a large extent dictate what will be discussed. Jones believed that the Prime Minister cannot dictate the outcome of debate in Cabinet by summing up against the sense of the meeting, although others have commented that Mrs Thatcher's habit of setting out her views at the outset, rather than waiting until colleagues had stated theirs, tended to modify Jones's point. He further argued that the absence of evidence of Cabinet revolts against Prime Ministers does not indicate subservience to their will but most likely that final decisions are agreed ones, reached after a process of adjustment and compromise.

The view that Cabinet ministers become totally immersed in the affairs of their own departments and that this contributes to the power of the Premier can be overstated. Ministers have to defend the whole range of government policy; interviewers on radio and television do not confine their questions to the departmental responsibilities of those being interrogated. As most ministers have one eye on what they can expect in the next reshuffle they do not restrict themselves to one area of expertise to the exclusion of all else.

Because Prime Ministers have no department of their own they will be at a serious disadvantage compared with their colleagues. This is particularly a weakness when policy is being formulated, and the Prime Minister is likely to be brought in when discussions have been completed and positions adopted. Despite the changes in recent years to the organisation of No. 10 Downing Street, the Premier lacks the kind of organisational support available to the President of the United States. The Cabinet Office serves the Cabinet as a whole and not just the Prime Minister, and civil servants are loyal to their departments rather than to one person, however eminent.

In matters of composition, there are significant constraints on Prime Ministers' freedom of action. Although they may appear at the height of their powers when first forming an administration, especially when bringing their party from opposition, appearances can be deceptive. They virtually have to choose the leading figures in the party. On taking office in 1964, 'Wilson's first concern . . . was to build a government that would keep the Party united. He began by appointing a Cabinet which made few concessions to his friends and many to his enemies.'[16] The two runners-up in the 1963 leadership contest, Callaghan and Brown, were carefully balanced in senior positions. Most of the other appointments went to those who had occupied the equivalent Shadow Cabinet post. Although he had criticised the size of Douglas-Home's Cabinet, Wilson's contained exactly the same number of ministers; this showed the need to conciliate powerful individuals and interests in the party. In February 1974 Labour won a surprise victory and Wilson formed a minority administration. By this time, 'teamwork' was the slogan (rather than the virtuoso performance of 1964). Most of the 1974 Cabinet were experienced veterans either of government or of the Shadow Cabinet who virtually chose themselves. The veteran left-winger Michael Foot was the only unexpected appointment. Tony Benn, now a born-again socialist, was kept as a concession to the left and to prevent him making mischief on the back benches.

Another party leader who brought the party out of opposition was Margaret Thatcher in 1979. Yet despite this, her position *vis-à-vis* the Cabinet was not strong. Most members were doubters, unconvinced by her arguments; later they were to be dubbed 'wets' and progressively removed. But for a while, Tory paternalists such as Jim Prior and Lord Carrington kept a wary eye on the Prime Minister.

However, this generalisation depends on the situation and the issues concerned. Heath in 1970 excluded Powell, who had been a member of Macmillan's Cabinet and a prominent member of the Shadow Cabinet. Powell's views on immigration were at variance with those of his leader and the 'Rivers of Blood' speech was the last straw. Powell never again held ministerial office. When forming his Cabinet in 1976 Callaghan dropped two senior figures, Barbara Castle and William Ross. The wide changes in the government and the entry of a number of younger people diverted party attention away from what in other circumstances would have been a risky operation. Thatcher in 1979 offered Heath a post she knew he would refuse and ensured her control over events by placing her supporters Howe, Joseph, Howell and Nott in charge of the crucial economic ministries.

Some have pointed out that some ministers are powerful enough to choose their own position, at least initially. According to some accounts, both Jim Prior and Lord Carrington demanded their respective departments in 1979. However, there seems little evidence for this. Prior wrote that on the Saturday after the general election he was invited to No. 10 and asked to serve as Employment Secretary. He went on to say that although surprised, he felt that for Margaret Thatcher to have made a change would have been too dramatic a shift in policy. Lord Carrington's account makes it plain that he was delighted with the post of Foreign and Commonwealth Secretary.

Sacking powerful figures can be dangerous. In the post-war period, very few of those dismissed or who resigned after disagreements with the Prime Minister were senior enough to pose a threat to the leadership. None of the ministers sacked in Macmillan's purge of 1962 were in the first rank. However, the dangers of such a wholesale disposal of ministers was illustrated by this episode. Far from it contributing to a reinvigoration of the government and the recovery of Macmillan's fading reputation, it was a significant factor in the decline of both. Even had it been Wilson's wish, he could not have sacked Callaghan after the devaluation defeat in 1967. Nor could Wilson or Callaghan have dismissed Denis Healey from the Treasury, although the possibility was considered in late 1976. Another obvious example is that of Tony Benn in the 1974–79 governments. Major's dismissal of Norman Lamont created a bitter and determined foe who constantly attacked his former friend and who acted as the focus for right-wing discontent from the back benches.

Prime Ministers often prefer to move those seen as threats. Mrs Thatcher moved Prior from Employment to Northern Ireland and Wilson shifted Benn from Industry to Energy. The humiliating downgrading of Howe in 1989 had disastrous repercussions for Mrs Thatcher a year later. However, this should not be over-stressed. Callaghan sacked Barbara Castle in 1976, and Mrs Thatcher, for a time, seemed to have almost total power to dismiss ministers.

Prime Ministers must be aware of the need for some kind of balance in their appointments. Factors such as youth versus experience, left and right, wet and dry must all be taken into account.

What has been referred to as 'ministerial government' is also a check on the power of the Premier. Departmental ministers have their own position to defend and their own agenda to pursue and will seek to resist prime ministerial interference. The British system is highly fragmented and the success of a minister is measured at least in significant part by his or her ability to defend the department, to secure for it as much resources as possible; their reputations are not particularly enhanced by their contribution to the collective good of the goverment, although a minister who too clearly neglects the whole will also not prosper.

Constraints from Parliament

The power to dissolve Parliament is a two-edged weapon. A successful dissolution is a source of strength but a wrong guess can mean the end of a career. A threat of dissolution as a weapon to enforce obedience on party dissidents lacks credibility, as Harold Wilson found in March 1967 when he warned backbenchers against rebellion. His comment that 'every dog is allowed one bite, but a different view is taken of a dog that goes on biting' was greeted with derision by the bulk of the parliamentary party and by most commentators. Nor was much credence placed on Major's suggestion that he would dissolve Parliament if the Maastricht legislation failed to pass. For one thing, the opposition would make much political capital out of an obvious and public split in the governing party, while rebels are unlikely to be cowed. Most MPs sit for safe seats and are unlikely to face defeat in their own constituencies. Even the possibility of de-selection is unlikely; constituency associations tend either to support their dissident member or to take a line of neutrality.

Other constraints

There are other factors which can either enhance a Prime Minister's position or act as a constraint, depending on the circumstances.

The media are increasingly important in shaping public attitudes to politicians in general and to the Prime Minister in particular. Prime Ministers want sympathetic attention, while the media wish to question and investigate. Post-war Premiers, with the exception of Attlee and Home, have made strenuous, even frantic, efforts to use the media through personal contacts, professional advisers, the lobby system, and controlled leaks (both used with particular ruthlessness by Bernard Ingham, Mrs Thatcher's Press Secretary). Most Prime Ministers have had periods of media success and failure; Macmillan's transition from 'Supermac' to 'Mac the Knife' is but one example.

Parliament, or more specifically the House of Commons, 'is the arena in which Prime Ministers are judged by fellow politicians. In the small intense world of Westminster they are scrutinized and tested by their own side as well as by the opposition. A Prime Minister's hold on the House is crucial to his/her hold on power.'[17] Prime Ministers who dominate the House give the impression, which filters through to the electorate via the media, that the government is in control and can be trusted with the nation's affairs. The Commons acts to reinforce the Prime Minister's authority. Yet when the Prime Minister and/or the government are in trouble, parliamentary scrutiny can be cruel. 'Each situation compounds itself. When a government is riding high a Prime Minister can enter the House with confidence, but when it is in trouble he/she will face a fierce interrogation knowing that they and the government are on trial.'[18]

The Prime Minister's power of patronage can be over-stated. Some have argued that the way to achieve high office is not to give loyal and silent support to the person to whom one owes appointment but to build up a following, to carve out a niche within the party, and to cultivate wider support among the public. In this way it will be politically risky for the Prime Minister to attempt to sack or force someone out of office. The Westland affair is an example; Michael Heseltine on the back-benches was a timebomb ticking under Mrs Thatcher. Loyal service is not enough to prevent dismissal. None of the ministers axed in 1962 had a reputation for being awkward or nuisances or opponents of the Prime Minister. They were removed because they were easy targets and appeared to have no significant following among the remaining leading Cabinet ministers or the MPs generally. Nor can a Prime Minister be guaranteed loyalty from those on whom honours and preferments have been showered. Many Conservative MPs knighted by Mrs Thatcher voted against her in November 1990.

It is also possible to overemphasise the Prime Minister's influence over policy. No one, not even a Prime Minister with a policy agenda as comprehensive as that of Mrs Thatcher, can survey the whole of an increasingly complex field. There is a host of pressures and a myriad of sources of policy initiatives, including the party, government departments, pressure groups, think tanks and so on. However much the Prime Minister may attempt to dominate the policies of his or her government, the pressure of time and of events limits what can be achieved. Despite what amounted to a state of permanent revolution under Mrs Thatcher, one of her constant lamentations was that much remained to be done. The Prime Minister will not necessarily be able to initiate or shape policy as he or she wishes. There are too many pressures to be accommodated.

Jones concluded that Cabinet government and collective responsibility are not defunct notions. The Prime Minister has to persuade not bludgeon. Though the leading figure whose voice carries most weight, the Premier is not the all-powerful individual that Crossman and others have described. 'A prime minister who can carry his colleagues with him can be in a very powerful position, but he is only as strong as they let him be.'[19]

The prime ministerial and Cabinet models assessed

Both the prime ministerial and the Cabinet government models have come under criticism for exaggerating and over-simplifying the complex pattern of behaviour and interactions between personalities, institutions and events.

The prime ministerial model has major weaknesses.

> This theory was never very subtle and, in the light of evidence now available, remote from the truth. It reflected Crossman's own penchant for dramatic generalization. The most telling rebuttal is Crossman's own voluminous diary, which provides day-by-day testimony of the vitality of Cabinet government, the influence of powerful ministers and the constraints on the Prime Minister . . . A simple distortion is easier to popularize than a complex truth.[20]

The capacity of Prime Ministers such as Macmillan, Wilson and above all Thatcher to dramatise themselves and to project an image of mastery created an illusion of unchallenged dominance.

However, the opposite thesis, that of Cabinet government, is equally simplistic, because it neglects the dominant position of the Premier. In reality, the Cabinet is mainly concerned with legislative timetabling, foreign affairs, public expenditure and what has been termed 'fire-brigade' issues, matters which need urgent though probably short-term consideration. Despite the various constraints under which he or she works, the Prime Minister is clearly the most powerful figure in the British political system. Although this power is not absolute, the real constraints are events which are totally beyond the control of any Prime Minister or any government.

Despite his advocacy of the Cabinet government model, Jones also conceded that the office 'has great potentialities, but the use made of them depends on many variables, the personality, temperament, and ability of the prime minister, what he wants to achieve and the methods he uses'.[21] This opens the way to an examination of the third perspective on the controversy.

The personality/circumstances view

Neither the 'presidential' nor the 'chairmanship' view takes much account of the differing personalities who have occupied No.10 Downing Street, nor the effect of circumstances and what Harold Macmillan referred to as 'events'. As Lord Blake put it: 'The truth is that the powers of the Prime Minister have varied with the personality of the Prime Minister, or with the particular political circumstances of his tenure'.[22] Prime Ministers differ widely in their personalities. Some, including Churchill, Heath and Thatcher, tended to dominate in Cabinet. Others took a more limited view of their role and, certainly in some areas of policy, let stronger ministers take the lead. Perhaps the clearest post-war example of a Prime Minister who tended to see himself as the chairman of a committee was Sir Alec Douglas-Home. However, Wilson during his second administration from 1974 to 1976 regarded his role more that of a centre-half than a centre-forward, allowing experienced colleagues considerable latitude in policy matters. Several commentators have pointed out the unhistorical nature of much of Crossman's analysis. In the nineteenth century some Prime Ministers (for example Disraeli and Gladstone) were dominant in their Cabinets, while others (such as Lord Rosebery) were not. In many respects Lloyd George displayed those 'presidential' characteristics which Crossman portrayed as a mainly post-1945 development.

Similarly, the situations faced by Prime Ministers differ and some are more fortunate than others. Supporters of Edward Heath emphasise the problems he had in coping with the massive disruptions caused by the aftermath of the Yom Kippur War; in comparison, they say, Mrs Thatcher was a lucky Prime Minister, at least until the end. However, temperament is a vital factor. While possession of the right temperament is no guarantee of success, its absence is a certain sign of failure. Perhaps the ability to make one's own luck is an aspect of temperament; successful politicians tend to be opportunists with more than a hint of ruthlessness.

Assessment of the debate

Though there is much evidence for all three approaches, none provide a complete answer. The evidence is limited, often ambiguous and open to conflicting interpretations. For example, both Crossman and Jones noted that Prime Ministers often ask party rivals to join the Cabinet, but while the former saw this as a weapon enabling the Premier to suppress opposition, the latter viewed it as a substantial constraint on prime ministerial power.

Barber pointed to three main factors involved in determining prime ministerial power.

(1) *The constitutional and political frameworks in which they operate* These only change slowly, and although they have flexibility they also impose constraints. Though there have been changes since 1945, for example in the election of party leaders, they have been amendments to the existing structure rather than new structures. No basic change, such as the creation of a Prime Minister's Department, has occurred. The office itself is an important factor. Bernard Donoughue believed that a Prime Minister's personal standing, especially in the

eyes of his Cabinet colleagues and of Whitehall, is basically a question of authority. 'All Prime Ministers have a degree of authority independent of personal stature. Some authority is intrinsic to the position of Prime Minister; it comes naturally and automatically with the office.'[23]

(2) *The circumstances they face* By contrast with the framework, circumstances are constantly changing in a manner difficult if not impossible to predict. Luck plays an important part in any Prime Minister's career, as does the ability to take advantage of good fortune. Major was lucky in being in the right place at the right time, but he also took good use of his opportunity. As a loyal supporter of Thatcher, as someone who seemed to have inherited her mantle and as someone who could reconcile the various factions in the party in a way not open to his two rivals, he showed the importance of luck in the timing of the contest, while he demonstrated opportunism in the way he and his supporters created a 'bandwagon' effect.

(3) *Their personality and personal qualities* Prime Ministers are judged partly on what personal resources they bring to the post and how well they use them. Political ability is an immense source of strength. Whatever criticisms can be made of Mrs Thatcher, her main claim to the support of her party was her ability to win general elections; her supporters often pointed to the contrast with her predecessor, who lost three of his four elections. Factors such as the ability to work hard, to identify clear aims, to take quick decisions and so on are all involved. Bernard Donoughue believed that successful Prime Ministers need three basic characteristics: strong ambition, unusual luck and above all remarkable physical stamina.

Time is another important element. Prime ministerial power is not a static thing; it can vary markedly during a period in office. As a generalisation, Prime Ministers are most powerful following a crisis successfully handled or immediately after winning a general election, possibly from opposition. But they can falter, perhaps from a mishandled crisis such as Suez or from the accumulation of misfortunes and miscalculations, such as those marking the end of Macmillan and Thatcher.

Prime ministerial power fluctuates; at times he or she will appear to have presidential powers, at others the constraints dominate. No one demonstrates that more clearly than Mrs Thatcher.

Margaret Thatcher as Prime Minister

At first sight no one could have been less a 'chairman (or woman)' figure than Mrs Thatcher. In opposition she claimed that her style of government would be markedly different from that of her predecessors. There is much evidence to support both the 'presidential' and the 'personality/circumstances' theories. The 'presidential' school, which saw a trend towards a more personal style of government, regardless of the actual incumbent, emphasised the increasingly centralised decision-making, while the 'personality' school stressed what they saw as the factors peculiar to Mrs Thatcher such as her dominant and distinctive character and the way she imposed her will on all around her.

However, George Jones painted a more complex picture. He queried 'whether the enemy of collectivism has eradicated collective Cabinet government'.[24] Pointing out that over the years the balance between prime ministerial domination and a more collegiate system fluctuates, he looked at episodes such as Westland. He concluded that Mrs Thatcher's actions were motivated by a desire to maintain the collective policy of the Cabinet and the party against a lone dissident, rather than being an example of personal power, as Heseltine claimed. Jones believed that Thatcher's well-known dislike of general discussions of strategy in Cabinet was neither new nor disturbing. She acted as the defender of collective government and of party strategy, rather than as a presidential figure, pushing her personal policy.

Mrs Thatcher's relations with the Cabinet fluctuated, largely in line with her own popularity and with that of her government. At no time did it consist only of her own supporters. A number had a substantial following in the party and among the electorate, acting as a significant constraint on her ability to get her own way. On the other hand, she is said to have interfered in departmental matters to a marked degree; she clearly had a personal agenda which covered more areas of policy than was the case with most post-war Premiers. In Cabinet meetings she usually announced her views at the start of a discussion, in effect challenging her opponents to make their position clear at the outset; previous Prime Ministers tended to allow discussion first and then to put forward their views in the summing up.

Commentators such as Peter Hennessy were critical of her 'quasi-presidential style', stressing the reduction in the number of Cabinet and Cabinet committee meetings and Mrs Thatcher's fondness for often informal consultation with close colleagues and advisers as a way of downgrading or bypassing the full Cabinet. This was particularly marked in economic policy-making, where she feared a hostile majority in Cabinet would block her policies. Jones saw nothing new in this development, which had originated in the last century. He claimed that such groupings were beneficial, in that they relieved the Cabinet of much work and left it free to concentrate on the critical matters and to survive as the central decision-taking body. He believed that such meetings did not detract from Cabinet government; rather, they enhanced it.

Jones provided a useful metaphor for understanding the office of Prime Minister. 'The office of Prime Minister is like a piece of elastic: it can be stretched to accommodate an activist, interventionist Prime Minister, but also contract to contain a more passive Prime Minister.'[25] This echoed Hennessy's view that what the Cabinet is or does depends on a mixture of personalities and situations. 'Cabinet Government remains a putty-like concept. A prime minister can make of it very largely what he or she will, provided colleagues do not baulk at their treatment.'[26] Jones ended by pointing out that as long as her style brought success it would be tolerated; if it was seen to have failed, she would be replaced by a leader with a different style.

In a later article,[27] Jones pointed to the impact of changing fortunes on the Prime Minister as her standing and that of the government plummeted in the polls. Shortly after the article was published the Prime Minister 'on probation' fell from office. The unpopularity of Thatcher and of the government unnerved Tory MPs and allowed the challenge, first from the 'stalking-horse' Sir Anthony Meyer and then from the serious contender, Michael Heseltine. Ministerial tolerance eventually snapped; resignations by Lawson and Howe (and the forced departure of Nicholas Ridley) fatally weakened her position. Although most of the Cabinet expressed support for the Prime Minister during the first round of voting, this eroded when they were called individually to No. 10. The lack of support convinced Mrs Thatcher that further resistance was useless, and she resigned.

The 'prime ministerial' versus 'Cabinet government' argument is a sterile one. A number of variables affect the power of any Prime Minister. They are the personality of the Prime Minister and his/her colleagues, the general parliamentary situation and political standing of the Prime Minister, the type of policy area involved, the degree of involvement in the issue by outside interests such as pressure groups and the media. The downfall of Thatcher and her replacement by Major brought about significant changes in the conduct of the Cabinet. But the change can be overestimated. Many of the developments of the Thatcher era represent the continuation of changes which are of long duration.

Notes

1 The Earl of Oxford and Asquith, *Fifty Years of Parliament*, Cassell, 1926, Vol. II, p. 185.
2 Walter Bagehot, *The English Constitution*, Fontana, 1963, p. 51.
3 Ibid., p. 52.
4 Ibid., p. 53.
5 Ibid.
6 Lord Hailsham, 'Elective Dictatorship', *The Listener*, 21 October 1976, p. 497.
7 Tony Benn, 'The Case for a Constitutional Premiership', in Anthony King (ed.), *The British Prime Minister*, Macmillan, 1985, pp. 221–2.
8 Rodney Brazier, *Constitutional Reform. Re-shaping the British Political System*, Oxford University Press, 1991, p. 9.
9 Michael Foley, *The Rise of the British Presidency*, Manchester University Press, 1993, p. 2.
10 Ibid., p. 18.
11 Ibid., p. 264.
12 Ibid., pp. 282–3.
13 *Times Literary Supplement*, 30 July 1993.
14 *Financial Times*, 28 September 1993.

15 Bernard Donoughue, *Prime Minister. The Conduct of Policy under Harold Wilson and James Callaghan*, Cape, 1987, p. 4.
16 Ben Pimlott, *Harold Wilson*, Harper Collins, 1992, p. 327.
17 James Barber, *The Prime Minister since 1945*, Blackwell, 1991, p. 56.
18 Ibid., pp. 59–60.
19 G.W. Jones, 'The Prime Minister's Power', in King (ed.), *The British Prime Minister*, p. 216.
20 Simon James, *British Cabinet Government*, Routledge, 1992, p. 92.
21 Jones, 'The Prime Minister's Power', p. 216.
22 Lord Blake, *The Office of Prime Minister*, Oxford University Press, 1975, p. 51.
23 Donoughue, *Prime Minister*, p. 13.
24 George Jones, 'Cabinet Government and Mrs Thatcher', *Contemporary Record*, Vol. 1, No. 3, Autumn 1987, p. 8.
25 Jones, 'Cabinet Government and Mrs Thatcher', p. 10.
26 Peter Hennessy, *Cabinet*, Blackwell, 1986, p. 4.
27 George Jones, 'Mrs Thatcher and the Power of the Prime Minister', *Contemporary Record*, Vol. 3, No. 4, April 1990.

5

The functions of the Prime Minister

This chapter surveys the functions and powers exercised by the modern Prime Minister. The much debated question of the extent to which government policy originates with the head of the government is also discussed, and a typology of prime ministerial policy-making is outlined.

Introduction

Attempts to define the functions and powers of the British Prime Minister and to establish a typology of prime ministerial policy-making come up against a basic problem. In many countries the role of the head of government is set out in some authoritative (though rarely comprehensive) form. Given the lack of definition in the British system of government, something deriving in large part from the absence of a written constitution, this is not the case in this country. There are few statutory references to the Prime Minister and nowhere a clear and authoritative account of what he or she is expected to do.

The tasks undertaken by the Prime Minister and the extent to which he or she will give policy leadership vary widely. Some Prime Ministers see themselves largely as political managers, keeping their governments together and ensuring the implementation of party policies rather than imposing an essentially personal agenda. Attlee, Wilson and Callaghan came into this category. In many ways John Major followed this tendency; although he had some policy initiatives of his own, he was essentially a party manager, seeking to balance the various factions and to keep his government from collapse. Others, such as Churchill, Macmillan and Heath, sought to give a clear lead in some areas of government policy, mainly relating to foreign or economic policy, but were content to follow agreed lines in other areas of business. Alec Douglas-Home, for several reasons, gave little lead in any policy area. Margaret Thatcher sought consciously to dominate virtually all areas of policy and to in effect personalise her government.

This means that the office is a highly flexible one, adjusting both to circumstances and to differing personalities. Obviously, there are many assumptions concerning the role of the Prime Minister. He or she is expected to impart a certain style to government, ranging from the imperious certitude of Thatcher to the retiring, publicity-shunning Attlee. Yet at the same time the job is highly malleable, allowing different Prime Ministers to interpret the job in their own way. There are very few duties he or she *must* carry out. Jim Callaghan, reflecting on first becoming Prime Minister, wrote:

> For the first day or two while I was making governmental changes there was a constant stream of Ministers coming and going, but once that was complete I sat back and realised I had nothing to do . . . For a brief period as I sat in the Cabinet Room I savoured the suspicion that as everyone else was doing the Government's work I could be the idlest member of the Administration if I was so minded.[1]

One reason for this is the absence of a written constitution. This means that Prime Ministers have been able to extend their powers without fearing accusations of violating the constitution. Ministers who attempt to limit the Prime Minister's authority or to accuse him or her of misusing their position directly challenge the head of government and so risk their own career. However, when the Cabinet chooses to exercise its constitutional superiority it can impose limitations on any Prime Minister, however powerful and imperious. To rephrase Asquith: 'The power of the prime minister is what the prime minister wants, and is able, to get away with'.[2]

The sources of prime ministerial power

(1) The Prime Minister has 'authority' which arises from possession of the office rather than from any particular skills or abilities; it is this which ensures the respect of colleagues (who are in reality the Prime Minister's subordinates) and the willingness of departments to follow his or her policies. The British Prime Minister is both head of the government and a party leader. Bernard Donoughue reflected on the changes which took place when Callaghan succeeded Wilson: 'It was very striking to observe how, from the moment Mr Callaghan became Prime Minister, other politicians who had been friends and life-long colleagues began to behave differently towards him. There is a charisma attached to the occupancy of No. 10.'[3] He or she is virtually always addressed as 'Prime Minister' except in private or with his or her closest and most trusted colleagues.

Ministers expect the Prime Minister to give a lead on important policy matters. Failure to do so will lead to criticisms from ministers (almost always taken up in the media) and may result in the government falling into factions and losing any sense of direction. The inability of Jim Callaghan to take a grip on the situation during the 'winter of discontent' left the administration rudderless and drifting out of control.

Developments since 1945, such as the growth of summitry and the pervasive influence of television, have exalted the position of Prime Ministers, who are now in many ways remote from their colleagues. The Prime Minister represents Britain, and the Cabinet is obliged to delegate their authority to him or her.

(2) Ministers are reluctant to combine against the Prime Minister. The argument that they will check him or her because they are rivals is not borne out by the evidence. In most clashes between a Prime Minister and members of the Cabinet, rivals and supporters are found on both sides of the argument. Very rarely will a Prime Minister pursue a policy to which senior colleagues are opposed; he or she will seek to 'square' the most significant and dangerous critics, perhaps by making concessions over other issues. Nor is it likely that ministers will oppose a policy they support on the grounds that the Prime Minister may be exceeding the authority of the past; complaints will only be made if the minister concerned disagrees with the policy the Prime Minister is pursuing.

(3) Despite the example of Mrs Thatcher, it remains difficult to remove a Prime Minister, as John Redwood found in 1995. Party leaders are elected by a wider franchise than in the past and it takes a combination of strong hostility to the Premier in the Cabinet and in the party, some focus of opposition, and the support of most leading ministers to mount a successful challenge. Mrs Thatcher fell because of a combination of circumstances: she had quarrelled with a number of leading colleagues, some of whom had left the government in a blaze of publicity, opinion polls registered the depth of her electoral unpopularity and Heseltine offered Tory backbenchers a viable alternative. The final blow was Sir Geoffrey Howe's resignation speech in the Commons, when the 'dead sheep' finally struck.

(4) The style and personality of the Prime Minister is also a factor. Though there was a marked contrast between the terse and businesslike Attlee and the loquacious Churchill, both got good results from their ministers because they were admired and trusted. Eden's meddling insecurity drove his colleagues almost to distraction. Wilson was admired for his brilliance (and for his ability to win elections) but never trusted, while Heath was regarded with a mixture of awe and fear but was never on close terms with his ministers. For some years, Macmillan dominated his government by sheer force of personality, and almost until the end of his troubled administration Callaghan's avuncular nature and generally sunny disposition kept his far from happy band of brothers rowing in the same boat. Mrs Thatcher's style and personality aroused deeply contrasting views. Admirers such as Nicholas Ridley and Keith Joseph saw her abrasive and sometimes brutal manner as what was needed to turn Britain around and restore a sense of national pride and purpose. Others, including several who were initially supporters, came to view her regime as almost Stalinist and as deeply flawed and counter-productive. John Major was both by temperament and inclination much more courteous and thoughtful, even though given to outbursts of fierce anger, as when he referred to his Cabinet critics as 'bastards'.

(5) Chairing the Cabinet and the most important Cabinet committees is also

important. Although they can rarely be used to flout a collective decision, they can be employed to steer, direct or nudge a decision in the way the Prime Minister wishes.

(6) The Prime Minister is the only member of the government in a position to take an interest in everything which is going on. He or she is uniquely involved in the flow of business, is in a position to intervene in the work of each minister, and can see the whole picture. There is both a personal and a political incentive to keep a grip on everything, as the Premier will be held politically responsible for the success or failure of the government as a whole.

(7) In a way possibly unique in democratic systems, the Prime Minister not only determines who will sit in the Cabinet, what they will do and what Cabinet committees exist and who sits on them, he or she also decides which departments exists and what their purpose is. This gives the Prime Minister domination over the administrative system and the ability to establish, abolish or alter the terms of reference of government departments and a host of other bodies.

(8) In some ways the media enhances the authority of the Prime Minister, who is in a unique position to put the government's case, to influence how commentators interpret events and so on. This is especially the case if he or she can gain the support of influential commentators and (perhaps crucially) powerful newspaper proprietors. However, it can also be a two-edged sword. Increasingly, what the media helped to create it can also help to destroy, as Mrs Thatcher found towards the end of her premiership.

(9) The power to appoint and to fire is the most crucial. This is reinforced by the desire for office of most politicians, which means that the Premier is in a powerful position. He or she can influence the behaviour of ministers, fearful of dismissal or hopeful of promotion, and of backbenchers, anxious to get the first foot on the rungs of office. Although this power is subject to all kinds of limitations, mainly of a political nature, it is the Premier's power of appointment and dismissal that, above all else, sets him or her apart from all other ministers.

Limitations on the office

(1) The principal constraint on the Prime Minister's power is the limited scope for independent decision-taking. Because of the lack of specific statutory powers enjoyed by the Prime Minister, he or she must largely act through others. Despite considerable prime ministerial influence on ministers' actions, the ultimate decision is theirs.

(2) The Prime Minister holds power by virtue of being a party leader, and there is always the possibility of being deposed and thus removed from office. All Prime Ministers realise that there are others after their job, including their closest colleagues.

(3) The usual human failings also limit Prime Ministers, even ones such as Thatcher: lack of time, lack of energy, lack of expertise, an inability to focus on everything at once. Wilson's tendency to act as though he were playing Space

Invaders, shooting at each blip as it flitted across the screen, was a defect, not a strength.

(4) Prime Ministers, unlike their counterparts in many other democracies, are limited by having a small personal staff. The total comes to around thirty, and only around eighteen are closely concerned with policy and the presentation of policy. There are two main reasons. First, most Prime Ministers have not wanted a larger staff. They have in general wanted to work with and not against their colleagues, they have seldom had a policy agenda of their own, and they have usually identified their success with that of the government as a whole. Thus a large personal staff would serve no useful purpose. Even Thatcher did not feel the need to create a Prime Minister's Department. She preferred to dominate by force of personality while relying on a small (though shifting) group of intimates to carry out her wishes. Second, there would be sustained resistance to any such move, being seen from a variety of perspectives as a threat to the collective nature of British government. Ministers especially would see their subordination to the Prime Minister as being institutionalised, depriving them of the possibility of exercising a collective check on an over-mighty Premier.

The powers and functions of the Prime Minister

The task of outlining the functions and powers of the Prime Minister can be dealt with in several ways. Donald Shell[4] outlined the work of the Premier under three headings: as head of government, as party leader and as national leader. Anthony King set out seven tasks which are mandatory 'in the sense that a prime minister who did not perform them or who delegated them to others would be thought to be shirking his or her responsibilities'.[5] Simon James[6] saw the Prime Minister's role as having two main facets: political and governmental. By combining their insights it is perhaps possible to get some idea of the multiplicity of tasks performed by the modern Prime Minister.

However, it is not really possible to distinguish clearly between the various aspects of the Prime Minister's job. The Prime Minister is a party politician who wishes to go on being Prime Minister until he or she chooses not to. In all his or her multifarious activities, the political element, the need to appeal to the electorate, cannot be far from the Prime Minister's thoughts. Obviously, there are clearly occasions when the party politician is uppermost: addressing the party conference, making a party political broadcast and so on. There are others where that aspect is largely absent. It would have been inappropriate (and highly counter-productive) for Mrs Thatcher to have behaved as a party politician when laying a wreath at the Cenotaph on Remembrance Sunday.

The Prime Minister as head of government

Appointing and dismissing ministers Perhaps the most significant power of the Prime Minister is that of appointing and dismissing ministers and conducting regular reshuffles, both planned and unplanned. Although as a constitutional formality this is done in the name of the sovereign, in reality (and despite the host of political factors which must be taken into consideration) these are matters for the Prime Minister alone. This function has grown over time rather than as a result of a conscious accretion of power. It began in the eighteenth century as the monarch ceased to appoint Cabinet members (except in a purely formal sense) but has grown in scope. As recently as the early post-war period senior ministers sometimes appointed junior ministers within their own departments, although they would consult the Prime Minister before confirming their choice. However, this is no longer the case and all appointments are made by the head of the government. This power extends to that of approving ministers' choice of PPSs. Prime Ministers also insist on sacking PPSs who step out of line by voting against the government or even by abstaining on a vote.

Prime Ministers who succeed someone of their own party obviously take over a team of ministers. However, they can, if they choose, make changes as sweeping as they desire (or can get away with). Leaders of the Opposition who win a general election to become Prime Minister bring with them a Shadow Cabinet, which in the case of the Conservative Party is appointed by the leader while in the case of Labour is elected by Labour MPs. Up to the present no incoming Prime Minister has been obliged to automatically appoint the members of the outgoing Shadow Cabinet, although practical considerations dictate considerable continuity. This position has changed, however. In 1981 the Parliamentary Labour Party altered its Standing Orders so as to limit the autonomy of future Labour Prime Ministers. Standing Order E says that:

> When the Party is in Office, the Cabinet shall continue to be appointed by the Prime Minister. On taking Office as Prime Minister, the Leader shall appoint as members of his Cabinet those who were elected as members of the Parliamentary Committee at the Dissolution and have retained their seats.

Despite this, Tony Blair omitted two members of the outgoing Shadow Cabinet in May 1997, ostensibly on the grounds that not enough Cabinet posts were available.

In addition to the power of initial appointment, Prime Ministers have to cope with ministerial resignations and retirements. A minister's resignation may be requested by the Premier; the usual formality is for a grateful and occasionally effusive exchange of letters, in which the departing colleague is thanked for his services to the nation and the party, while he or she expresses gratitude for having been given the opportunity to serve and protests undying loyalty to his or her leader.

Whereas ministerial reshuffles used to occur mid-way through a government's life, they are now an annual feature of the political scene. A particularly dramatic example occurred in June 1995. The Cabinet reshuffle which followed Major's re-election as Conservative Party leader was also more extensive than had been thought likely. Overall, Major promoted several of the more loyal right-wingers, whilst excluding Redwood and his supporters in what was seen as a risky exercise in party management. The most dramatic part of the reshuffle was the elevation of Major's former rival for the leadership, Michael Heseltine, to be First Secretary of State and Deputy Prime Minister, a post with no constitutional authority. He was given a major coordinating role in government and headed ten Cabinet committees, charged with producing election-winning policies to be embodied in the next manifesto. Downing Street was at pains to point out the significance of the appointment. It was announced that he would 'assist the Prime Minister generally and will have specific responsibility for the competitiveness agenda and the working of government and its presentation of policy. He will chair a number of cabinet committees and will be an ex-officio member of Cabinet committees generally.'[7] It is an open question whether Major enhanced Heseltine's position out of weakness, a desperate throw of the dice to gain the support of his most dangerous rival, or whether it was a shrewd move to neutralise him, to throw him some bones in order to keep him on board and to compensate him for his failure to reach the top of the 'greasy pole'.

Chairing the Cabinet The Prime Minister is solely responsible for calling and chairing Cabinet meetings although he can delegate this power to some other member of the government should this be necessary, for example in case of illness or absence from the country. This prerogative is jealously protected. In March 1968 there was a furious row between Harold Wilson and his Foreign Secretary, the volcanic and highly excitable George Brown, over what Wilson saw as Brown's attempt to convene an irregular (and partial) Cabinet meeting to discuss an economic crisis. Fears of a Cabinet coup (similar to that in 1916 when Asquith was ousted in favour of Lloyd George) led Wilson into an unusual display of temper. Shortly after this incident, Brown resigned, the matter having developed into an argument about Wilson's style of government.

The power to chair meetings involves deciding whom to call to speak, what interjections to allow, what items to put on the agenda, control of the supply of papers and the supervision of the writing of the minutes, which are issued under the Prime Minister's authority. The summings up of discussions constitute the formal decisions of the Cabinet and are known as 'Cabinet Conclusions'. In Cabinet the Prime Minister has the advantage of having gone over the matter with the minister beforehand. Formal votes are rare, although Wilson had a propensity to call for a show of hands, and there have been suggestions that on occasions Prime Ministers have summed up against the sense of the meeting. Similarly, control over the agenda has been used to prevent discussions of certain matters. Wilson kept devaluation almost completely off the Cabinet agenda from the formation of the government in 1964 until mounting crisis forced its discussion in 1967. The solitary exception was on 19 July 1966; according to some commentators, Wilson refused to circulate the minutes of that meeting, even to the Cabinet ministers who attended it. The Prime Minister's control over Cabinet even extends to apparently trivial matters such as the seating arrangements, which involve complex considerations of power and precedence, as well as more human elements.

The precise manner in which Prime Ministers deal with their Cabinets will vary considerably. This depends partly on personal style, partly on political circumstances and can vary over the period in office of any particular Premier. Prime Ministers must remember that they can lead only up to the point that the Cabinet will follow; there is a breaking point even for such a supine group as that surrounding Mrs Thatcher for most of her premiership. The Prime Minister is also responsible for ensuring that collective responsibility is observed, not only in the Cabinet but in all ranks of the administration.

Cabinet committees The Prime Minister appoints all members of Cabinet committees and decides their terms of reference. It is clear that many decisions are in practice taken by committees and then presented to Cabinet for ratification. So the ability of the Prime Minister to decide who sits on which committees and what matters are discussed is obviously of crucial importance. Recent Premiers have even gone outside the official structure of Cabinet committees to ensure that certain matters are dealt with by those sympathetic to his or her position.

The machinery of government Prime Ministers must also involve themselves in highly complex and often controversial issues regarding the organisation of government business, ranging from the structure of central departments to the establishment of executive agencies in the Civil Service and the creation of new quangos (quasi-autonomous non-governmental organisations). Though these matters rarely hit the headlines they raise issues of the greatest importance for the public good and engage the Prime Minister as head of the government, concerned to serve the public interest not just in the present but to take decisions which will have an impact long after the Prime Minister has departed his or her office. Decisions taken now about the structure of the education service, the debate about the organisation of the National Health Service, the extent to which government functions are carried out by executive agencies (involving a much-reduced central departmental core) are all examples of decisions which have long-term consequences for the people of this country and in which the Prime Minister must have a possibly crucial imput.

But the head of government is also head of party and will be concerned not just with the public good but with his or her party's fight for re-election (and for his or her own hold on power). So considerations of party ideology, the need to appeal to voters and issues regarding the distribution of posts must also weigh on the Prime Minister's mind.

The Civil Service The Prime Minister is responsible for appointments to the two most senior grades in the Home Civil Service (Permanent Secretary and Deputy

Secretary) and for the highest positions in the Diplomatic Service. In making domestic appointments, the Prime Minister is advised by the Head of the Home Civil Service (who in turn is advised by the Senior Appointments Selection Committee, a group of senior officials). For posts in the Foreign Service, advice will be given by the Foreign Secretary, the Permanent Secretary to the Foreign Office and the Foreign Office Senior Selection Board. Traditionally, the Prime Minister would accept official advice and select from a short list, but Mrs Thatcher took a close interest in senior appointments, using the 'is he one of us' test, by which is meant that she preferred a certain type of person, one who would show zeal and enthusiasm for the policies she was determined to pursue rather than the traditional type of civil servant, marked by disinterestedness and even scepticism. While some critics have accused Thatcher of politicising the Civil Service, others have doubted that this has taken place.

Patronage The Prime Minister is responsible, directly or indirectly, for a host of appointments in British public life. They include senior judges, the archbishops and bishops of the Anglican Church, senior military officers, the Governor of the Bank of England, members of the governing bodies of the BBC and the IBA and many others. This power of appointment extends to certain university posts in the gift of the crown. Although some of these appointments are in theory made by other ministers, the Prime Minister's power to influence them is considerable; it is unlikely that a minister would resist a clearly expressed preference from No. 10. The Honours List, with awards ranging from life peerages to more humble honours such as the MBE, although in theory emanating from the monarch, in reality is dominated by the 'advice' of the Prime Minister.

There is an important political aspect to the granting of honours. Conservative Prime Ministers make awards for 'political and public services' and use them to reward supporters and allies; virtually all Conservative MPs end their Commons service with a knighthood and may well receive a life peerage. Life peerages are also given to others who have given help to the party; much controversy was created over the apparent link between awards to businessmen whose companies gave substantial donations to the Conservative Party. Although Labour Prime Ministers did not make overtly political awards, critics pointed to the substantial number of trade union leaders who used to grace the House of Lords on their retirement; the reliance of the Labour Party on donations from affiliated unions was seen to be analogous to company donations to the Tories.

Military and security matters The chiefs of the armed forces are appointed by the Prime Minister and retain the right of appeal to him or her over matters relating to defence expenditure. Some Prime Ministers have taken a close and direct interest in military matters. During the Second World War Churchill was also Minister of Defence, by no means an honorific title, and he again took the post for the first few months of his peacetime administration. His appointment of the war leader Earl Alexander of Tunis, a political novice, to succeed him was a way of ensuring that he had continued influence in an area of vital concern. Thatcher at the time of the Falklands conflict and Major during the Gulf War presided over special Cabinet committees and Mrs Thatcher in particular adopted a hands-on approach to the conflict, although without alienating the military leaders, unlike Anthony Eden, whose continued interference in military matters during the Suez expedition was deeply resented by service chiefs.

The Prime Minister is head of Britain's security services and since 1989 has been responsible for the appointment of a Commissioner to oversee the security services. Successive Premiers have refused to give a public account of this aspect of their responsibilites, but it is clear that in both formal and informal terms the Prime Minister is in overall control of their activities.

Parliamentary duties Before the Second World War Prime Ministers would also act as Leader of the House of Commons, which entailed being responsible for the business of the House and thus spending long periods of time on the government front bench. In the post-war period, Prime Ministers have spent ever-decreasing amounts of time in the Commons. Although the Prime Minister will be expected to speak in the debate in answer to the Queen's Speech at the start of each session of Parliament and in No Confidence debates and to make Statements, for example after attending international conferences, interventions by Prime Ministers in other debates are becoming increasingly rare. The Prime Minister has to attend the Commons for short periods on Tuesday and Thursday afternoons to answer Prime Minister's Questions, although he or she can delegate the responsibility when ill or out of the country. These are now the high point of the parliamentary week and often attract attention in the media, unlike the usual run of parliamentary debate.

The Prime Minister and the monarch The Prime Minister is the sovereign's principal adviser. Although he or she no longer writes a letter summarising the Cabinet's proceedings (until the middle of the First World War the only record of what the Cabinet decided) the Prime Minister, while Parliament is in session, still has a weekly audience with the Queen and is likely to be invited to spend some time with the Royal Family on the Queen's Balmoral estate. The present Queen has now been served by ten Prime Ministers; although relationships between Queen and Premier have been shrouded in confidentiality they are rumoured to have varied from the correct to the cordial. She is said to have been particularly close to her first Prime Minister, Winston Churchill, and to have been on friendly terms with her two Labour Premiers, Harold Wilson and James Callaghan. During Mrs Thatcher's time it was often thought that tension existed between the two, at least in part because of the Prime Minister's indifference to the Commonwealth, whose titular head is the Queen. However, after her retirement Mrs Thatcher was made a Lady of the Garter, an honour in the personal gift of the Queen, so it is likely that the rumours were exaggerated, though probably not without some substance.

There are certain occasions when the Prime Minister formally 'advises' the Queen, who is constitutionally obliged to follow that advice. One such occasion concerns the dissolution of Parliament. During the First World War the Prime Minister acquired the sole right to advise the monarch, within the terms of the 1911 Parliament Act, as to the date of the general election, and although he or she may consult Cabinet colleagues, party officials and 'spin doctors' the responsibility is his or hers alone. A correct decision will enhance the authority of the incumbent, a wrong one will in all likelihood mean a hasty exit to the House of Lords.

The Prime Minister and the media A significant part of the success or failure of Prime Ministers in the post-war period has been their ability to cultivate the media, especially television, and to create an 'image' to which the electorate will respond. An important aspect of the longevity of Mrs Thatcher was the support she enjoyed from sections of the media, especially the Conservative-supporting tabloids, for whom she could do little wrong, at least until the end. More recently, the attempts by Tony Blair to cultivate the Murdoch-owned papers have indicated the importance Labour now attaches to relations with formerly hostile sections of the press.

The Prime Minister as party leader

A marked trend in British politics in recent decades has been the domination of the governing party's election campaign by the Prime Minister (mirrored by the opposition parties' concentration on their respective leaders). The Prime Minister, especially in the case of the Conservative Party, takes responsibility for the writing of the manifesto, tends to monopolise media coverage and attempts to determine the nature and direction of the contest. Much of the media portray the election as a battle between the Prime Minister and the Leader of the Opposition, rather than as one between parties.

The relationship between a Conservative Prime Minister and his or her party differs from that existing in the Labour Party. Conservative leaders (in or out of office) appoint the party Chairman and, although leaving day-to-day matters to that person, usually continue to keep a close watch on developments. Some Tory Prime Ministers have had a rather detached relationship with the party, both inside and outside Parliament. Heath grew almost to dislike the party he led and his lack of sympathy for the bulk of Tory MPs, was a crucial factor in his fall. Although initially Margaret Thatcher cultivated close relations with her MPs towards the end she too lost contact, something which counted against her when Heseltine made his move in November 1990. A Labour Prime Minister has a more formal connection with the party machine outside Parliament in that, as party leader, he is *ex officio* a member of the NEC and attends its monthly meetings. Callaghan in particular found this a daunting prospect as the party outside Parliament moved to the left in the late 1970s. Traditionally, Tory leaders took a rather detached attitude to the annual conference, turning up only on the last afternoon (after the official ending of the conference) to make a valedictory speech. Heath was the first to attend the entire conference and his example has been followed since. Conference was seen as an opportunity for the mass party to declare its support for and loyalty to the parliamentary leadership, although in recent years a rather more critical mood has been observed and the leadership has come under sustained pressure, especially over Europe. Labour Prime Ministers, especially Wilson and Callaghan, were on occasions given a rough ride by conference, where attempts were made to assert the primacy of the extra-parliamentary party over the leadership. Attempts were made to bind the Parliamentary Labour Party to follow conference decisions, something both stoutly resisted. Tony Blair appears to exert a firmer control over the party at all levels than any previous Labour Leader. Whether this will continue now he has joined Macdonald, Attlee, Wilson and Callaghan in Labour's Pantheon remains to be seen.

The Prime Minister as national leader

In a constitutional monarchy the Prime Minister must walk something of a tightrope. He or she must know when to seek the limelight and when it is more proper to leave it to the titular head of state. While the Queen leads the nation's homage at the annual Service of Remembrance by laying the first wreath of poppies, the Prime Minister attends on behalf of the government. Generally, the Queen (or some other senior member of the Royal Family) takes the salute at military parades, even if the Prime Minister is also on the podium. The constitutional niceties are generally clearly understood and do not cause problems. However, Mrs Thatcher's decision to take the salute at a military parade following the end of the Falklands War at which no member of the Royal Family was present caused some comment but little controversy in those fervid times. The Prime Minister will have a number of roles of symbolic importance when he or she needs clearly to express the feelings and aspirations of the whole nation. Occasions such as royal weddings or funerals require the Prime Minister to move a Loyal Address in the Commons and it fell to John Major to announce the separation of the Prince and Princess of Wales. The Prime Minister also is expected to sum up the public's feelings when some disaster happens.

Of greater significance is the role the Prime Minister now plays in international diplomacy, a comparatively recent addition to his or her tasks. Before the Second World War it was rare for a Prime Minister to attend international gatherings and most holders of the office only went abroad for holidays. Foreign relations were left to Foreign Secretaries. Neville Chamberlain began the vogue for personal diplomacy by visiting Hitler in Germany, taking his first air journey in the process. Summit meetings were still not common in the 1950s and

1960s, and Churchill fought a long and unsuccessful battle with his Cabinet for permission to go to Moscow to try to ease East–West tensions. But in the 1970s the pressure for British Prime Ministers to attend international meetings of all kinds grew, and since then they have been expected to attend gatherings of various international bodies, most notably regular meetings of the European Union as well as the biennial Commonwealth summit.

This kind of activity now takes up an ever-increasing part of Prime Ministers' energy as Britain's role in the world has declined. To some extent this is due to the changing pattern of international relations, to the fact that Britain is a member of many more inter-governmental organisations than used to be the case. It is also a factor of modern communications; flying to New York to address the United Nations is a routine operation and need not involve absence from Britain for more than absolutely necessary. But domestic political considerations cannot be ignored. A reputation as a world statesman (or woman) is likely to enhance the Premier's standing with the electorate, something Mrs Thatcher realised and used to her advantage. However, involvement in international affairs, the chance to shine and to be the centre of attention, can also be highly attractive, especially when things at home are going sour and the electorate refuses to take the Prime Minister at his or her own evaluation. Towards the end of her career the lure of the international stage preoccupied Mrs Thatcher and led her to minimise the growing discontent at home.

The Prime Minister and policy-making

Post-war Prime Ministers have varied widely in the extent to which they have been policy-makers. They have stretched right across the spectrum, from Mrs Thatcher at one end to Sir Alec Douglas-Home at the other. Thatcher saw her role as establishing the basic policy for her government and she did not hesitate to intervene in any policy area she chose. At the other extreme, Douglas-Home had few policy interests of his own outside foreign affairs, so he left the initiative to his ministers.

Policy-making and policy-influencing take much of the time and energy of a modern Prime Minister. Various factors determine the nature of prime ministerial involvement. To some extent the personality of the Prime Minister and the view he or she takes of the nature of the job will be a factor. Someone such as Margaret Thatcher with an almost messianic determination to change Britain would be bound to have strong views across almost the whole range of government policy and to have no inhibitions about intervening in departmental responsibilities wherever she thought it necessary. Other Prime Ministers have had less ambitious aims; they have tended to be interested in certain areas of concern but to allow their ministers to take the initiative in matters in which they were not directly involved. Some Prime Ministers have chosen to restrict the areas in which they have made policy on the basis of their own specialised knowledge or previous experience. Attlee's long involvement in Indian affairs led him to take the lead in the planning for independence in 1947. The Prime Minister's perception of the importance of the issue, either in terms of the national interest or in relation to the success or otherwise of the government, will also be a factor. Jim Callaghan's intervention in the education debate (symbolised by his speech at Ruskin College) is an example of this tendency. Sometimes Prime Ministers may be forced into a policy-making role because the minister responsible proves politically unreliable; Wilson's involvement in industrial strategy was in part related to the need to keep a close check on Tony Benn. In some cases, the tendency of a minister to tread on too many toes and bring the government into disrepute may be a factor. John Major's need to rebuild the bridges broken down with such abandon by his Education Secretary John Patten is a case in point.

The economy

Policy concerning the state of the economy and Britain's place in the world are areas in which virtually all post-war Premiers have had a continuing interest. There have been exceptions; Attlee had little expertise in economics, something which showed clearly when he mishandled the 1947 crisis, and he left policy-making in this area to his Chancellors, especially Sir Stafford Cripps. Douglas-Home made no secret of his lack of competence in economic management; his famous quip about doing the sums with the aid of matchsticks, though refreshingly candid, was used with ruthless effect by Wilson, anxious to show the contrast between the modernising Labour Party led by a trained economist and what he called the accident-prone Tories, led by the bumbling fourteenth Earl of Home. 'Ironically, therefore, Home's economic limitations served only to underline that a Prime Minister could no longer avoid a significant involvement in economic policy-making.'[8]

In general, however, Prime Ministers have taken a leading role in both economic and foreign affairs. During the Suez crisis Eden was very clearly in charge of the Foreign Office. Harold Wilson gleefully took advantage of the resignation of George Brown as Foreign Secretary in 1968 to replace him with the more pliable Michael Stewart. Edward Heath took personal charge of the negotiations which led to Britain joining the European Economic Community (EEC). Heath's appointment of the inexperienced Anthony Barber to replace Iain Macleod was probably influenced by his desire to dominate economic policy-making, plus the realisation that his government lacked another figure of Macleod's stature. On the other hand, Prime Ministers on occasions have had to share the limelight with powerful colleagues. Wilson had to take George Brown on his tour of European capitals during the abortive negotiations for membership of the EEC in 1967. At other times, the political situation has made the Prime Minister dependent on a powerful colleague. After the resignation of Jim Callaghan over devaluation in 1967, Wilson had no realistic alternative to making Roy Jenkins Chancellor of the Exchequer, just as in 1993 the weakened position of John Major meant that he needed a strong man like Kenneth Clarke to replace the discredited Norman Lamont.

Prime Ministers since 1945 have varied widely in their experience of economics. Winston Churchill (arguably one of the worst finance ministers of this century), Macmillan, Callaghan and Major were all Chancellors before entering Downing Street. Harold Wilson was the only Premier to have been educated as an economist. Heath had had experience in several ministries concerned with the economy. Attlee, Eden and Douglas-Home had little economic background, while Margaret Thatcher immersed herself in the arguments about economic management during her time as Leader of the Opposition.

Prime ministerial involvement in economic management has grown throughout the post-war period, but especially since it came to be recognised that Britain's declining economic health needed the personal attention of the head of government. Attlee's lack of direction was his only major weakness. Churchill found post-war economic problems baffling and deeply resented the restrictions placed on foreign and defence policy by Britain's much reduced circumstances. The Chancellor, R. A. Butler, chaired the Cabinet Economics Committee in place of the Prime Minister, and it was he rather than Churchill who took the (rather short-lived) credit for the apparent success of the government's economic strategy. Eden, a poor delegator, clashed with both his Chancellors, Butler and Macmillan. He was inconsistent in his views about the economy and, conscious though resentful of his lack of experience and confidence in this area, left the chairmanship of the Economic Committee to successive incumbents of No. 11 Downing Street. His growing preoccupation with the Middle East led him to leave economic affairs in the hands of Harold Macmillan. This enabled Macmillan to strengthen his own position as pressure from the United States grew, itself a factor in Eden's fall.

Macmillan was the first Prime Minister to take a continuing and open interest in economic policy-making. There were several reasons for this development. The Suez crisis revealed the limitations a weak economy put on Britain's international role. As Chancellor, Macmillan was converted from a 'hawk' to a 'dove' by American pressure on sterling. In addition, Macmillan had firm views on the management of the economy. His determination to avoid a recurrence of mass unemployment led him to a commitment to economic growth even at the expense of a higher rate of inflation than the Treasury thought prudent. His dismissal of the resignation of the entire Treasury ministerial team as a 'little local difficulty' is symptomatic of this attitude. Finally, the increased coverage of politics by the media, especially television, focused attention on the Premier, who was increasingly held responsible for all aspects of government policy.

Alec Douglas-Home inherited many economic problems but sought to distance himself from them, partly because he realised his own limitations and partly because he believed his ministers should get on with their jobs. He allowed his Chancellor Reginald Maudling, criticised then and later as indolent and complacent, to chair the Economic Committee, although he claimed to talk regularly with him. Home's successor, Harold Wilson, was determined to play a leading part in economic affairs. Initially he was in a strong position. He was a trained economist, his colleagues lacked experience after thirteen years in opposition and at first he had public backing for his dynamic 'First 100 days' strategy. Wilson took a direct part in the management of the economy, especially the decision not to devalue:

> He fostered the view that the government was capable of reshaping the country's economic destiny, in which public expenditure would play a prominent part. Yet after the warm public response to his early dynamic approach Wilson was to learn that the government's capabilities were less than he had suggested and that personal involvement exposed the Prime Minister to criticism when things went wrong.[9]

Edward Heath was also committed to changing the history of Britain and initially followed a series of policies known as the 'Selsdon programme', aimed at reviving the British economy in ways that threatened the Butskellite consensus. However, the 'U-turn' ended Heath's dreams and he spent the remainder of his time in office in a desperate attempt to cope with ever-growing economic catastrophes. In office again from 1974 to his retirement in 1976, Wilson took a more relaxed view of what his government could do. He tended to let economic problems simmer and to avoid discussion in Cabinet. He knew that the seriousness of the situation had to become manifest before his colleagues would do anything to reduce the level of public expenditure, a problem he basically left for his successor to solve. Callaghan's experience showed both the strength and the weakness of a Prime Minister in terms of making economic policy. He played a central role in the sterling crisis of 1976, taking the lead in discussions with the IMF and negotiating with foreign governments in an effort to prop up the pound. He supported the Chancellor, Denis Healey, in his battles with IMF officials, Cabinet colleagues and an increasingly restive party. Yet Callaghan led his government to an ignominious defeat after the 'winter of discontent' seemed to rob him and his colleagues of the will to rule.

If Margaret Thatcher ever had doubts about the rightness of her economic policies they were closely hidden. As she saw it, her central mission was to transform the economy, to reverse the long decline and to force the British people to 'stand on their own two feet' and in the process to become 'leaner and fitter'. For much of her time she faced a majority in Cabinet which was hostile to or least sceptical of her economic policies. She outflanked the opposition within her own ranks by a series of strategies: appointing her supporters to Cabinet posts concerned with economic management, placing reliable civil servants in key posts, using sympathetic advisers such as Sir Alan Walters, often to second-guess her Treasury ministers. Her preference was for working with *ad hoc* groups, especially her version of the 'economic seminar', in order to bypass her more sceptical Cabinet colleagues as well as official Treasury advice. Above all, personal leadership and conviction was the key to her domination of

Table 5.1 *Relationships between Prime Ministers and Chancellors*

	Chancellor as political figure in own right	Chancellor lacks independent political base
Harmonious relationship	Chancellor enjoys autonomy and support from Prime Minister	Chancellor faithfully executes Prime Minister's policies
Difficult relationship	Clashes over policy, ultimate breakdown of relationship	Prime Minister lacks confidence in loyal Chancellor, dismissal likely

Source: Wyn Grant, *The Politics of Economic Policy*, Harvester Wheatsheaf, 1993, p. 69

economic policy-making during her time as Premier. In the end, however, it was the failure of economic policy – the inability to deliver low taxation, low interest rates, rising living standards for 'middle England' and quality public services – which caused the Conservative Party to dismiss her from office.

John Major played a not inconsiderable role in the economic policies of the Thatcher era, first as Chief Secretary to the Treasury and then, briefly, as Chancellor. However, he was able to disengage himself in the public mind from the errors and excesses which marked her last years in office. The Conservatives won the 1992 election largely because they were able to convince the electors that they were a new government led by a man untainted by the past. However, the débâcle of Britain's forced exit from the ERM and the sacking of Lamont dealt Major's reputation a severe blow. He appeared to have no alternative to appointing Kenneth Clarke to replace Lamont and their unity on economic management seemed to be of the 'sink or swim' variety. This draws attention to the crucial importance of the relationship between the Prime Minister and the Chancellor of the Exchequer. When this relationship breaks down, economic policy-making is damaged and the national interest may suffer long-term harm.

Table 5.1 provides a typology of relationships between Prime Ministers and Chancellors. A harmonious relationship does not mean that the two are agreed about all aspects of economic policy or that they are on friendly terms. 'It does mean that they are broadly agreed about policy objectives and mechanisms to achieve them; that they have defined their respective spheres of responsibility; and that they are prepared to support each other's authority when it is challenged in Cabinet or elsewhere.'[10] A relationship of friction means disagreements about policies, mutual mistrust and a lack of support. The end result is likely to be the resignation or dismissal of the Chancellor.

In some situations the Chancellor is a minister of independent political standing and has an effective working relationship with the Prime Minister, one based on mutual respect. The Prime Minister is prepared to allow considerable freedom of action to the Chancellor while at the same time offering support and guidance when needed. A good example was the relationship between Jim Callaghan and Denis Healey; it was particularly fruitful because Callaghan had been Chancellor and so appreciated the pressures Healey was under. In other cases, there have been Chancellors who have lacked an independent power base and who have been largely content to follow the Prime Minister's wishes. Grant instanced Derick Heathcoat Amory, appointed by Macmillan after Thorneycroft and his Treasury colleagues resigned over the level of public spending. Similarly, Sir Geoffrey Howe, Mrs Thatcher's first Chancellor, was the loyal executant of her policies; only later did his disenchantment with her grow to such a pitch that he resigned, precipitating her downfall. There have also been examples of Chancellors who have lacked both an independent position and the confidence of the Prime Minister. The unhappy and unsuccessful Selwyn Lloyd, sacked by Macmillan in 'the night of the long knives', is one such.

The final category is of an independently minded Chancellor with his own ideas about economic policy clashing with a Prime Minister with similar strengths. In his memoirs Nigel Lawson recounted his version of the events which led to his dramatic resignation in October 1989, an episode which, although it came as the culmination of an growing gulf between Thatcher and himself, was triggered by increasingly public criticisms of his economic policy by Sir Alan Walters, the Prime Minister's unofficial adviser. Lawson's often-quoted resignation letter emphasised the need for full agreement between Prime Minister and Chancellor. In her memoirs, Mrs Thatcher typically downgraded the significance of the affair; to her, it was not a matter of high principle but an excuse for Lawson to resign before the magnitude of his errors at the Treasury became apparent. In the same passage she referred to her disappointment at not being able to appoint as Chancellor Nicholas Ridley, one of the few remaining Thatcherites in her Cabinet. In a side-swipe at John Major, her eventual choice to follow Lawson, who was reluctant to move from the Foreign Office, Thatcher wrote 'I told him that we all have to accept second best occasionally. That applied to me just as much as to him. So he agreed with good grace.'[11]

Foreign policy

Foreign policy is the other area to have claimed a significant share of Prime Ministers' time and commitment. Most post-war Premiers have had direct experience in this area. Eden, Macmillan, Home, Callaghan and Major (for a very short period) were all former Foreign Secretaries and Heath had been a Foreign Office minister. Churchill's interest in foreign and imperial affairs had been a life-long preoccupation; he was probably the last Prime Minister to see this aspect of policy as pre-eminent over the needs of the economy. He regarded most domestic policy issues as 'a matter of drains'. Mrs Thatcher had had little or no ministerial involvement with the outside world but travelled widely as Leader of the Opposition. As Prime Minister she quickly achieved a major reputation on the world scene. Labour Prime Ministers have tended to have a more limited involvement in foreign affairs prior to reaching the top. Attlee had been a member of the Simon Commission on Indian government but otherwise lacked direct experience, while Wilson's acquaintance with foreign affairs was limited to the world of international trade. Blair's experience has been even more restricted.

Just as most post-war Premiers have taken a continuing and sometimes dominating interest in economic management, so have they involved themselves in foreign affairs. All have chaired the Cabinet's Foreign and Defence Committee. In some ways this is a paradox. When Britain was at the height of its importance as a Great Power Prime Ministers often left the Foreign Secretary a great deal of discretion. Yet since 1945 Prime Ministers have had a close and continuing involvement with the outside world as Britain's world role has declined in significance. This is partly because the world has become a more complex and threatening place and partly because of Britain's involvement in international bodies such as the United Nations, the North Atlantic Treaty Organisation (NATO) and the European Union.

The trend is also related to domestic political considerations. All post-war Premiers have been forced, whatever their initial inclinations, to seek to make an impact on the world scene. This has been partly because of the logic of circumstances, the desire to avoid war or to make a contribution to ending international conflict; until recently, the shadow of nuclear war was one of the factors conditioning involvement on the world scene. Attlee took over from Churchill as the Potsdam Conference oversaw the ending of the Second World War, and then took direct charge of the negotiations to bring about Indian independence. In 1950 he flew to Washington to persuade President Truman not to give in to growing clamour to use nuclear weapons in Korea. Churchill clung to office in the vain hope that his international prestige and memories of the joint struggle against Germany could persuade the Russians to come to an international summit. Wilson, while expressing public support for the American role in Vietnam, made strenuous efforts behind the scenes to end the conflict.

Length of time in office can be a factor. Experience in foreign affairs obviously can lead to greater effectiveness on the world scene. Success in the international field also has a domestic spin-off. The televised visit of President Eisenhower to Downing Street for a chat with Harold Macmillan about old times and the world situation was a curtain-raiser to the Conservatives' successful election campaign in 1959. A factor in the success of Mrs Thatcher was her reputation as an international stateswoman. Television pictures of her triumphs abroad and of her meeting other world leaders had an impact on many voters and helped to ensure her continued hold on power. Immersion in foreign policy can also be related to lack of success at home. Prime Ministers may consciously seek foreign triumphs in the hope of diverting attention from problems at home or they may bask in the plaudits of an international audience unaware of or unconcerned with matters of more pressing interest to British voters. When

Callaghan returned from an economic summit early in 1979 he gave the impression that the domestic chaos of the 'winter of discontent' was a minor matter when seen from the perspective of Guadaloupe. Although he did not *say* 'Crisis, what crisis?', he certainly gave that impression. Mrs Thatcher's growing preoccupation with foreign and European affairs led her to take her eye off the ball and ignore the growing unease on the Tory back benches which was a crucial factor in her downfall. While it may be a cliché to say 'It's the economy, stupid', domestic considerations are what voters most respond to.

In terms of foreign affairs post-war Premiers have had mixed fortunes. Eden's career was ended by the disaster of Suez, Churchill presided over the continuing transition from Empire to Commonwealth and Wilson was much more attached to the notion of Commonwealth than he was to membership of the European Community. On the other hand, some Prime Ministers are associated with triumphs on the international scene. Attlee and the withdrawal from Empire, Macmillan's 'wind of change' speech and Heath's successful negotiation of British entry to the EEC are examples, and it is likely that history will show that Mrs Thatcher played a significant role in the ending of Communism.

Since 1945 Prime Ministers have had a number of policy preoccupations in the foreign and defence fields. Attlee, Churchill and Eden all took a close interest in what used to be called Imperial affairs, but Eden's catastrophe over Suez led subsequent Premiers to realise the inevitability (and even the desirability) of the end of Empire and, with few exceptions, to delegate responsibility for colonial independence and Commonwealth relations to other ministers. Mrs Thatcher's hostility to the Commonwealth, although never articulated in public, was well known. All Prime Ministers have taken responsibility for Britain's nuclear deterrent into their own hands. Attlee took the decision to manufacture the atomic bomb in a small committee and kept the details a closely guarded secret. Although Churchill was more open with his Cabinet, he did not reveal the development of the hydrogen bomb. Macmillan undertook personal negotiations with Kennedy which led to Britain obtaining the Polaris missile. Both Wilson and Callaghan, faced with a Cabinet and party with a strong unilateralist element, kept nuclear matters in the hands of a small group of like-minded colleagues. A number of decisions were rushed through by the use of various devices; the details of the cost of the 'Cheveline' programme, an updating of Polaris, were skilfully hidden from the Cabinet. Relations with the super-powers were another preoccupation. Most post-war Premiers made strenuous efforts to maintain the 'special relationship' with the United States. Churchill was accorded the rare honour of addressing a joint session of both Houses of the US Congress, Macmillan's relations with Kennedy were warm and mutually beneficial, while those of Margaret Thatcher and Ronald Reagan can be described as a mutual admiration society. On the other hand, Eden and Heath and to some extent Major showed less interest in the connection. The fraught relations with the Soviet Union were also a preoccupation of Prime Ministers such as Churchill, and he and Macmillan vainly tried to arrange summit meetings, while Wilson and Thatcher made several visits to Moscow and other parts of the former Communist bloc.

In the same way that relations between Prime Ministers and their Chancellors fluctuated, so the connections between the head of the government and successive Foreign Secretaries have performed several roles. Attlee both liked and trusted Ernest Bevin and left him very much in charge of the Foreign Office. Eden was an automatic choice for Churchill, although the relationship was complex and somewhat destructive. Heath respected Home and had much reason to be grateful for his predecessor's loyalty and professionalism. And in his second period as Prime Minister, Wilson largely left Callaghan alone. At other times the relationship was less than cordial. Eden feared that Macmillan would seek to frustrate his aims and so quickly replaced him with the more dutiful Selwyn Lloyd, and the relationship between Wilson and Brown had both political and personal tensions which eventually led to Brown storming out of the government. The growing rift between Thatcher and Howe was a proximate cause of her downfall.

Patterns of prime ministerial involvement in policy-making

Simon James[12] pointed to the three possible roles played by Prime Ministers when intervening in a policy area. The first is as a *co-ordinator*, ensuring that the initiatives of different departments do not conflict with each other and that the issues are brought forward for discussion at the right time. The second is as an *arbitrator*, involving settling disputes on matters on which he or she has no particular view and wishes merely to reach an acceptable outcome. Third, the Prime Minister may be a *protagonist*, pushing some particular policy line about which he or she feels strongly.

There are many methods by which Prime Ministers involve themselves in policy issues. In some cases departmental ministers may take the initiative, perhaps to ensure the Premier's support should colleagues try to resist an initiative or to win resources such as money or parliamentary time. Under all Prime Ministers, getting the backing of No. 10 Downing Street has been a crucial aspect of success, although this was most marked during the time of Mrs Thatcher. In this way, Prime Ministers can inject their ideas into the policy-making process at an early stage and can often help the departmental minister concerned, immersed in detail and pressed by civil servants to satisfy their needs and concerns, to take into account wider governmental and party perspectives.

Other issues may come to the Prime Minister's attention through the Cabinet and its various committees. Clashes between ministers, such as that which led to the resignation of Heseltine and Brittan over the future of the Westland helicopter company, may require prime ministerial involvement, sometimes in things which are not initially of great significance. Parliamentary debates and Prime Minister's Question Time may provide ideas which can be taken up later;

the reactions of government backbenchers to government activities also are sources for policy initiatives. The No. 10 Policy Unit, Prime Ministers' 'kitchen cabinets', the various party research organisations and (increasingly) the work of various 'think-tanks' all provide ideas to feed into the policy-making process. Reports of enquiries of various kinds, such as Royal Commissions, also may generate initiatives which Prime Ministers may adopt (and may also claim as their own), while the media often thrust things upon prime ministerial attention. Personal contacts of many kinds are another way of providing ideas, bringing pressure and allowing Prime Ministers to indulge in initially private musings which, in the fullness of time, may result in a government initiative.

Notes

1 James Callaghan, *Time and Chance*, Collins/Fontana, 1988, p. 403.
2 G. W. Jones (ed.), *West European Prime Ministers*, Frank Cass, 1991, p. 35.
3 Bernard Donoughue, *Prime Minister. The Conduct of Policy under Harold Wilson and James Callaghan*, Cape, 1987, p. 13.
4 Donald Shell and Richard Hodder-Williams (eds), *Churchill to Major. The British Prime Ministership since 1945*, Hurst, 1995, Chapter 1.
5 Anthony King, 'The British Prime Ministership in the Age of the Career Politician', in Jones (ed.), *West European Prime Ministers*, p. 31.
6 Simon James, *British Cabinet Government*, Routledge, 1992, Chapter 4.
7 Quoted in the *Guardian*, 6 July 1995.
8 James Barber, *The Prime Minister since 1945*, Blackwell, 1991, p. 98.
9 Ibid., p. 99.
10 Wyn Grant, *The Politics of Economic Policy*, Harvester Wheatsheaf, 1993, p. 69.
11 Margaret Thatcher, *The Downing Street Years*, Harper Collins, 1993, p. 717.
12 James, *British Cabinet Government*, p. 113.

6

The Prime Minister and the wider world: relations with Parliament, the party and the electorate

This chapter examines the relations between the Prime Minister and Parliament to assess to what extent the ability of the Prime Minister to dominate Parliament is a key element in his or her success. Another aspect is the relationship between post-war Premiers and the parties they have led. The ups and downs of the interaction between Prime Ministers and the electors will also be considered.

Introduction

There is a complex and shifting relationship between the Prime Minister and Parliament, his or her party and the electorate. Success in one area leads to success in another. Electoral popularity usually leads to an increase in party support for the Prime Minister both in the country and in the Commons. The loyalty of government backbenchers is crucial to the Prime Minister's ability to dominate the Commons. This in turn is picked up by the media and relayed to the electorate, reinforcing the impression of a Premier and government in charge. Similarly, a setback in relations with one group can lead to a loss of support in other areas, with potentially disastrous results. Loss of electoral support can lead to rumblings of discontent in the party. Government backbenchers begin to fear for their seats and their careers. Their support at Prime Minister's Question Time becomes less fervent and their leader finds it harder to score points in battles with the Leader of the Opposition; mutterings in the corridors become more vocal, to the delight of journalists anxious for a story. Briefings (initially anonymous but becoming more and more public) about the possibility of a change of leader fill the press, television and radio. This further diminishes the support for the government among the voters and the demand grows for a new face in No. 10.

This process can be seen in the downfall of Margaret Thatcher. A series of policy errors in the late 1980s contributed to a sharp decline in support for the Conservative goverment, fuelled by growing public disenchantment with her style of government. Poll reverses became of such a magnitude as to lead many Conservative MPs to fear a massacre at the next election. Opinion grew at Westminster in favour of a change of leader, leading her not to contest the second round of voting.

The Prime Minister and Parliament

The relationship between the Prime Minister and Parliament has changed considerably since the end of the Second World War. This reflects wider social changes which in turn have had an impact on the political system, such as the decline of deference and the lack of trust in politicians generally. In particular, media treatment of politics and politicians has changed out of all recognition. Television has to an increasing extent created the public perception of the Prime Minister and more generally of Parliament, as demonstrated by the virtual disappearance of serious coverage of debate at Westminster even in the broadsheet papers.

In turn, there have been changes both to the composition of the Commons and to the behaviour of backbenchers. MPs are less willing to follow their leaders, more prone to rebellions in the division lobbies and infinitely more likely to make their views known to the eagerly waiting cameras and microphones on Palace Green. Prime Ministers are less able to rely on the almost unthinking loyalty of their backbenchers than was the case in the earlier post-war period, a change which came during the Heath government.

Although post-war Prime Ministers have spent a decreasing amount of time in the Commons and have contributed less and less to its proceedings, parliamentary support is still a vital aspect of their survival. An important element is the ability of Prime Ministers to create the image of a successful administration, that the government is in control. To do this they have to convince the various audiences to the parliamentary theatre: their own government colleagues and backbenchers, the party in the country, the media in all its manifestations, and above all the electors. In parliamentary terms, the most successful and dominant Prime Ministers are those who can convince the Opposition of its own impotence and irrelevance, as Harold Macmillan was able to in his duels with Hugh Gaitskell and as Mrs Thatcher succeeded in doing for much of her time in office. Various factors contribute to this dominance: the sheer authority of office, especially if achieved by winning a general election, the personality of the Prime Minister, the support he or she has in the party (both in the House and in the country), the ability of the Leader of the Opposition (especially at Prime Minister's Question Time, now almost as much a test of the Prime Minister-in-waiting as of the real incumbent), the morale of the opposition in general, the degree to which the media supports the head of government and finally the nature of electoral opinion.

At other times Prime Ministers have lost their hold on the House. This most often happens at a time when the Premier is perceived to have mishandled a crisis or a scandal. Eden was given a torrid time during the Suez crisis and on occasions completely lost his grip on the House, sometimes having to be rescued by the Speaker. Although for most of his time as Prime Minister Harold Macmillan dominated the Commons, towards the end he lost much of his dominance as he was hit by the Profumo Affair and then by gathering economic clouds; it was his misfortune to have to face Harold Wilson as Leader of the Opposition, who was a far better parliamentary performer than was his predecessor Hugh Gaitskell. Even Mrs Thatcher had her moments of danger. As she left No. 10 for the censure debate on the Westland affair, she said to one of her advisers 'I may not be Prime Minister by six o'clock tonight'. Rather more unusual is the Prime Minister who never succeeds in dominating the House. Most commentators are agreed that Alec Douglas-Home was unable to exert any real control over the House of Commons, a result of his inexperience in that forum, the demoralised state of his party and the formidable debating skills of Wilson.

Prime Ministers and Parliament since 1945: parliamentary style

Post-war Premiers have varied in their affection for the Commons as a place and for Parliament as an institution. Churchill had an almost romantic attachment to the Commons and was steeped in its history and traditions. When the Chamber was rebuilt after wartime bomb damage he refused to allow its size or shape to be altered for fear that its almost club-like atmosphere would be changed. Most post-war Premiers have paid tribute to the Commons as an institution and have testified to the influence it has had on their lives. Perhaps for this reason, few Prime Ministers have been much interested in parliamentary reform. Under Attlee there were some significant changes to the committee system and minor reforms to the Lords, including a further reduction of its powers to delay Commons' legislation. Macmillan introduced some changes to the Lords, which included the introduction of life peers and the right of hereditary peers to disclaim their titles. Richard Crossman, Leader of the House under Wilson, was responsible for further reforms of the committee system, although few of his changes became permanent. Margaret Thatcher promised changes while Leader of the Opposition and so had little choice but to allow Norman St John Stevas, her first Leader of the House, to bring in a system of departmental select committees in what has been the most important reform of Parliament since 1945. Mrs Thatcher opposed the changes but was defeated and then lost interest in the process. She resisted the televising of the Commons, ostensibly because of fears that it would adversely affect the atmosphere of the Commons and bring about a deterioration in Members' behaviour. In reality she was worried that it would bring advantages to the Labour Party, faced with an overwhelmingly hostile press. Under Major there were tinkerings with the select committee system but no really significant changes.

It is not easy to analyse the varying parliamentary styles of post-war Premiers. Attlee was terse, not using two words where one would do. Yet throughout his premiership he exercised a quiet, almost schoolmasterly authority over the House. He proved to be more than a match for Churchill. Exploiting Churchill's frequent absences from the House, he 'dealt with Churchill's criticisms one by one, with a cool, clinical dialectic which, now he had rattled Churchill and roused the House, was the ideal weapon for the occasion'.[1]

Churchill's parliamentary style was the reverse of that of Attlee and he dominated the Commons by force of personality and the magic of his language. During the war his grip on the Commons was almost unchallenged. Despite this, he remained aware of its power to unseat even the most dominant leader and paid attention to the concerns of MPs and was keenly aware of their constitutional powers. Although he easily defeated the motion of censure in July 1942, he took it very seriously and went to great pains to sooth the fears of those who were concerned at the direction the war was taking. At the same time, he expected the Commons to give him its support in the great struggle for the survival of the nation and after July 1942 was never in any kind of danger of defeat on a significant issue. Opinions differ as to his effectiveness during his administration from 1951 to 1955. Some regard him as a giant, dominating the Commons by force of personality, oratorical ability and the sheer weight of history. Others think he was something of a spent force except in set-piece debates, usually about foreign affairs. Especially after his serious illness in 1953 increasing deafness limited his effectiveness.

During his brief premiership, Anthony Eden rarely mastered the House and after Suez he was treated harshly by MPs. On a number of occasions he was so badly heckled by the Opposition that he had to be rescued by the Speaker; his own side more than once sat in embarrassed silence. Eden was not used to the uproar on the Opposition benches, being more accustomed to being listened to in polite silence. He was not physically well-equipped for the situation; his persistent ill-health was compounded by lack of sleep. His physical demeanour showed the strain; he often seemed vacant and his mouth hung open. When he returned from his convalescence in the middle of December 1956 the knives were out. In his last speech in the Commons on 20 December he denied there had been collusion with France and Israel to attack Egypt and then went on to alienate those who had opposed the landings and those who were against the cease-fire. This sealed his fate and he went three weeks later.

Harold Macmillan based his predominance over the Commons and over the political scene generally on his ability to rally the party after the traumas of Suez. For a while he towered over his contemporaries. He was witty, erudite and polished, and had oratorical skills which often reduced his opponents to impotence. Early in his time as Prime Minister he was given the nickname 'Supermac' by the left-wing cartoonist Vicki. This attempt to satirise and denigrate Macmillan backfired and came to symbolise his capacity to dominate the political scene generally and the Commons in particular. However, later things turned sour and Vicki gave him a new name, 'Mac the Knife', a reference to his dismissal of seven Cabinet ministers. Setbacks in the country were reflected in a weakened hold over the Commons, something which coincided with the growing effectiveness of Wilson, who succeeeded Gaitskell as Leader of the Opposition in February 1963.

Sir Alec Douglas-Home rarely dominated the Commons. He was unique amongst post-war Premiers in that he had most of his parliamentary experience in the Lords, having succeeded to his father's earldom in 1951 after a short time in the Commons. He did not have the full backing of his party and showed up badly against Harold Wilson as Leader of the Opposition.

Harold Wilson became a national political figure by living down his early reputation as a dull, almost bureaucratic member of the Attlee government, developing formidable skills as a parliamentary debater. As Prime Minister Wilson initially dominated the Commons. He towered above his inexperienced colleagues and outmatched both Home and Heath, particularly at Prime Minister's Question Time. However, soon after the triumphant 1966 general election Wilson's hold on the Commons and on his own party decreased sharply and he never regained his predominance. His parliamentary style during his government from 1974 to 1976 was far less dominant. This partly reflects Wilson's physical and mental exhaustion and growing disillusion with the task; it is also related to the increased confidence and assertiveness of his leading colleagues. He lost many of his parliamentary skills, the capacity to rally his supporters and to score off the Opposition. His speeches lacked fire; they got longer, sometimes trivial and tended to bore the House.

Before becoming Prime Minister Edward Heath was not regarded as a particularly effective Commons performer. In part this was due to his having been a whip for nine years, during which time he was a silent observer of the scene. He thus failed to acquire experience of making speeches and of interjecting in debates and so learning how to dominate, charm and humour Members. He rarely shone as Leader of the Opposition in his duels with Wilson. However, as Prime Minister he won grudging approval because of his thoroughness in preparing for debate, his authority and competence, although he was seldom an exciting performer.

James Callaghan had a long apprenticeship for the job of Prime Minister. He could command respect in the House, where he looked comfortable and at ease, and generally dominated his opposite number, Margaret Thatcher, whom he patronised, especially at Prime Minister's Question Time. As with other post-war Premiers he admitted to hating Question Time, fearing being caught off-guard. His avuncular manner served him well until the end, when his inability to control the situation left him open to devastating attacks from Conservative members.

Margaret Thatcher's dominance of the Commons was aided by the weakness of her opponents. Although he had built up a formidable reputation as an orator, Michael Foot was no match for the rampant Thatcher and was regularly humiliated, especially at Question Time, as was his less experienced successor Neil Kinnock. Her impact on Parliament, about which she was highly conservative, was personal rather than institutional. She was the first Premier for twenty years to recommend hereditary peerages (a practice not followed by her successor) but showed no interest in reform of the Lords. Although the large Conservative majority in the Commons voted loyally for the legislative measures of the Thatcher era, she had less control over organisational matters. She was hostile to the increases in Members' pay and the allowances paid for secretarial and research help, and resisted the election in 1983 of Bernard Wetherill as Speaker.

John Major's relationship with the Commons was mixed. As Peter Riddell pointed out:

> Mr. Major has been particularly sensitive to the mood of Parliament, in part because his rise up the ministerial ladder during the 1980s was based upon his ability to read the mood of his fellow Tory MPs. He was extremely skilful in handling MPs, understanding their personal and constituency interests. He has often been described as one of nature's whips, with his preference for conciliation rather than confrontation.[2]

The attention he paid to forging contacts with a wide range of Conservative MPs paid rich dividends during the leadership contest in autumn 1990 and again when he resigned as leader in 1995 and successfully offered himself for re-election. However, he was not a natural orator and his ability to dominate by force of personality was limited. After the unexpected election victory in 1992 his government was beset by difficulties and his party deeply split, especially over Europe. His small majority was only one of his problems. While Thatcher could largely take opinion in the Commons for granted, Major was forced to cultivate various groups of MPs, the Ulster Unionists as well as his own backbenchers. There was some increase in the assertiveness of Conservative backbenchers, a decline in the willingness to take the government at its own evaluation. However, the essential relationship between the executive and the legislature largely remained the same; party lines continued to determine the behaviour of the overwhelming mass of Members. The crucial element was unrest among Tory backbenchers rather than pressure from the Opposition or from Parliament as an institution, which was seen by ministers as something to be circumvented rather than as a body capable of obstructing the government. This can be seen in the contemptuous manner in which Sir Richard Scott's criticisms were brushed aside.

The changing pattern of relations between the Prime Minister and Parliament

The part played by Prime Ministers in the working of Parliament has changed over time. Dunleavy, Jones and O'Leary considered the roles played by Prime Ministers in the Commons between 1867 and 1987, scrutinising four prime ministerial responsibilities: answering questions, giving ministerial statements, delivering speeches and making minor interventions, such as impromptu responses to speeches. Their general conclusion was that 1940 was a dividing line; although there were variations, Prime Ministers before that date 'were often multi-faceted parliamentary performers who would, for example, both make a speech in a debate and then intervene subsequently. But in the modern period PMs have tended to attend the Commons only for a set and specific purpose, especially the effectively mandatory Prime Minister's question time.'[3] This is partly because prior to 1940 most Prime Ministers who sat in the Commons were also Leaders of the House, with responsibility for managing Commons business, making it very likely that they would have to intervene frequently in one way or another. The exception was Lloyd George who was never Leader of the House during the coalition governments he headed between 1916 and 1922. In 1940 Churchill relinquished the post of Leader and since then Prime Ministers have left the day-to-day running of both Houses to other ministers. Since that date there has been little variation among Prime Ministers in terms of answering parliamentary questions. In all other respects there have been differences which became sharper from 1976 when first Callaghan and then Thatcher became less active in the Commons. In terms of the number of parliamentary days between any type of intervention, Dunleavy, Jones and O'Leary conclude that the most active Prime Ministers in the pre-1940 period were Gladstone, Balfour and Chamberlain. In the post-1940 period Churchill, Eden and Home were active Premiers, while Thatcher and Macmillan appear as the least active. Figure 6.1 summarises prime ministerial activities in Parliament since 1867.

Whatever reasons there might be for this, it should not be seen as a sign of the decreased importance of Parliament. Although not a policy-making body, it is the place where ministers are held accountable for government policies. To a large extent political reputations are made and lost in the Commons. Success in the parliamentary arena is generally hard-won and even the most dominant performer has to strive to achieve it. Churchill rehearsed assiduously, even for his 'impromptu' interventions. Wilson always wrote his own Commons speeches (although he made use of speech-writers for other occasions).

Prime Minister's Question Time

Most Prime Ministers have found Question Time an enormous trial. Macmillan was said to have felt physically sick before his time came, Wilson deeply disliked the whole performance, Thatcher prepared in great detail for the twice-weekly event, ate very little before getting to her feet and generally dominated the process. Sarah Hogg and Jonathan Hill, both of whom worked in No. 10 under John Major, have described how he prepared for Prime Minister's Question Time. The basic routine closely followed that of Mrs Thatcher. At 9.00 a.m. on the days he had to answer in the Commons he worked through a note prepared overnight by one of his Private Secretaries, followed by the media summary given to him by the Press Secretary. All the key staff were present and all were

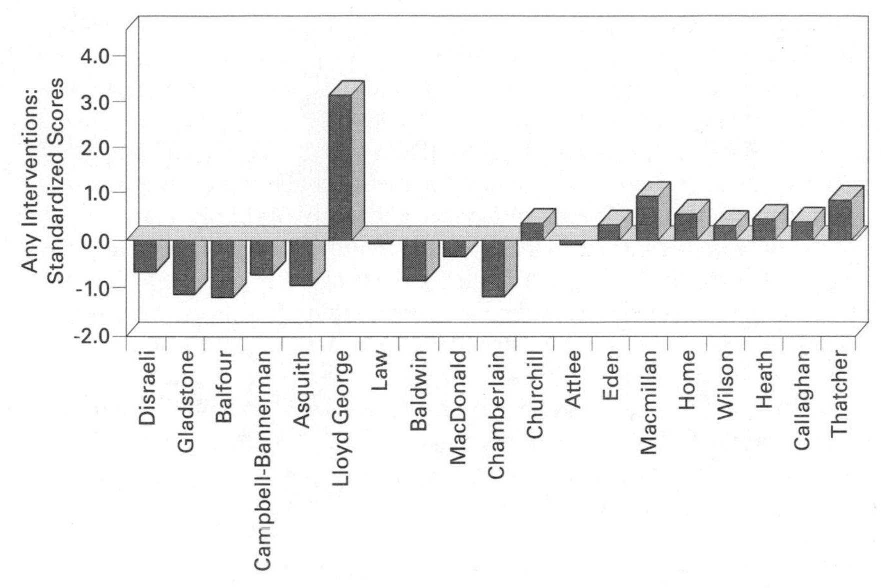

Figure 6.1 Prime ministerial parliamentary activity: parliamentary days between any activity (from Patrick Dunleavy, G. W. Jones and Brendan O'Leary, 'Prime Ministers and the Commons: Patterns of Behaviour, 1868–1987', *Public Administration*. Vol. 68, No. 1, Spring 1990, p. 127)

encouraged to participate. During the morning the various topics likely to come up were worked on by his advisers, who included both civil servants (who dealt only with government business) and his political advisers (who dealt with the more partisan aspects). Major spent his lunchtime reading the results of his advisers' work, alone except for his Private Secretary for Parliamentary Affairs and the Political Secretary. This was the opportunity, in effect, to rehearse his response, to 'get comfortable with the line he was going to take, think it through for himself'.[4] The whole team met in the hall just before 3.00 p.m. to be whisked off to the Commons in scenes familiar from countless television news broadcasts. They all gathered in his room in the Commons for any last minute queries the Prime Minister may have had and fired practice questions at him. He then entered the House, the Press Secretary went to his seat in the gallery, while the rest of his advisers crammed into the officials' box in the corner of the Chamber. There was usually a post mortem where the team were asked for their evaluation of his performance; unlike Margaret Thatcher, Major was said to prefer candour to flattery. Tony Blair has indicated that he will seek to make changes to Question Time, perhaps by changing it from a twice-weekly and highly artificial occasion into a thirty-minute question and answer session.

Although dating back to the nineteenth century, the present practice was established in 1961. Questions are taken at 3.15 p.m. for fifteen minutes on Tuesdays and Thursdays. These two short periods are the high-point of the parliamentary week, especially the exchanges between the Prime Minister and the Leader of the Opposition. The Chamber is always packed and the occasion usually attracts more public and media attention than all the rest of the week's business put together. Most questions are in the form: 'To ask the Prime Minister if he will list his official engagements for [the day of the sitting]'. This open question allows the questioner to ask a supplementary about almost any aspect of government business. Meticulous planning by the Prime Minister and his advisers usually enables him to spot the supplementary and to provide an answer which will show the incumbent and the government in as good a light as possible. Only rarely do questions really seek information; the aim of opposition MPs is to embarrass the Prime Minister, while government backbenchers usually seek to assure their leader of their undying loyalty. During Question Time the Leader of the Opposition is allowed three questions, after which other party leaders join the fray. This is in many ways a ritualised battle, with much 'righteous indignation' being generated. Sometimes the animosity is real. It is unlikely that there was a warm personal relationship between John Major and Tony Blair.

The fixing of Prime Minister's Question Time in its current form has also had the effect of giving an increased role to the Leader of the Opposition. By the end of the 1970s it had become established that it was for the leader of the main opposition party alone to question the head of the government. Michael Foot intervened at *every* Question Time, making it a twice-weekly battle. Kinnock extended the practice by asking multiple supplementaries and taking an increasing share of the time involved. Since then the Leader of the Opposition has intervened at every Question Time, unless the Prime Minister is absent, in which case the Deputy Leader of the Opposition faces the government spokesperson. Until 1995 the Leader of the House stood in for the Prime Minister, but after the reshuffle following John Major's successful re-election campaign the Deputy Prime Minister, Michael Heseltine, took questions.

The number of questions for the Prime Minister has grown enormously. Macmillan began the practice of making Question Time the centrepiece of the parliamentary week and answering practically any question. By the 1960s some 1, 200 questions were being asked each session, a figure which rose to around 2, 000 by the early 1970s. In the 1989–90 session over 13, 000 questions were put down for oral answer. Several factors have contributed to this explosion. One is the change in style of questions. In the earlier period they were specific, which meant that the Prime Minister knew what he was being asked. However, specific questions have become rare. The present system gives the widest opportunities for supplementary questions, the real point of the exercise, and also avoids the question being passed on to other ministers. In any case, Prime Ministers are reluctant to pass questions on, perhaps for fear of seeming to avoid an issue (or perhaps fearing the ability of the departmental minister concerned to deal adequately with the matter). Another is the opportunities Question Time gives to backbench MPs to gain publicity, to reassure their constituents that they are still alive and the interests they serve that they are active on their behalf.

Question Time is a trial of strength and a battle of wits. If the Prime Minister flounders or shows signs of nerves or embarrassment it will reflect badly on his or her reputation. It can also have a wider significance. It may mean that the goverment is in difficulties or has lost its sense of direction. The reaction of government backbenchers is crucial. If they are loudly supportive the Prime Minister will be seen to be in charge, but if they sit in stony silence it will demonstrate that they are unhappy and unsure of the government's grip on affairs. Although it is comparatively rare for Prime Ministers to be seriously caught on the back foot, Question Time does occasionally reveal problems for the administration. During the 1980s there was a growth in organised barracking, with the whips co-ordinating attempts by backbenchers on both sides to drown out the other side. Neil Kinnock in particular suffered from this activity, adding to his difficulties in commanding the House.

The importance of Question Time is evidenced by the enormous care the Prime Minister and his team of advisers take in their preparation, especially in trying to spot the supplementaries from friend and foe alike. The No. 10 Policy Unit, the Private Office, the Press Office and other parts of the Prime Minister's team will be involved. The detailed preparation involves much contact with departments to find out what they are doing. This involves a network of contacts between the No. 10 staff and the departments and is one of the ways in which prime ministerial control over the machinery of government has grown in recent years. The main effort will be to try to work out the likely supplementaries of opposition MPs in order to avoid the Prime Minister being caught off-guard. However, questions by government backbenchers cannot be treated lightly, especially if the MP concerned is a known malcontent (perhaps over Europe) or to have a particular bee in his or her bonnet. The practice has grown up of 'planting' friendly questions which sympathetic government backbenchers can lob at the Prime Minister. This allows the Prime Minister to be fully briefed about the matter in question, to make in effect a mini-statement. It also takes up time which might be devoted to more searching questions from the Opposition.

Statements

The fixed nature of Question Time makes this activity more than four times as common as any other type of parliamentary activity by the Prime Minister. This has changed very little over the period since the Second Reform Act, the only major exception being Lloyd George. The pattern of prime ministerial statements to Parliament is quite different, in that they have become *more* frequent and uniform since 1940. Gladstone, Disraeli and Balfour made reasonably frequent statements (on average one every thirty–forty days). Then Campbell-Bannerman and subsequent Premiers made statements around once every ninety days. The change came with the 1940s. Churchill made thirty-nine statements during the Second World War, perhaps because he was also Minister of Defence. His example was followed by all but one post-war Prime Ministers, who made statements on average between every nine and sixteen days, in the main about overseas summits, strategic defence issues, and security and intelligence service scandals. The exception was Mrs Thatcher, who made statements on only seventy-nine days in twelve years in office, reaching the lowest post-war figure of under five a session in 1985–90. Her statements were confined almost exclusively to international affairs, particularly related to the various summits (including those on Europe) which she attended.

Speeches

Generally, pre-1940 Premiers made speeches in the Commons more frequently than those of the later period, although there are exceptions. Post-war Premiers made speeches on average half as often as those of the earlier period. Over the period as a whole and as compared with post-1940 Prime Ministers, Thatcher stands out as making few speeches, around once every forty-five parliamentary days. She left it to Cabinet colleagues to make all but the most unavoidable Commons speeches. Excluding the obligatory debate on the Queen's Speech, Thatcher made only twenty-three speeches of fifteen minutes or more from 1979 to 1990, of which more than half were on foreign affairs. Whereas her three predecessors spoke primarily on domestic issues, she spoke only eleven times on the economy or on social themes.

There have been fewer changes to the rules governing speeches than for the other types of activity dealt with above. Prime Ministers speak in the debate following the annual Queen's Speech and on major items of legislation. They may also be forced to attend when the Speaker allows an emergency debate (a fairly rare occurrence) or to answer a No Confidence motion. On these occasions the Prime Minister is almost always debating with the Leader of the Opposition.

Interventions in debates

Over the whole period studied by Dunleavy *et al.*, intervening in debates was the second most frequent prime ministerial activity in Parliament. Prime Ministers responded to questions once every 2.4 days, intervened in debates every 8.3 days, while making statements or speeches only every 21 to 24 days. However, the picture is distorted by the great reluctance of Thatcher and to a lesser extent Callaghan to intervene in impromptu or unscripted debating situations. Mrs Thatcher intervened about once every hundred days during her time in office. This was a radical departure from the previous norm, especially for post-war Tory leaders. Non-Tory Premiers all made less interventions than their Tory counterparts and only Macmillan's pattern was similar to that of Thatcher.

There are several explanations for the distinctiveness of Mrs Thatcher's contributions in Parliament. First, like Lloyd George and to some extent Churchill, she strongly preferred to run the government itself rather than to appear in Parliament. Second, she became Leader of the Opposition during

Callaghan's time as Prime Minister, and she might have been influenced by his lack of activity in this area. Third, she much preferred to present herself in public only in well-scripted and carefully controlled situations. Her lack of activity in making statements or speeches, plus the effort she put into preparing for Question Time, the only unavoidable parliamentary chore, add weight to this interpretation. The fourth possibility was that she was the first woman Prime Minister, who found herself in an overwhelmingly male environment. She clearly did not find the club-like, almost public school atmosphere to her taste. She lacked the taste for the repartee which characterises the Commons and her sense of humour was not strongly developed. The infrequency of her appearances in the Commons made it hard for Opposition Leaders Foot and Kinnock to attack her except at Question Time, where she had the built-in advantage of the last word. Barber adds another possibility: 'that Thatcher avoided unrehearsed situations because the degree of bitterness in the House had risen sharply as she set out to break the post-war consensus in her crusade against socialism'.[5] Although Mrs Thatcher dominated the Commons when things were going well, she was vulnerable in times of trouble, as over Westland.

Thus debating interventions have become less frequent, especially in the post-war period. In contrast to the other types of activity surveyed, post-war Prime Ministers have behaved in highly variable ways about intervening in debates. The pressure of government business seems to keep modern Prime Ministers out of the Chamber except for Question Time and set-piece statements and speeches, which are themselves much less frequent than in the past. The attention paid by the media to presentation and image means that there is enormous pressure by party managers and spin doctors to avoid a slip or a damaging confrontation with the Leader of the Opposition. This probably means that reverting to the previous pattern is unlikely, whoever is Prime Minister.

Parliamentary management

Despite the withdrawal of Prime Ministers from the day-to-day control of the Commons, parliamentary management in its broader sense is still an essential task of the Prime Minister. The term is an imprecise one and means the Prime Minister's ability to get his or her own way and to avoid setbacks and pitfalls. It is affected by a number of considerations such as the stature of the Prime Minister, the differing party cultures (for example, the traditional deference paid to Conservative Party leaders compared to the more critical attitude to leadership taken by Labour MPs), the balance between the government and the opposition, and the way backbenchers behave. As will be discussed later, there have been major changes in the way ordinary MPs react to leadership.

The ability of the Commons to hold the government to account has declined. The Prime Minister usually has no difficulty fending off attacks by the Leader of the Opposition and is aided by the whips' practice of planting 'soft' questions on compliant government MPs. Attacks by Opposition MPs are usually brushed aside, increasingly by the device of failing to answer the question and criticism by individual Opposition MPs is rarely dangerous. The Prime Minister therefore needs to take more care to cultivate his or her own side than to placate the Opposition. He or she is aided by the natural feelings of loyalty of government backbenchers, allied to the wish of many of them for office or honours.

Parliamentary management is achieved in several ways. One is the availability of patronage in the form of posts in government, the awarding of honours such as knighthoods and peerages or appointment to positions in the gift of ministers, such as membership of quangos and other bodies. Some of these carry salaries, others are of a more honorific nature but still eagerly sought by party supporters. Prime Ministers have varied in their ability and willingness to use patronage as a way of ensuring loyalty on the benches behind them. One of Heath's failings was his unwillingness to use it, either in the form of frequent ministerial reshuffles or the awarding of knighthoods and peerages. This can be compared to Thatcher's frequent government changes, allowing the hopeful to believe their day would come, and the largesse she poured on her supporters and those discarded from her administrations.

Patronage in the form of posts in government has grown considerably since 1945, especially at middle and lower ranks. Approximately one-third of goverment MPs hold ministerial office at any one time, constituting the so-called 'payroll vote', and ensuring their loyalty in the division lobbies. In addition, many others will be aware of the need for good behaviour if they are to achieve ministerial office, although the extent to which this conditions behaviour has changed, as will be discussed below.

Prime Ministers have both formal and informal links with their backbenchers. The primary channel is the whips' office. One of the tasks performed by the whips is that of keeping the Prime Minister in touch with the views of backbenchers whilst at the same time rallying support for the government. They also advise the Prime Minister on more junior appointments to the government. The Chief Whip attends Cabinet although he or she is not a member. The Prime Minister works closely with the Leaders of both Houses who are responsible for managing government business. In the Conservative Party the Chairman, who is usually though not invariably a member of the Cabinet, also has a significant role in party management on behalf of his leader.

Backbench organisations are also significant. The attitude of the 1922 Committee to Conservative Prime Ministers is usually cordial and supportive, although relations can break down. It is the 'men in grey suits', the Executive of the 1922 Committee, who will organise the election to find a successor. In the Labour Party relations between Labour Prime Ministers and the parliamentary party have fluctuated according to the political circumstances and the personalities existing at any particular time. Attlee was generally popular and trusted by most Labour backbenchers. Wilson was initially admired but mounting difficulties led to criticism of his trustworthiness among sections of the parliamentary party. Tension between Callaghan and his enemies in the PLP related more to policy differences than to the often intense personal dislike felt for his predecessor.

Another important factor is the size of the government's majority. A large majority is likely to make the task of management easier and to ensure that legislation is passed in the form desired by ministers. However, a large majority cannot guarantee the administration against setbacks: Wilson suffered two embarrassing rebuffs by his own side in 1969, on trade union and Lords reform, and Mrs Thatcher had to withdraw a measure to liberalise Sunday trading in 1986. These examples are rare. Possession of a large majority means that it needs a substantial rebellion by government backbenchers to threaten defeat. However, it can also free backbenchers from the constraints of the whips and encourage them to vote against the government without fear of endangering the government's life. Since the time of the Heath government defeat in the Commons has been shrugged off, particularly if followed by a successful Confidence vote. This has been one of the factors altering the behaviour of backbenchers.

On the other hand, a small majority does not necessarily pose insuperable difficulties. In 1964 Wilson had a majority of only five (quickly reduced to three by a by-election defeat) but he was able to survive for eighteen months and to get his considerable legislative programme through virtually unscathed. The possibility of imminent defeat, followed by a general election at a time not of the government's choosing, concentrated the minds of Labour backbenchers and forced them to repress their suspicions about the direction of government policy. Churchill in 1951 had an overall majority of seventeen and found little difficulty in avoiding defeat and governing with few scares.

A small majority can be used as an excuse. Since 1992 John Major's majority of twenty-one was steadily whittled away and he faced constant mutterings and even rebellions from various sections of the parliamentary party, especially over Europe. Several pieces of legislation were lost, most notably a proposal to increase VAT on domestic fuel, and others, for example the planned privatisation of the Post Office, were abandoned. Ministers tended to explain their parliamentary difficulties in terms of the small majority. However, this is an oversimplification. On most issues Tory backbenchers continued to support their government, perhaps after sometimes public agonising and the extracting of concessions from ministers, as was the case following the publication of the Scott Report. The longer the party has been in power, the more disenchanted and disaffected MPs there are sitting behind the leader. Sacked ministers are resentful, while those who have given up hope of preferment have no compelling reason to profess a loyalty they no longer feel. 'As Mr Major vividly remarked in his leaked 1993 comments: "Where do you think most of this poison is coming from? From the dispossessed and the never-possessed. You can think of ex-ministers who are going around causing all sorts of trouble. We don't want another three more of the bastards out there."'[6] The difference in the situation is in the nature of party discipline, related to behavioural changes by MPs.

The threat of punitive action against MPs is not as effective as in the past. It is probable that prime ministerial threats of a dissolution when faced by rowdy and rebellious backbenchers were never very effective in restoring discipline, but since the 1960s, with a volatile electorate and no guarantee of a successful appeal to the country, Prime Ministers have risked having their bluff called. Threats are likely to have the opposite effect. The withdrawal of the whip is a sanction which has lost much of its force. John Major was forced to restore the whip to the eight Eurosceptic backbenchers because of the threat to the government's majority in the Commons; no assurances of 'good behaviour' were given by the rebels.

There have been significant changes in the relationship between leaders and led in both major parties. In an analysis of voting behaviour in the Commons throughout the post-war period, Philip Norton drew attention to a sea-change which occurred in the 1970–74 Parliament.[7] The earlier period had been characterised by strict party discipline. There were very few government defeats in the Commons; they were on matters of little substance and few backbenchers on either side voted in the other lobby. The Prime Minister could generally rely on the loyal support of his followers. Prime Ministers saw their backbenchers as 'lobby-fodder' whose only real function was to give largely unquestioning support. However, the Parliament of 1970–74 saw a marked increase in backbench dissent. There was a sharp increase in the frequency of revolts and in the number of MPs involved, and the government was defeated on a number of occasions, some of significance. Norton concludes that this was a reaction to the style of Edward Heath, although growing ideological cleavages in the party also contributed. During the 1974–79 Parliaments the trend continued. For much of the period the Labour government was in a minority and suffered many defeats. Norton's provisional findings for Parliaments since 1979 indicate that MPs continued to behave in ways more akin to those of the 1970–74 and subsequent Parliaments than to those of the pre-1970 period. Although Prime Ministers expect backbenchers to give their support, this is less likely to be forthcoming than in the pre-1970 period.

To some extent the relationship between the Prime Minister and his or her followers is a factor of the popularity of the Premier and the government with the voters. It is much more likely that the relationship will be a warm and supportive one if the Prime Minister has just won an election or is perceived to be likely to win the next one. However, a Prime Minister seen to be an electoral liability is in danger of losing the support of his or her backbenchers. The dramatic loss of support suffered by John Major and his government after the forced exit from the ERM in September 1992 was echoed in the unrest over his leadership among Tory backbenchers, a process which culminated in his dramatic resignation of the Tory leadership in 1995; his re-election was less a ringing endorsement than a recognition that no more credible alternative was on offer.

However, there are other factors at work. Party leadership and management demands that the Prime Minister should be a 'good House of Commons man', approachable and sociable. Prime Ministers have varied in the degree to which they have established informal avenues to their supporters in the Commons. Some have found it easy to mingle in the bars and tea-rooms and to use these contacts both as a way of building support and of discovering what anxieties were being expressed. It was also useful as a way of learning about possible plots against their leadership and of discovering which backbenchers should be brought into the government or consoled for disappointment by some kind of honour or award.

The significant change in the relations between Prime Minister and followers came at the time of Heath. Criticism grew among his colleagues for what increasingly was seen as aloofness and almost contempt for the mass of the parliamentary party. His parsimony with honours and his reluctance to reshuffle the government and hence bring in new faces were both held against him. He lacked the social niceties of his predecessors, failed to show any interest, real or feigned, in the lives of Tory backbenchers, their families or their needs, so that when the time came he had little in the way of regard or affection with which to fend off the criticisms of his leadership which led to his replacement by Mrs Thatcher. She initially learned from the experience of her predecessor and tried to build relationships with her supporters. She was conscious that she was elected by the parliamentary party and tried to ensure her accessibility both in the Commons and other places. In the end, though, she too lost touch with those on whom she depended. In the leadership campaign in 1990 Mrs Thatcher expressed surprise that she was asked to canvass support among her backbenchers. She became less diligent with the party as she became more preoccupied with the world and her place in it. Such a process is inevitable: 'for all Prime Ministers time and generation pose problems. The longer they stay in office, consumed with affairs of state and often drawn from an older generation than many of their followers, the more difficult it becomes for them to avoid remoteness from their backbenchers and even ministerial colleagues.'[8]

Prime Ministers and their parties

The relationship between Prime Ministers and their parties is a vital component of the political system. The Prime Minister is usually head of the majority party in Parliament; the few exceptions to this rule have been the product of war or other types of crises. The leader needs the party, but the party also needs the leader; the leader's vote-winning power is a significant and growing part of the appeal of his or her party. A Prime Minister who is perceived by the party and the public as successful and likely to win the next election will be supported and sustained by the party and to a very large degree, especially in the Conservative Party, can do what they will with the party organisation. On the other hand, a leader who offends a significant section of the party, especially at the parliamentary level, or who is perceived to be an actual or potential electoral liability, is likely to have their licence withdrawn. Again, this is more true of the Conservative Party, with its greater appetite for political power, than it is for the Labour Party. A constant danger for Prime Ministers is the tendency to forget they are party leaders and to ignore the need to manage, conciliate and sooth the feelings of the party faithful.

Parties are complex organisms which operate at a number of levels: governmental, parliamentary, central and regional and constituency. This complexity makes different types of demands on leaders and some Prime Ministers may shine at some levels and be less successful at others.

Prime Ministers and party structures

The differing party structures have affected party leaders in a variety of ways. The Conservative Party has a 'top down' structure which places considerable power in the hands of the head of the party, while the Labour Party's organisation is more complex and its ethos less inclined to invest its leader with the almost mystical aura surrounding the Tory counterpart. Despite the argument of R. T. McKenzie[9] that in practice there is little difference in the way Labour and Conservative Prime Ministers have exercised power, most critics have agreed that traditionally Labour Premiers have had a harder job with the party organisation than have their Conservative counterparts. In the case of the Conservative Party the extra-parliamentary party is organised in a hierarchical fashion which emphasises the claims of the leadership. The wide-ranging powers the Conservative leader enjoys over the party organisation, for example the power to appoint the Chairman of the party and other leading officials, the inability (and unwillingness) of the annual conference to bind the leadership in terms of policy and the tendency of party activists to see the party's success in terms of the party leader, all differentiate the Conservative Party from Labour. However, there is a heavy price to pay for this concentration. Electoral success is the condition for his or her continuance in office. Labour leaders have faced often bitter criticism from within, but the Labour Party has never forced one from office or elected a new leader until a vacancy has occurred. For a while following the fall of the Callaghan government it looked as though the left had won the battle for supremecy and had imposed a variety of checks on the leadership and on the PLP which would fundamentally alter the relationship and make the leader responsible to the extra-parliamentary party. However, Kinnock, Smith and Blair, arguing that such a change would probably ensure the unelectability of Labour, persuaded conference to reverse most of the gains the left made during the leadership of Michael Foot. Commentators from a variety of perspectives are generally agreed that Tony Blair is the most powerful leader the party has had, with a largely supportive PLP, a secure majority on the NEC and a conference which mirrors the determination of the party membership to do nothing which would imperil victory. In comparison, John Major faced a degree of opposition from his party, both inside and outside Parliament, more reminiscent of Labour leaders of the earlier period.

Until recently the differing roles played by conference was one of the features distinguishing the two parties. The Labour left, particularly during the Bennite ascendency in the early 1980s, tended to argue that conference was the final source of authority, especially in terms of policy-making. Even those in the party who disagreed with this fundamentalist argument accepted the importance of conference as a sounding-board for the views of party activists from the unions and the constituencies and as a vital part of the organisation. Conservative leaders, on the other hand, have been supported by all elements in the party in their denial that the annual conference has any power to bind them in any way; thus the Tory conference has been seen as a rally of the faithful, united in their determination to support and sustain the leadership and to work whole-heartedly to ensure the return of the Conservative Party to government. These differing views of the role and significance of conference have been reflected in the patterns of attendance by party leaders. Labour leaders have always attended annual conferences in their entirety; to fail to do so would be seen as an unacceptable slight to the mass party. Until 1965 their Tory counterparts turned up to the last afternoon (after the official ending of the conference) to deliver a rousing peroration without in any way conceding the right of conference to a position of significance. Heath broke this tradition in 1965 and since then Tory leaders have been present throughout the proceedings of conference, although still not conceding it any formal power. However, in recent years there have been significant changes in the way the party conferences have operated. In the Labour Party the leadership has gained a firm grip over the proceedings of conference, while Conservative conferences have been the scene of often bitter arguments over policy, especially concerning Europe.

Prime Ministers and their parties since 1945

Until the 1960s Conservative leaders were seen by the party faithful as remote and inaccessible figures, separated from the mass membership not just by the office they held but by a yawning social gulf. The aristocratic or upper-middle-class backgrounds of Churchill, Eden, Macmillan and Home added to the gap between leaders and led. This changed with the election of Heath, a man from a very different social background, and was accentuated by Mrs Thatcher, who took great pains to cultivate the grass roots and to speak to them in a language they could understand, uttering sentiments close to their hearts. John Major similarly tried to keep in touch with Conservative activists but was faced with deep divisions in the party and criticised by many for weak and divisive leadership.

Initially Churchill was seen by many in the Conservative Party as an opportunist who changed his party to suit his own ambitions. This taint never entirely left him; some Conservatives, especially on the right, never entirely trusted him. It was only when he became leader following Chamberlain's death that he asserted his domination over party, Parliament and the public. Churchill was given to moods of deep depression (which he referred to as his 'black dog') and at times felt that the bulk of the Conservative Party hated him. The changes in the Conservative Party, its transition to a mass popular party, owed little to Churchill's efforts, being the work mainly of Lord Woolton, David Maxwell-Fyfe and Butler. Churchill remained somewhat aloof from these party developments, as he did from the Tory establishment generally. Churchill's frequent appeals for an end to party bickering, which implied that the Tories were as much to blame as their opponents, did not help relations.

Eden was initially highly popular, both with the bulk of the parliamentary party and with party members. This was because of his reputation as a statesman, his (public) closeness to Churchill and his success in winning the 1955 election. However, this quickly turned sour as a result of the Suez fiasco and few mourned when he left No. 10. Macmillan, in contrast, was one of the great party managers of this century. He inherited a battered and deeply demoralised party which was widely expected swiftly to be driven out of office and transformed it into a self-confident organisation, sure of its right to rule. His skill as a party leader lay in holding the various groups in the party together while keeping it in touch with social change. As well as being a good communicator with his government colleagues and the parliamentary party, Macmillan was also effective in communicating with party organisers and workers in the country, and at least until the end could rely on the traditional loyalty of the rank and file, even if increasingly those at the top had doubts about his leadership. Yet Macmillan, like Churchill, had little in common with their aspirations and prejudices. Macmillan has been regarded by some commentators as the most intellectually gifted of twentieth-century Premiers and in some respects despised many of the attitudes of the increasingly middle-class Conservative Party. This gap widened after he left office, and he spent the last years of his life in increasingly public disagreement with the Conservatism of Margaret Thatcher.

As party leader, Heath was hampered from the start by the fact that the parliamentary party was divided about him. Like Mrs Thatcher, he lost the support of the parliamentary party; in addition he succeeded in alienating many Tory activists by his aloof manner which barely concealed the contempt he felt for many of the rank and file. His insensitivity to the needs of party management were shown by those he appointed as Party Chairmen. Heath was a dominant leader, as shown by his dismissal of Sir Edward du Cann. Later, du Cann's election as Chairman of the 1922 Committee was a sign of growing unrest in the party, signs which Heath failed to notice.

The same was true of Heath's relations with the parliamentary party. He felt that as Prime Minister he was entitled to command loyalty. He did not help his Chief Whip by circulating in the Smoking Room and other meeting places. In fact, when Heath did turn up he tended to do more harm than good, and one of Pym's jobs was to keep him away as much as possible. He grew more and more angry and impatient with the attempts of his friends to tell him how he was regarded by many Tory backbenchers, and appeared rude, insensitive and increasingly isolated.

Mrs Thatcher was a Prime Minister who equated party interest with the national interest. When she became leader she did not have a close knowledge of how the party machine functioned. She had been on the Conservative front bench in the Commons for most of her time as an MP and like most of her predecessors she had never held senior office in the party organisation. In contrast with Heath, Thatcher was close in her thinking and prejudices to those who attended Tory Party conferences. She made a point of attending a variety of gatherings attended by activists so that she became well informed of their views and could respond to them at the annual conference. In this way she kept in close touch with grass-roots opinion; this was a basic component of her populist style. However, as Barber pointed out, this willingness to listen and respond had its dangers. At the 1987 conference there was a groundswell of support for the demand that the poll tax be immediately introduced in England, instead of being phased in over some years, as was the original intention:

> Fired by . . . enthusiasm, the conference rose in support of 'the Big Bang', and for Thatcher, who was already inclined that way, the temptation was too great. She went with the conference tide instead of listening to the voice of caution from Cabinet colleagues like Nigel Lawson. It was a disastrous mistake.[10]

She also used conferences to gain support for her views and to isolate her enemies in the party. Meetings of the party's Central Council were used for the same purpose. It was unprecedented for a leader to mobilise support in the extra-parliamentary party as a way of consolidating his or her position within the Commons.

In her early days as leader and as Prime Minister she made efforts to keep in close touch with backbench opinion in the Commons. Guided by successive PPSs (and especially the politically astute Ian Gow) she would tour the Commons tea-rooms and invite herself to join groups of her supporters. However, as with most other post-war Prime Ministers, the increasing cares of office and length of time in office, which especially in a Prime Minister long in office tends to separate them from newer intakes of backbenchers, brought this to an end. Mrs Thatcher did not repeat Heath's meanness over honours. She gave out knighthoods to Tory MPs at the rate of six or eight per year; by the end, virtually everyone with more than ten years' service had been knighted. However, as she found, gratitude has its limits and many of those honoured by her failed to give her their support when the time came.

When Major took over, the party was in a downturn after a period of domination. The party organisation was in a muddle and there were criticisms of Thatcher's last Chairman, Kenneth Baker, especially for what was seen to have been his financial incompetence. This led to efforts by Norman Fowler to rectify the situation. Central Office was slimmed down and savings made, largely by making staff redundant. The role of the party in policy-making declined even further; ideas came largely from the No. 10 Policy Unit under Sarah Hogg, who was given responsibility for writing the 1992 election manifesto. An important role was played by Jonathan Hill, appointed as Major's Political Secretary and head of the Political Office in March 1992. His job was to act as a bridge between the Prime Minister and the party machine.

Like Mrs Thatcher, John Major used gatherings of party activists to try to bolster his position as he came under increasing criticism following the forced withdrawal from the ERM. Before the 1993 conference he faced the possibility of a challenge to his leadership:

> Major toured the country speaking to closed gatherings of the party activists trying to build his support in advance of the conference and the new session of parliament. In the event the party conference passed without any serious eruption, and so was judged a success from the leadership's point of view. But the contrast between the lofty dignity and distance preserved by Churchill, Eden or Macmillan and the sight of Major cavorting around the country courting the party faithful was striking.[11]

Only four of Labour's post-war leaders have become Prime Minister. Attlee's relations with his party can be contrasted with those of his two successors as Prime Ministers. One of his great strengths was that he was not associated with any of the various groups in the party. He became deputy leader because nearly all of those more senior to himself had been defeated in the 1931 disaster and succeeded Lansbury in 1935 because of the inability of his rivals to agree on a candidate. The same thing happened when Morrison tried to organise a challenge in 1945. Attlee was associated with no cabal in the party and was close to no one, except to Bevin, who was to prove the rock against which all plots against him foundered. Thus he had no debts to pay, no faction to favour.

For much of his time, Wilson was an outstanding leader of his party, although later the suspicion he increasingly incurred among many sections of the party sowed the seeds of distrust and disunity which came to a crisis in the late 1970s. Although initially Wilson's relations with the bulk of Labour MPs were close and he was regarded with a mixture of awe and affection, this was transformed into dislike and distrust which spread right across the spectrum of Labour Party opinion. Although many felt gratitude for his having kept the party together and winning three of the four elections it fought under his leadership, there were few regrets when he retired.

Wilson's relations with the rank and file of the party were initially close. His image of 'ordinariness', despite getting one of the best degrees in his period at Oxford, was not entirely a pose. Wilson was indefatigable in his desire to meet Labour Party activists. Throughout the time he led the party he spent part of most weekends travelling round the country speaking at party meetings. This contact gave him very real pleasure and encouraged him in his battles, real or imaginary, with London-based intellectuals and with the press, which became increasingly critical of his leadership. Later, however, his leadership became divisive and many members felt he had betrayed the party.

Jim Callaghan similarly faced opposition from the left which by the late

1970s had achieved a dominant position throughout the extra-parliamentary party. Callaghan lost patience with the NEC; he declared that attending meetings was like being in purgatory. His main aim was to keep the Labour Party together. Although distrusted by the left he did not face the personal hostility and even hatred many felt for his predecesor. Callaghan regarded the conference as a body which needed to be told the truth about Britain's perilous economic situation, even at the expense of ruffling some powerful feathers. However, although Callaghan was elected as Wilson's successor largely because it was thought by many in the party that he was uniquely qualified as a conciliator, one who could keep the party together and reconcile the unions, the task proved too great for him.

Tony Blair came to the leadership following the death of John Smith. He rapidly achieved a dominance of the party unparalleled in Labour's history. His project of modernisation included persuading the party to accept the extension of one member one vote, which in turn facilitated the abandonment of Clause Four and the acceptance of many of the assumptions of the Thatcher era such as the salience of the market and the need for reform of the welfare state. Labour's sweeping victory in the 1997 general election should make Blair's task of leading the Labour Party the most straightforward since Attlee. However, Labour has traditionally provided many pitfalls for its leader, so Blair needs to ensure that channels of communication between party and government remain open.

Prime Ministers and the voters

In the increasingly presidential style of electioneering in Britain, the Prime Minister of the day plays a part of great significance. He or she has several roles:

Calling elections

The Prime Minister decides the date of the election. Although it is a clear convention that the responsibility is the Premier's alone, close colleagues may be consulted. The ability to control the timing of the election, a luxury given to all post-war Premiers except Jim Callaghan, can be crucial. Several elections have been won because of the successful manipulation of the economy. Popular, vote-winning policies can be brought forward and unpopular ones put off until after the election, and the Prime Minister's reputation as an international statesperson can be utilised. Some post-war Premiers have made the correct decision and emerged with a strengthened majority or with a majority sufficient for another term: Eden in 1955, Macmillan in 1959, Wilson in 1966, Thatcher in 1983 and 1987 are in this category, although in most cases the euphoria did not last long as troubles swept over the governments they led.

Yet the right to choose the election does not confer an overwhelming advantage on the Prime Minister of the day. Of the fourteen elections held between 1945 and 1992 the government won eight and the opposition six. Some Prime

Ministers have mis-timed the election or been forced into one against their will. Attlee's decision in 1951 was badly mis-timed. Heath gambled in February 1974, somewhat against his inclinations, because of the energy crisis. Senior figures in the party feared that delay would result in a loss of support and so Heath was persuaded to dissolve. Most commentators are agreed that equally wrong was Callaghan's decision not to hold an election in the autumn of 1978 when the polls suggested that Labour had a chance of winning or at least of emerging as the largest single party. Callaghan's view was that the public still remembered the traumas of the IMF loan in 1976 and that more time was required for the better economic news to sink in. In the end, opinion poll evidence that the Conservatives were still ahead of Labour, although by a much reduced margin, led Callaghan to make his surprise announcement that there would be no election that autumn. On the other hand, John Major's decision to play it long and delay the election until April 1992 proved successful, partly because it allowed the Conservatives the opportunity to distance themselves from Margaret Thatcher and to convince voters that Major headed a new government.

Election campaigns

The Prime Minister plays a central part in his or her party's fight for re-election. This has a number of dimensions. Tory leaders are responsible for the party manifesto; although the writing is done by teams of advisers the final draft is issued under the personal authority of the head of the party. In the case of Labour, the manifesto is a joint responsibility of the Cabinet or Shadow Cabinet and the Home Affairs Committee of the NEC. In most cases, the views of the head of the party are paramount and what goes into the manifesto has their approval. In 1983, however, the influence of the left-wing dominated NEC was paramount in what came to be called 'the longest suicide note in history'.

The roles played by the Prime Minister in the actual campaign have varied over time and according to the situation of each election. Although campaigns have become highly professional and media-dominated, this was not true in the past. The party leaders issued a general message to the voters and departed for a national tour of speeches, with a few press interviews on the way, perhaps returning to London for the odd radio broadcast, while other senior figures in the party were left to take responsibility for the campaign. Nowadays this would be inconceivable. The demands of the media dominate the election schedules of all the party leaders. The security threats to the lives of party leaders, especially the Prime Minister and to a slightly lesser extent the Leader of the Opposition, and the need to protect them from hecklers and a potentially hostile press, mean that in general they speak only to carefully selected audiences of the party faithful. An exception to this highly professional and stage-managed organisation was John Major's decision to use an old packing case as a platform from which to address the voters of Luton in 1992. According to Hogg and Hill it had been discovered in the back of the battle bus taking Major and his entourage round the country. In what was a rather chaotic walk-about Major decided to climb on the case in order to try to combat an attempt by the Socialist Workers' Party to drown him out. 'And that is how an old packing case became the Prime Minister's secret weapon.'[12]

Prime Ministers have sometimes taken direct control over the election campaign, sometimes sidelining the party professionals. More usually, however, the Prime Minister's personal staff and the professionals from party headquarters have worked closely together, although not always in perfect harmony. Although the Conservative Party's professional organisation in Central Office has been generally more efficient, better staffed and financed than that of the Labour Party, this has not prevented friction breaking out, as in the 1987 election campaign.

Personalities in elections

To a very large extent, general elections focus on the respective personalities of the Prime Minister and the Leader of the Opposition and their claims to the confidence of the voters. This is not a new phenomenon. The battles between Gladstone and Disraeli centred on the differing personalities of the two men. In 1945 Churchill attempted to use his reputation as the great war leader to his advantage, contrasting himself with the rather colourless Attlee, whom he dubbed 'a sheep in sheep's clothing'. It was the sheep rather than the British bulldog which emerged victorious on this occasion. This approach to the voters ended when the television age focused attention on personality, style and the ability to create an image. Since 1959, the first election in which television played a significant role, attention has been increasingly focused on party leaders. They have dominated party political broadcasts; the famous 'Kinnock the Movie' of 1987 and John Major's car journey back to his Brixton roots, with his gasp of amazement that the house in which he had lived for a time was still standing, are two examples. The need to ensure that the images presented to the public are those the party leaders choose has meant the virtual demise of the public meeting with its constant risk of the leader being put on the defensive or made to look foolish by a heckler.

David Denver analysed the impact of party leaders on voting intentions. He drew attention to the changes in electioneering style since the early post-war period. The contrast between the pre-television era and the modern, highly professional and media-dominated battles of today is a reflection of the fact that campaigns are now focused on party leaders. Strenuous efforts are made to ensure that policy is presented in ways that will appeal to voters and that leaders present the right image. Mrs Thatcher was advised by a variety of media and public relations specialists who helped her choose the right clothes, the correct hair-do and to lower the pitch of her voice in order to get away from her slightly school-mistressy tone. Under Kinnock the Labour Party abandoned its red flag motif in favour of the less threatening red rose. Some commentators have claimed that these and other developments have made British elections more 'presidential', with elections largely as contents between party leaders. However, it is not clear what impact party leaders have on election results.

Most observers are agreed that there has been a change in electoral behaviour from aligned to dealigned voting. This means that party identification has declined in significance in determining people's votes. In the period of alignment the salience of the party leader in deciding how people voted was low. Party identification overrode any temporary issues regarding who the preferred party's leader was. Assessment of the party leader by voters was conditioned by the party choice of the voter; in other words, if Conservative voters approved of Macmillan as Prime Minister it was because they were Conservative voters. They did not vote Conservative because they approved of Macmillan. This is less true in the era of dealignment. 'With the erosion of the importance of long-term factors, however, we might expect an increase in the electoral impact of party leaders. The competence, personality and image of individual leaders might be regarded as akin to issues that could swing votes in the short term.'[13]

In the pre-television period the influence of party leaders on voting was minimal, partly because voters had little knowledge of or contact with political figures. This began to change in the 1960s but the impact of party leaders remained small. The television age has changed the picture. The mass media began to focus on the party leader, emphasising personality and style as much as if not more than policies. In the late 1970s opinion polls began to discover marked differences in public perceptions of which leader would make the best Prime Minister. These factors increased the likelihood that the issue of leadership would begin to affect voting intentions.

The impact of party leaders in recent elections has been mixed. In 1979, although voters preferred Callaghan to Thatcher, the Conservatives won the election. Although Callaghan was popular with voters, Mrs Thatcher was not very unpopular and so her party was preferred over Labour. The impact of personality at this election was not great. In 1983 Foot was a significant electoral handicap for Labour, although Thatcher was not an unqualified bonus for the Conservatives; less than half the voters thought her the best choice. Although in 1987 Kinnock was less unpopular than Foot had been in 1983, he still had a negative impact. In 1992 the Tories benefited from Thatcher's replacement by Major, and polls showed that the 'Kinnock factor' harmed his party. Polling evidence for the 1983, 1987 and 1992 elections can be seen in Table 6.1.

Ivor Crewe has traced the slump in Conservative fortunes after the 1992 general election. The period up to 15 September 1992, 'Black Wednesday', when Britain was forced out of the ERM,

> was the longest electoral honeymoon for a post-war British prime minister. Despite the deepening recession, Conservative support bounded back and remained remarkably buoyant up to and through the election it unexpectedly won in April 1992. John Major himself was widely liked and trusted, despite – or perhaps because of – his grey ordinariness.[14]

Table 6.1 *Best and worst person for Prime Minister, 1983–92*

1983		*1987*		*1992*	
Thatcher	+21	Thatcher	+8	Major	+30
Foot	−50	Kinnock	−13	Kinnock	−37
Steel	+33	Steel	−2	Ashdown	+5
Jenkins	−4	Owen	+7		

Notes: The figures given are the percentages saying that a leader would make the best Prime Minister minus the percentage saying that he/she would be the worst.

Source: material reproduced by kind permission of Professor Ivor Crewe

By contrast, the period after Black Wednesday

> has turned out to be the longest electoral nightmare for any post-war British premier. Conservative support has plummeted in the polls. The government was humiliated in local and Euro-elections and crushed in every by-election. Voters decided that Major was not decent and dependable but weak and useless. Conservative backbenchers and editors blamed their party's misfortunes on him and called for his head.[15]

Crewe examined two connected assumptions about a 'Major factor'. The first was that Major was the architect of the Conservatives' recovery and electoral victory, and the second was that he was primarily responsible for the slump in their fortunes. He concluded that the initial improvement was much more related to Thatcher's departure than to Major's arrival. However, once Prime Minister, Major's popularity soared, running far ahead of his government's. This was based on public approval of his leadership style; 'caring', 'concerned for the country as a whole' and 'likeable' were adjectives used about him. 'Honest John' had replaced the 'Iron Lady'. The change of leader allowed the party to present itself to voters as a new government.

During the 1992 election campaign there was a concerted campaign in the Conservative press to boost John Major and denigrate and belittle Neil Kinnock. Major was more of an asset to the Tories than Thatcher had been in 1987 and it is likely that were it not for his leadership the Conservatives would have fared worse. However, Crewe's view was that Major's personal impact on the vote was probably small. Broader factors, including the gradual shift to the right of the electorate and the Tories' reputation for economic competence, were the explanations for the result of the 1992 election.

Then began the deepest and longest electoral slump in modern British political history. Confidence in the government and the Prime Minister sank to unprecedented lows. 'Black Wednesday' destroyed Tory claims to competence in economic management and Major, who took Britain into the ERM and who insisted that withdrawal would be 'fool's gold', could not divorce himself from the fiasco. Since then the voters have taken every opportunity to demonstrate their anger with Major and his government.

Several explanations for the slump in Tory popularity have been put forward. To a considerable degree Major contributed to the position. Polls showed him to be the least respected Prime Minister since polling began. 'Incompetent', 'indecisive' and 'ineffective' were all words used about him in the period following 'Black Wednesday'. However, this judgement was more on his policies than on his personality; his political reputation declined more than his personal one and he continued to run ahead of his party. He remained liked as a man even if not as a politician. This is one reason why Tory backbenchers gave Major a substantial majority in his contest with Redwood in 1995. The voters, however, were unforgiving and time ran out for Major and his bruised and embattled party.

Notes

1 Kenneth Harris, *Attlee*, Weidenfeld and Nicholson, 1984, p. 319.
2 Peter Riddell, 'Major and Parliament', in Dennis Kavanagh and Anthony Seldon (eds), *The Major Effect*, Macmillan, 1994, p. 47.
3 Patrick Dunleavy, G. W. Jones and Brendan O'Leary, 'Prime Ministers and the Commons: Patterns of Behaviour, 1868–1987', *Public Administration*, Vol. 68, No. 1, Spring 1990, pp. 136–7.
4 Sarah Hogg and Jonathan Hill, *Too Close to Call. Power and Politics – John Major in No. 10*, Little, Brown, 1995, p. 33.
5 James Barber, *The Prime Minister since 1945*, Blackwell, 1991, p. 59.
6 Kavanagh and Seldon (eds), *The Major Effect*, p. 50.
7 Philip Norton, 'Parliamentary Behaviour since 1945', *Talking Politics*, Vol. 8, No. 2, Winter 1995/96.
8 Barber, *The Prime Minister*, pp. 61–2.
9 R. T. McKenzie, *British Political Parties*, Mercury Books, 1963, 2nd edn.
10 Barber, *The Prime Minister*, p. 50.
11 Donald Shell and Richard Hodder-Williams (eds), *Churchill to Major. The British Prime Ministership since 1945*, Hurst, 1995, p. 160.
12 Hogg and Hill, *Too Close to Call*, p. 227.
13 David Denver, *Elections and Voting Behaviour in Britain*, Harvester Wheatsheaf, 1994, 2nd edn, p. 108.
14 Ivor Crewe, 'Electoral Behaviour', in Kavanagh and Seldon (eds), *The Major Effect*, p. 99.
15 Ibid.

7

The Prime Minister and the media

This chapter examines the complex relationship between post-war Prime Ministers and the media. Attention is paid to the growing concentration on news management and the work of the so-called 'spin doctors' in recent years. What some critics have seen as the almost obsessive relationship between Margaret Thatcher and the media will be examined and the role of the Prime Minister's Press Secretary is also considered.

Introduction: the media in post-war British politics

The influence of the media has grown since 1945. Television in particular has come to dominate the coverage of political events and largely to shape and determine their conduct and content. The precise impact of the media preoccupies politicians, the media and commentators alike. Politicians and their advisers agonise over how to use the media, while newspapers and television organisations alternatively advance claims to exert great influence with voters or, perhaps for fear of a backlash, disclaim any such thing. The tabloid headline in 1992 'IT'S THE SUN WOT WON IT' may have stopped just short of a claim to omnipotence, but was a clear hint that the Conservatives should remember where power lies. Yet as things turned sour for John Major's government, the *Sun* apologised to its readers for recommending a vote for the Conservatives, a reminder that ultimate power to elect and defeat governments lies with those same people who decide which newspaper to buy. Newspapers are commercial organisations and in the end need to temper their ideological preferences to the necessity not to alienate their readers (and advertisers).

The relationship between the media and politicians is a complex and shifting one. Journalists tend to see their role as one of scrutinising politicians in an attempt to get at 'the truth', an attitude typified by some contemporary television interviewers who clearly start with the question 'why is this lying bastard lying to me?'. Increasingly they see themselves as holding the politicians accountable, as speaking for an electorate deprived of any realistic method of bringing their rulers to book. Politicians, on the other hand, fluctuate between a desperate need to court the media, to be noticed and if possible praised, and an often angry response to probing which regularly takes the form of attacking the media for misusing its power. On a number of occasions governments have put pressure on the media to present things from their point of view. Examples include threats made to the BBC at the time of Suez and the Falklands War and the use of the law to prevent the voices of IRA sympathisers being heard on the air.

There has been a long record of hostility between both Labour and Conservative Prime Ministers and the BBC. Both Churchill and Eden became convinced that the Corporation was honeycombed with Communists; Churchill instructed the party's broadcasting officer to set up a monitoring unit to check for left-wing bias, a tactic used later by Norman Tebbit when Chairman of the Conservative Party. Although initially Harold Wilson enjoyed good relations with the BBC, he later came to feel there was a conspiracy by what he saw as Tory sympathisers such as the commentators Ian Trethowan and Bob McKenzie. At the Labour Party conference of 1968 Wilson acknowledged the applause of the delegates by saying 'Thank you for what the BBC, if it's true to its normal form, will tonight describe as a hostile reaction'. This was echoed in a speech by Jonathan Aitken in March 1995 when he renamed the BBC the 'Blair Broadcasting Corporation', a speech cleared by No. 10 after Major declared himself 'very keen' on its contents. Mrs Thatcher was the Prime Minister who launched the most sustained attack on the BBC, which stood for everything she detested politically: independence, public service and a suspicion of commercialism. There was a deliberate policy designed to ensure that the BBC's reporting of the 1987 election campaign did not offend the party; according to several commentators, the ploy succeeded.

On the other hand, the relationship between politicians and the media is sometimes much more cosy. During the Thatcher era there were close links between Downing Street and the editors of most of the Tory-supporting papers. Particularly during election campaigns Conservative Central Office co-ordinated its efforts with several newspapers, especially the tabloids. News stories and editorial comments were shaped in order to maximise party advantage. Mrs Thatcher's gratitude was expressed by a liberal sprinkling of peerages for complaisant owners and knighthoods for editors and even for some journalists. However, what the press gives it can also take away. John Major initially basked in a warm glow of press approval; soon after 'Black Wednesday' this turned into almost universal vituperation. Scarcely a Tory paper had anything good to say about the Prime Minister; even the usually super-loyalist *Daily Express* became bitterly critical of Major's leadership (or rather, of what was seen as his lack of leadership).

Television has gradually become the principal method of political communication. The public service tradition of the BBC for many years ensured that political matters were treated with kid gloves. This began to change with the advent of commercial television; brash young presenters such as Christopher Chataway and Robin Day had a much less deferential attitude to politicians, even daring not to call them 'sir' and refusing to let them speak from prepared briefs and determining the questions in advance. Gradually politicians adjusted to the new medium. Whereas Attlee ignored its existence and Churchill expressed unqualified contempt for what he referred to as 'tee vee', Eden was widely praised for his televised election broadcasts during the 1955 general election campaign. During the Suez campaign he became the first Prime Minister to speak directly to the nation on television. Macmillan achieved considerable mastery over the medium and used it imaginatively and to marked political effect, as when he invited President Eisenhower for a 'fireside chat' just before he dissolved Parliament in 1959; the image of the two old friends discussing world affairs as though they were equal partners had an impact on the outcome of the election. After that, no Prime Minister could affort to ignore television.

Prime Ministers must decide how much priority to give to public communication in all its forms, and especially to the mass media. In the pre-television age, Parliament was the main arena (with the added advantage that it was the forum for party management), with the party outside Parliament also making demands on the time of the Prime Minister. The advent of mass communication has added to the Prime Minister's need to communicate. Thus the Prime Minister must be an active communicator; the alternative is either to give the impression of drift or surrendering the initiative to the opposition or to party rivals.

In the post-war period the public's perceptions of Prime Ministers have come increasingly from their visibility on the broadcasting media rather than from press reports of such things as speeches and appearances at mass rallies. Virtually all aspects of a Prime Minister's style, appearance and personality have become the stuff of television coverage of politics. The manner in which Prime Ministers have handled media relations has revealed much about their political styles. Some have (at least initially) welcomed the media while others have remained resistant. Some Prime Ministers, such as Macmillan and Wilson, were natural communicators, while others such as Douglas-Home, Heath and Major were not. Others, in particular Thatcher, learned to master the arts with the aid of others.

How Prime Ministers came over on the screen increasingly affected how people voted, leading politicians to spend more and more time and effort on managing the media. This in turn increased the importance of the Press Secretary, especially Bernard Ingham. Thus there is a strong link between presentation and substance. How a policy will be received by the media is an important factor both in the adoption of that policy and of the various alternatives which might be possible. This was as true of Attlee as of Major. Thus it is the scale of the involvement rather than the involvement itself which has changed.

Post-war Prime Ministers and the media

Prime ministerial concern with the media is not new. Lloyd George sought to influence newspaper magnates with a liberal use of honours, a tradition continued by many of his successors, especially Mrs Thatcher. Baldwin mastered the new medium of radio with ease; his fireside chats were the British equivalent of those of F. D. Roosevelt, the American President during the Depression years. His successor Neville Chamberlain came back from a meeting with Hitler proclaiming 'Peace in Our Time' and waved a piece of paper for the benefit of newsreel cameras from BBC television, then in the early stages of its development. Churchill's wartime radio broadcasts did much to inspire the British with a will to win.

The period since 1945 has seen the interaction between politics and the media grow to the point where it is sometimes difficult to see where one ends and the other begins. By the end of the 1950s, as television rapidly became the main source of political news and information, presentation became crucial and the ability to manage the media a vital aspect of political and personal success. However, manipulation is not all one way and the parties' 'spin doctors' devote their considerable talents to ensuring that their leader or their party is presented to the best possible advantage.

Post-war Prime Ministers have varied in their relationship with the media. Some have achieved considerable success, at least initially. The bulk of the press treated Churchill with awed respect. Macmillan was the first to see the potential of television and Wilson dominated the media for a while by promoting an aura of competence and modernity combined with a refreshing openness, a 'cheeky chappie' man-of-the-people ordinariness. Callaghan projected a strong, reliable image, at least until the end. Others struggled. Although Eden was initially treated with considerable deference, even before Suez the *Daily Telegraph* called for 'the smack of firm government'. Alec Douglas-Home was a poor communicator and Edward Heath was always uneasy with the media. More commonly, media relations with Prime Ministers have been a mixture, with periods of success and failure. Macmillan's transition from 'Supermac' to 'Mac the Knife' and Wilson's from a dominant force to virtually a hate figure are two examples. Although Mrs Thatcher dominated much of the media for most of her time as Prime Minister she was often uneasy, especially in probing and unscripted interviews. She preferred easy targets like BBC radio's *Jimmy Young Show* to the more expert interviewers of the *Today* programme.

Madgwick[1] pointed out that the media performance of the Prime Minister is influenced by five factors:

1 The broadcasting media have to provide non-partisan coverage of politics. In contrast with the press, radio and television make an effort to give cover-

age to the main political views – even if minority opinions are somewhat under-represented.

2 In the post-war period the press has had a heavy Conservative bias. Only one mass-circulation paper, the *Daily Mirror*, could be relied upon to support the Labour Party, especially after the disappearance of the part-TUC owned *Daily Herald*.
3 The advantages conferred by the media in terms of publicity means that Prime Ministers have had to make increasing efforts to pay attention to appearance, voice, mannerisms and so on. In particular, they have to be quick on their feet, to have the ability to react quickly to whatever is thrown at them by interviewers and journalists.
4 The government has a built-in advantage in terms of news management. Governments do things while the opposition only reacts. This provides the opportunity to project the Prime Minister as a world leader, above petty domestic considerations. But this can rebound if things go wrong or if the Prime Minister can be made to appear to be neglecting domestic considerations, fates which overwhelmed both Callaghan and Thatcher.
5 A high exposure to the media can be risky, even for Conservative politicians. 'Banana skins' can occur, as with Wilson's 'pound in your pocket' and Callaghan's 'crisis, what crisis?'. Mrs Thatcher usually managed to avoid banana skins and even when they did occur could generally rely on the Conservative newspapers to minimise or even ignore them.

Attlee's dislike of the media was genuine. He rarely read the newspapers and even more rarely gave interviews. Although he appointed Francis Williams as the government's Public Relations Manager, he took little interest in the process of news presentation let alone media management, then in its infancy. He had no interest in television and refused requests by the BBC to make an appearance. Eventually his attitude to the press and television cost votes in the 1950 and 1951 elections when he refused to project himself and his party.

Churchill was similarly cavalier in his attitude to the media. He disliked television, although he was more aware of the importance of the newspapers. Initially he abolished the post of Public Relations Adviser, saying that the place for pronouncements about policy was the House of Commons rather than to journalists. Ministers were strongly discouraged from talking to the press, which led to general dissatisfaction with the poor flow of information. There was a feeling that the government appeared rudderless. By the early months of 1952 Churchill was prevailed upon to think again, and an Adviser on Government Public Relations was appointed, leading to a resumption of the lobby system, even though Churchill adamantly refused to have a Press Office in No. 10. Churchill was never publicly interviewed on either radio or television. Suez and a more critical public opinion changed all this.

Eden had a more positive attitude to television and took a close interest in managing relations with the BBC. He met reporters from time to time and worked hard to gain newspaper support over Suez. In the 1955 election campaign the Prime Minister took a leading part in his party's party political broadcasts, taking professional advice about presentation. He appeared in television and radio broadcasts. He was very good on television, where he spoke directly to the cameras. However, soon after the election criticism grew in the normally loyal Tory papers such as the *Daily Mail* and *Daily Telegraph*. Eden was an innocent in his handling of the press. Speculation that all was not well with the government found its way into the press as the result of an interview by R. A. Butler. In December 1955 a Press Association journalist asked him, 'Mr Butler, would you say that this is the best Prime Minister we have?'. Butler answered 'Yes'. This was widely seen as a disparagement of Eden. Press criticism grew. A leading article in the *Daily Telegraph* of 3 January 1956 said: 'Most Conservatives and almost certainly some of the wiser Trade Union leaders, are waiting to feel the smack of firm government'. Randolph Churchill's column in the *Evening Standard* was full of personal venom against Eden. The Prime Minister decided to confront his critics and he issued a statement denying he was going to resign. He followed this by a speech declaring his intention to continue in office. Eden had over-reacted; he was always too sensitive to press criticism. Relations soured over Suez, especially with the BBC. Enraged by the corporation's decision to give Gaitskell the right of reply, he considered commandeering the BBC, although nothing came of it.

For much of the time, Harold Macmillan proved himself to be a master at media presentation, quickly seeing the importance of gimmicks, such as the large white fur hat he wore on his visit to Moscow in 1959. After initial hesitation the Tory press saw him as the saviour of the party and gave him unstinting support. Macmillan also used the economic and social changes of the time to his advantage, welcoming the spread of television, both as a sign of growing national prosperity and as a way of appealing to voters in their own homes. Macmillan saw the potential of the medium, which appealed to the 'actor manager' in his makeup. His first break-through as a 'performer' came in an interview with Robin Day in February 1958. Then came an impromptu interview by the American commentator Ed Murrow, in which Macmillan emerged as a favourite fireside performer. One observer thought this was the first time the public had seen the Prime Minister not as an Edwardian caricature but as a masterful and dominating statesman. The 1959 election was the first to be dominated by television. The Conservative Party had been preparing for a long time and Macmillan was fully involved in the planning. However, as with most post-war Premiers, the good relations soured. Towards the end press attacks on Macmillan took their toll. His dislike of the press grew during his premiership and never left him. He hated the personal intrusions and he kept the press lords at a distance.

Sir Alec Douglas-Home did not enjoy a honeymoon with the media of however short a duration. Much of the press was critical of the manner in which he became Prime Minister and his physical appearance on television was a significant handicap, as it proved a gift to press cartoonists and satirists in other parts of the media. Douglas-Home made little mark in relations with either television or the newspapers but was the first Prime Minister in effect to be destroyed by television. 'His performance may not really have affected voters in the close-run election as badly as his party colleagues judged, but it was their judgement that mattered, and it weighed in Home's decision to stand down as Conservative leader in 1965.'[2]

In many ways Harold Wilson stands comparison with Margaret Thatcher for the intensity of their relationships with the media. During Wilson's time and partly as the result of his efforts media management changed dramatically. Initially he was prepared to meet the media on its own ground, being more accessible to journalists than had been previous Premiers, and he used television with great success. He brought Anthony Wedgewood Benn, a former television producer, into Labour's inner circle, giving him a key role in managing public relations. An informal group of public relations and advertising men came into being and opinion polling was welcomed by Wilson. He applied their findings to his performances, especially on television. He appeared in a relaxed manner on television shows, even breakfasting with the young David Frost. However, when his policies came under attack Wilson blamed the media, especially television, which he came to see as part of a conspiracy against the Labour Party and especially against himself. Wilson's attitude to the press also changed. One of his worst political faults was an inability to let an inaccurate press report pass. He felt the need to issue an elaborate and often pedantic explanation which drew even more attention to the original story. This was similar to Margaret Thatcher's obsession with secrecy; her attempt to ban *Spycatcher* also gave the book both the 'oxygen of publicity' and greater credibility than it probably deserved. Trevor Lloyd-Hughes, Wilson's first Press Secretary, was at first supplemented by Gerald Kaufman, a party loyalist, and then replaced by another Labour loyalist, Joe Haines.

Edward Heath antagonised Fleet Street. From the start he had been written off as a failure, and this hardened his heart. His victory in 1970 convinced him that he did not need the support of the newspapers and he did not shower honours on friendly editors or even proprietors. He did have some firm friends in the press but he regarded most journalists as supporters of Labour, even if they no longer favoured Wilson. He blamed 'commentators' for his own inability to change the nation's attitudes. However, he avoided getting into conflict with the BBC, thinking it beneath the dignity of his office to get into public rows with the Corporation, however much he resented some of their programmes. At the end he suffered the fate of virtually all post-war Prime Ministers. Heath became convinced that the media were biased against him and were determined to misrepresent and undermine him and his government.

Heath disliked anything that smacked of image-building; the facts would speak for themselves. Although he had been groomed in Opposition by people from advertising, in office he discarded them. He was a much less effective television performer than his predecessor. In addition, his method of media management was different from that of Wilson. He appointed a career diplomat as Press Secretary, partly because of the importance he placed on entry to the EEC, providing him with all the information he asked for but giving no guidance on how to use it, what sort of 'spin' to apply. Heath was at his best with the correspondents of the foreign press, whom he found intelligent, well-informed and less inclined, as he saw it, to twist his words and misrepresent him. He had a low opinion of the Fleet Street lobby correspondents, which he did not bother to hide. He felt there were too many of them and that they lacked intelligence and were seeking to distort his words and actions.

There were no new developments during Wilson's second term as Prime Minister, nor were there under Callaghan, who also chose a civil servant as Press Secretary. While he proved adept at handling interviewers, he lacked Wilson's general sensitiveness to the importance of media relations as a method of political management.

Of all the post-war Prime Ministers Margaret Thatcher had the most complex and intense relationship with the mass media. To some extent she was the creation of media men such as Gordon Reece, who helped to transform her from dowdy suburban housewife into mega world stateswoman, an almost regal figure yet one who never lost the carefully crafted common touch. Her media relations had several distinctive features. She enjoyed beating interviewers at their own game and readily agreed to appear on programmes such as those for housewives and children, which previous Premiers had ignored. She preferred the radio studio to that of television. Picture opportunities were eagerly exploited. The 1982 Falklands War provided many such, both of the war itself and of the Prime Minister directing and commenting on it at home. In the 1983 election campaign they abounded, especially those showing the Prime Minister wearing different kinds of industrial hats. This aspect of her relations with the media continued for the rest of Margaret Thatcher's time in office. Sometimes the surreal aspect took over, as when she was filmed and photographed vigorously picking up the rubbish which had just been thrown down for her to collect! A development of the Thatcher years was the use of the 'sincerity machine' or Head-Up Display Unit. It was a highly sophisticated electronic autoprompt system, first used in Britain by President Reagan in his speech to the Houses of Parliament in June that year. The text of the speech was projected from two hidden television cameras onto transparent lecterns on either side of the speaker. That enabled the speaker to look at the audience while reading the speech. Major did not take to the new method, and after a systems failure at a Conservative Party conference its use was abandoned. Thatcher used patronage to reward those who supported her and applied the 'is he one of us?' test in making key appointments to bodies such as the BBC. Industrial relations law was framed with at least one eye on the interests of media moguls such as Murdoch. Media management was at its height over crisis situations such as the Falklands, both to try to win popular support and to avoid the screening of images which might have disturbed the public. Her Press Secretary, Bernard Ingham, became one of her closest advisers.

The importance of Gordon Reece in ensuring the success of Margaret Thatcher and in laying the foundations for the Conservatives' long domination of British politics cannot be over-stated. He influenced Thatcher's relationship with the media, and especially with television, from the moment she became Tory leader. Reece had spent much time working in the United States and had learned much from American politics about how to 'package' a candidate. His strategy was to soften her image and appeal to the 'target voters': Labour women, skilled workers and first-time home-buyers. He commissioned public opinion polls after each of her television broadcasts. He told her that her voice was too shrill, she was too aggressive and hectoring, and that her appearance was austere and dowdy. He taught her various techniques to practise, such as humming to lower the pitch of her voice. He advised her what clothes to wear and changed her hair-style and make-up. He developed very close ties with the editors of the Tory press, which continued to give Mrs Thatcher virtually unstinting praise until almost the end of her career. Reece also introduced the Saatchi brothers to the Conservative Party. They ran the fastest-growing advertising agency in Britain and concentrated on selling Thatcherism as though it were a product. Their campaign 'Labour isn't working' registered an impact in the opinion polls and was a significant factor in Callaghan's decision not to call an election in the autumn of 1978.

Another important figure was Christopher Lawson, who had spent time in the United States observing Reagan's techniques of political marketing and persuasion. He found that 'attitudinal surveys' among voters showed support for 'Victorian values' such as imperialism, thrift, duty and hard work. These quickly became a theme of Thatcher's speeches and persisted throughout the rest of her time as Prime Minister. Mrs Thatcher's chief speech-writer, Sir Ronald Millar, was another significant influence. He became increasingly important as she came to attach great significance to her set-piece speeches, especially those at party conferences, which received maximum television coverage. From Millar came one of the most telling phrases she ever uttered: 'U-turn if you want to, the Lady is not for turning'.

Initially Major enjoyed the support of the bulk of the press. During the 1992 general election campaign Major was endorsed by most newspapers, who compared him favourably with the Leader of the Opposition, Neil Kinnock. During the campaign, time with journalists took up much of the Prime Minister's energies. There were interviews with most of the national daily and weekend newspapers, appearances on the main political programmes on television and radio, endless phone-ins and interviews for the regional media. 'He made himself more available to the media than any previous party leader and was much more accessible than Neil Kinnock, who was kept well away from the press.'[3] Initially Major, a modest person with a genuine dislike of the personality cult which surrounded Mrs Thatcher, resisted making a party political broadcast about his rise to fame, feeling a distaste for the Kinnock version in 1987. However, he allowed himself to be persuaded into allowing John Schlesinger, director of *Midnight Cowboy*, to make the film, costing £250, 000.

However, after the 1992 election the government suffered a seemingly never-ending series of public relations disasters. The Tory press turned against Major and loudly called for his replacement before the next election. A *Sun* headline screamed 'What fools we all were', proclaiming that Major had the leadership qualities of a lemming, and apologising for the advice to vote Tory in 1992. Such attacks on a Conservative leader had not been seen since the attempt to oust Baldwin in 1930. 'Major seemed . . . to have a kind of anti-Midas touch: everything he touched turned to dross . . . No prime minister since Churchill, arguably, seemed so unaware of the need for an active communications strategy, or else so incompetent.'[4] While in Mrs Thatcher's time news management from No 10 reached a high degree of effectiveness, Major proved himself highly unsuccessful in this respect. The 'bastards' episode symbolised his ineptness, as did later examples, including the row over BSE. Though there is no necessary connection between the government's low electoral standing and press hostility to the Prime Minister, it is difficult to believe that it is wholly fortuitous.

Many reasons have been advanced for the unparalleled unpopularity of the Major government: the legacy of a succession of wrong policies, having been too long in office, the intellectual exhaustion of Conservatism, above all the inadequacy of Major's leadership. However, one reason for the Prime Minister's problems was the failure of Gus O'Donnell, Major's first Press Secretary, to be more assertive. When he returned to the Treasury (at his own request) he was replaced by a similar figure, Chris Meyer, former head of the Foreign Office news department. In January 1996 Meyer left the post to become ambassador in Bonn. He was replaced by another career civil servant, Jonathan Haslam, who had previously been Deputy Press Secretary in Downing Street. Like his predecessors he attended daily meetings on the co-ordination of government policy, chaired by Michael Heseltine, and withdrew when overtly party political matters were discussed.

Prime Ministers and the press

Although broadcasting has always been subject to a degree of public control and thus to direct political pressure, newpapers have been largely free from direct government interference. Both parties have used prime ministerial patronage to ensure support from newpaper owners and editors. In the 1960s Harold Wilson conferred several peerages on men prominent in the Mirror group of newspapers and Conservative Prime Ministers have made routine use of peerages and knighthoods. Churchill had the support of the press barons of the time, most notably Beaverbrook of the Express group. Even after press proprietorship became increasingly international and conglomerate, Conservative Prime Ministers have continued to woo them by the use of honours, reaching a peak during the premiership of Mrs Thatcher. Such partisanship has overwhelmingly favoured the Conservative Party. Labour Prime Ministers have had to deal with a hostile press while trying to ensure the support of those papers which have either favoured Labour or been prepared to be even-handed. In every general election since the war until 1997 the Conservative-supporting papers had well over half the circulation, especially after the defection of the *Sun* in 1974.

However, 'As Conservative Prime Ministers in particular know, a Conservative press is no guarantee of support for any given policy – or Prime Minister for that matter. Who needs enemies, John Major might well have thought, almost as soon as he won the 1992 election, with friends like the Conservative tabloids?'[5] Even before the Suez crisis the *Daily Telegraph* criticised Eden, the papers were undermining Macmillan by 1962, there was little support for Home, and Heath's leadership was constantly questioned by the Conservative Party's 'friends' in the press. Mrs Thatcher found she could not rely on newspaper support at the end and Major's honeymoon was of short duration.

Harold Wilson had a difficult relationship with the press. At the 1964 election he established a close relationship with most of the journalists, even those from normally hostile newspapers. At the end of the campaign journalists presented Wilson with a book as a mark of their esteem. Later, he gave parties for journalists at No. 10 and mingled easily. Unused to this novel intimacy, they expressed their gratitude and wonderment in glowing reports. The March 1966 election was the last time that he enjoyed the approval of the bulk of the press. As the papers turned against him and the government the relationship between Wilson and most journalists became intensely personal and full of venom. During 1967 a 'Wilson must go' campaign began in sections of the press, including some previously loyal to the Prime Minister. The instigator was Cecil King, Chairman of the International Publishing Company, which in effect controlled the *Daily Mirror*. King published a signed article in the *Daily Mirror*, calling on Labour MPs to get rid of Wilson. This rebounded as Labour MPs closed ranks against press criticism and the *Daily Mirror* board sacked King, although the criticism of Wilson did not stop.

In June 1969 Joe Haines became his Press Officer; he became increasingly influential in the Wilson 'kitchen cabinet'. 'There has seldom been a prime ministerial press officer, Bernard Ingham included, who got on worse with the press. Yet Wilson listened to him, which was one reason for the lobby's jealous resentment . . .'.[6] Press enmity towards Wilson grew. The press took the view that Wilson was unfit to hold high office. This affected public perceptions; Wilson became an unsuccessful Prime Minister in part because the press saw him as such, a fate which eventually befell Mrs Thatcher after a long period of press sycophancy.

For much of his time as Conservative Party leader, Edward Heath also had a troubled relationship with the press. To the immense frustration of journalists there were no leaks, no gossip and no stories of plots by his ministers. Newspapers concentrated on drawing readers' attention to his shortcomings. The poor press Heath received was a contributory factor in his removal as party leader in 1975.

Mrs Thatcher was aided by a good press which continued for most of her time in office:

> [Her] great adventure was accompanied for the most part by reliable cheerleaders ... the Thatcher era coincided with a broad retreat from the days when newspapers considered it their primary duty to make life difficult for those in power. Too much was at stake, or so some editors and proprietors seemed to believe, for anyone to interfere with the heroic task Mrs Thatcher had set herself, the regeneration of Britain.[7]

She generously rewarded her supporters in the press and proved herself to be highly skilful in media management.

Initially, John Major had a good press from the Conservative-supporting papers. Although in the 1992 campaign the Conservative newspapers were not as supportive of Major as they had been of Thatcher, in the end they all called for a Conservative victory under decent, likeable John Major. However, the honeymoon was short-lived. The tabloid's frenzied pursuit of sleaze was given free rein and the ability of John Major's personality to cope with the misdeeds of his ministers and assorted Conservative MPs became the object of much press speculation. Even Major's gamble in resigning the leadership and standing for re-election did not gain the respect of the Conservative press. The *Daily Telegraph* accused him of 'ceaseless fudge, muddle, compromise and obfuscation', while *The Times* declared there could be no escape for the Tory Party without a new leader. Rupert Murdoch's *Sun* bitterly attacked the Prime Minister: 'Major could not lead a cinema queue. He is damaged goods, a loser.'[8] The most prominent of the press proprietors – Rupert Murdoch of News International, Lord Rothermere of Associated Press and Conrad Black of the Telegraph group – turned against him; their contempt was shared by their editors and reflected in the editorials which, although read by few readers, remain highly influential with politicians and other opinion-formers. Although these proprietors still distrusted Labour, some at least took Tony Blair to their hearts, Murdoch going so far as to invite him to Australia to address News International editors from around the world.

Prime Ministers and television

Although the newspapers remain important, in the post-war world television has come to dominate the world of political communication. Political television had a slow and uncertain start. In 1949 the BBC invited the Prime Minister and the Leader of the Opposition for the first time to make television broadcasts to the nation. Both refused, Churchill partly for the reason that it would be 'intolerable' to have to consider how he would appear to the viewers. In fact, at the end of his term as Premier, Churchill agreed to a screen test, to be conducted in the strictest secrecy. He hated it, and it was not shown publicly until many years after his death. Since then, how they look on television has become a prime consideration for Prime Ministers and their advisers.

The first televised party political broadcasts came in 1951. Increasingly television took over from the radio, especially as ITV pioneered new forms of political broadcasting. Newscasters such as Christopher Chataway and Robin Day became more probing as the public came to expect to see their leaders on the television. Prime Ministers and the political system generally were increasingly forced to adapt to the requirements of the medium. Election campaigns came to be shaped by the demands of television rather than the other way around. In the 1964 election Wilson learned that in order to make most effective television use of heckling, he had to repeat the heckler's point before demolishing it so that the television microphones could pick up the exchange. 'Walkabouts' for the camera replaced nation-wide tours and the party leaders dominated television coverage of their parties' campaigns. Televised press conferences and set-piece studio interviews also became standard. The indifference and even hostility of Attlee and Churchill to television can be compared with the strenuous efforts of more recent Prime Ministers and Leaders of the Opposition to court the media.

Television has had a number of effects on the political process and on the role of the Prime Minister.

(1) Parties have had to give an increasing amount of attention to the demands of the television cameras. The nature and direction of election campaigns have come increasingly to be influenced by advertising and marketing people. A growing trend has been to use eminent people from the worlds of entertainment and advertising as advisers. Labour's 1987 election campaign was widely praised for its professionalism; Hugh Hudson, the director of *Chariots of Fire*, made a party political broadcast about Neil and Glynis Kinnock which was so popular that it was repeated later in the campaign. Mrs Thatcher made extensive use of advice from the world of advertising and the media. The change of image transformed Mrs Thatcher from suburban middle-class housewife to world stateswoman; the phrase 'power dressing' will always be associated with her time in office. After a period in which Labour under Michael Foot rejected most of these developments, the party set up a Shadow Communication Agency consisting of sympathisers from the media and advertising. Peter Mandelson emerged as the 'spin doctor' who advised Kinnock, Smith and (perhaps above all) Tony Blair.

(2) This has increased in prominence the part played by the leader of the party. In recent elections, media coverage of the party has been dominated by the party leader. In the 1992 campaign, John Major was quoted a total of 469 times on radio and television news programmes; the nearest figure on the Conservative side was Chris Patten with 95 mentions. Kinnock obtained a

figure of 452 mentions, while John Smith was his nearest rival with 91. Yet media concentration on the respective party leaders as opposed to the parties they led was not new. As early as 1964, 'campaign news was heavily concentrated upon the party leaders, and . . . the 1966 general election was particularly "presidential" in this respect.'[9]

(3) To some extent, television has affected the type of person likely to be chosen as a party leader and thus as Prime Minister. It has decreased the importance of Parliament as a training ground for Prime Ministers. In future television may be the avenue for advancement, as has been the case in some Commonwealth countries and in the United States. The 'presidentialism' of Thatcher demonstrated the importance of media domination as a way of gaining and consolidating power. Also, increasingly it has become apparent that television is affecting the type of person chosen to represent the parties, from constituency level upwards. One of the reasons why Robin Cook did not enter the race for the Labour leadership following the death of John Smith was his appearance; his rather gnome-like face was thought to be a potential vote-loser for the party, certainly in contrast to the viewer-friendly Tony Blair.

(4) Although some commentators see television as a significant factor in the 'presidentialisation' of British politics, the political parties are ambivalent about promoting their leaders as quasi-presidential figures. The tradition in Britain of party voting and the belief that elections are about electing a government rather than a Prime Minister is deeply engrained in the British political culture. British party leaders emerge over a long period and have already built up an identity, an image, in a way that is not true in the United States, where many presidential hopefuls appear out of nowhere. 'So although television may direct particular attention to the party leaders it cannot focus entirely on them, or even predominantly on their personalities rather than their policies.'[10] Too marked a concentration on the leader may only achieve a hostile reaction from voters, who may feel that discussions of policy, of what the parties may or may not do, are being ignored. Media 'hype' may come to be resented; there is some evidence that 'Kinnock the Movie' aroused a feeling that the issues were being avoided, or personality being offered as a substitute for arguments about the merits of party politics.

Prime Ministers and television since 1945: a chronological survey

The central place played by television is a commonplace of modern British politics. Table 7.1 shows the age of post-war Prime Ministers when television restarted after the war and when each took office.

The first appearance by a British Prime Minister was in September 1938 when Neville Chamberlain's return from his meeting in Munich with Hitler was televised live. Television then closed down for the duration of the war but when it reappeared it found the political climate rather frosty. Neither Attlee nor Churchill bothered to learn anything about the medium. In the 1950 and 1951

Table 7.1 *Prime Ministers and television*

Prime Minister	*Born*	*First took office*	*Age on first taking office*	*Age when television restarted (07.06.1946)*
C. R. Attlee	03.01.1883	26.07.1945	62	63
W. S. Churchill	30.11.1874	[10.05.1940]		
		26.10.1951	76	71
A. Eden	12.06.1897	06.05.1955	57	48
H. Macmillan	10.02.1894	10.01.1957	62	52
A. Douglas-Home	02.07.1903	19.10.1963	60	42
J. H. Wilson	11.03.1916	16.10.1964	48	30
E. G. Heath	09.07.1916	19.06.1970	53	29
L. J. Callaghan	27.03.1912	05.04.1976	64	34
M. H. Thatcher	13.10.1925	04.05.1979	53	20
J. Major	05.04.1943	28.11.1990	47	3
A. C. L. Blair	06.05.1953	02.05.1997	43	—

Source: adapted from Colin Seymour-Ure, *The British Press and Broadcasting since 1945*, Blackwell, 1996, p. 204, 2nd edn.

general elections all three party leaders rejected the idea that party political broadcasts should be on television as well as on radio.

However, during Churchill's time as Prime Minister television ownership began to spread beyond the prosperous middle class. He started to recognise its potential as a medium of political communication and a Conservative Party report on the new medium impressed the Prime Minister. In 1954 the Conservative conference was televised and Churchill arranged that his speech on the last day should go out on the evening news.

Eden took a very different attitude. Initially, he was a great success on television, becoming the first national leader to speak to the nation direct. He took part in his party's political broadcasts during the 1955 election campaign, taking over the last broadcast for a solo performance, a tactic never before tried. It was a great success and set a pattern for the future. Eden was the first party leader to fight a modern election campaign, giving the broadcast media preference over public meetings.

Harold Macmillan was an early television star. He always claimed to be nervous and likened it to 'going over the top' during the First World War. Initially he was not a success. His appearance was shabby, with school-masterish spectacles, an unkempt moustache and uneven teeth. Then his appearance was transformed. The glasses had disappeared, his teeth regular and gleaming, the moustache under control, with a new suit completing the image of the first political television personality. He was the first to realise that the techniques learned at the hustings over a political lifetime were no longer adequate; indeed, they could be a positive disadvantage. Macmillan realised that television was more of a conversation than a speech. He became highly skilled and always seemed relaxed.

Macmillan was a great success on television during the 1959 election campaign. He was the first Prime Minister to develop a television 'image', unflappable, urbane and dominant, an Edwardian dandy. However, Macmillan was soon to discover that mastery of television is an ephemeral advantage. By 1961 his image came to seem cynical and out of touch; he seemed like a rather faded comedian playing himself. The first BBC satirical programme, *That Was The Week That Was* found the Prime Minister an ideal target and contributed to Macmillan's transition from 'Supermac' to 'Mac the Knife' (and to the ruthless debunking of his successor, Sir Alec Douglas-Home). When Macmillan, in an effort to restore his credibility after the Profumo Affair, allowed the television cameras to film him on the grouse moors, it backfired. Voters saw a rather dreary and faded old man; the contrast between the classlessness of Labour's new leader, Harold Wilson, and the upper-class pretentions of Macmillan was marked. When he announced his resignation in October 1963, the succeeding battle for the Tory Party leadership meant that 'the customary processes of consultation' would happen under the glare of the television lights.

Alec Douglas-Home's relationship with television was a disaster. He had virtually no experience of the cameras and his appearance was markedly untelegenic. He was nervous in interviews; his tongue would dart in and out like a lizard and he frequently licked his lips. He was frequently compared to a ventriloquist's dummy. Home commented on his relations with television. 'I had an unpromising start. I asked the lady applying the powder whether she could make me look better than I did on TV. She said "No, because you have a head like a skull". I said "Doesn't everyone have a head like a skull?" She said "No", and so that was that.'[11] As far as possible, he tried to pretend that television did not exist, preferring open-air meetings during which he addressed at most a few hundred people, turning down the opportunity to talk to a mass audience. Alec Douglas-Home failed to achieve even a degree of competence let alone mastery over television. Newsreel pictures of Douglas-Home shooting on his extensive Scottish grouse moors were picked up by *TW3* and did much to characterise the final year of the long Conservative domination of British politics. The general feeling that Home was a poor television performer was a factor in his decision to resign the leadership in 1965.

Wilson had a long apprenticeship as a television performer and determined to learn how to use the medium to his and his party's advantage. He regarded television as an essential part of his and his party's fight for power. The bulk of the press was anti-Labour and Wilson believed that television could help redress the balance, allowing voters to see that he was not the ogre some at least of the Tory papers made him out to be. He wanted to build an image as a young, credible alternative Prime Minister. In this he was much helped by his secretary, Marcia Williams. She stopped him making points by raising his fist, reasoning that this might appear threatening to the television audience, and got him to hold his pipe instead. She encouraged him to rest his face on his right hand, which showed his wedding ring to the camera. Wilson took J. F. Kennedy as his model, realising the need to use short paragraphs and phrases which would be picked up by the news programmes. He discovered that BBC news and ITN would regularly carry part of his speech live, so he waited for the red light on the cameras and then produced what has come to be known as a 'sound-bite'. In this, as in many other aspects of his relations with the media, Wilson was ahead of his time.

Initially he had very close relations with the broadcasting authorities, as he did with the bulk of the press. He would go to endless trouble to get things right, to produce the best stories and the most vivid images. He adapted easily to the requirements of the small screen, taking instructions from the professionals without resentment. Michael Foley saw a link between television and the emergence of 'presidential' politics in Britain. Wilson was the first Prime Minister to give rise to a comparison between British politics and the presidential nature of the American system. In this, television played a key role. Wilson was the first British political leader to see the importance of the mass media as a crucial way of taking his case to the people and enlisting their support. Television, at least initially, helped create Wilson's populist image as a pipe-smoking man of the people, full of Yorkshire common-sense and grit.

This picture also threw into sharp relief what Labour saw as the Edwardian grouse-moors complacency of Douglas-Home and the hierarchy of the Conservative Party. Wilson planned election campaigns in terms of the needs both of the party and the broadcasting media, something which involved a centralised control which maximised the appeal of his leadership and the electability of his party.

Yet Wilson's honeymoon with television was of short duration. He quickly became convinced that the BBC was hostile and was run by people of right-wing views, the mirror image of Conservative attacks during the time of Eden and later of Mrs Thatcher. The row between Wilson and the BBC intensified after Labour's win in the 1966 election, as Wilson's obsession that the BBC was a nest of Tory supporters grew. Wilson's television appearance after the devaluation of the pound in 1967 was a public relations disaster. He seemed almost to rejoice in the decision, which had in fact been forced on a government after strenuous resistance. This foreshadowed the situation following Britain's exit from the ERM in the autumn of 1992. Neither Wilson nor Major recovered from their respective setbacks and from the insensitive ways in which they were presented almost as triumphs of government planning. Back in power in 1974 Wilson largely ignored the BBC, convinced that it was pursuing an unceasing vendetta.

The case of Edward Heath demonstrates the importance of media skills. He was chosen as Conservative leader in 1965 partly because his background and meritocratic rise would, it was hoped, modernise the party's image. However, he failed to project himself on television, coming across as stiff and uncomfortable, something which he failed to rectify until after his ousting from the Tory leadership in 1975. Once in office Heath did not use film-makers and advertising people, feeling that as Prime Minister he did not need 'packaging'. He could be very effective on television with an interviewer he respected and on a topic he felt deeply about, such as Europe. However, on domestic matters he was less convincing; he forgot the lessons he had learned about presentation, and his voice took on the stiff, wooden quality his advisers had spent so much time and trouble trying to correct. He tended to speak *at* people, rather than *to* them. By the end of his time in office his use of language had become highly technical and virtually incomprehensible, while Heath himself was too exhausted to speak clearly.

Jim Callaghan seemed comfortable with the new methods of mass communication, feeling that he had little to learn. However, his downfall came about partly because of a disastrous mishandling of television. At the height of the 'winter of discontent' Callaghan went to the Guadeloupe summit of world leaders. Satellite pictures showed Callaghan and his fellow heads of government sitting in the sun on the beach while strike-bound Britain was gripped by icy weather. Interviewed at the airport on his return, Callaghan was asked what he was going to do about the crisis. The Prime Minister replied: 'Well, that is a judgement that you are making and I promise if you look at it from outside – and perhaps you are taking a rather parochial view at the moment – I don't think that other people in the world would share the view that there is mounting crisis'. The *Sun*'s headline 'CRISIS – WHAT CRISIS?' did the government and Callaghan himself great damage in the election which followed soon after.

Margaret Thatcher's initial unease in front of the cameras never entirely left her. Despite her later mastery of the medium, she never came to terms with television set-piece interviews, declaring at the time of the 1987 election 'I hate them. I hate them. I hate them.' As Prime Minister Mrs Thatcher and her advisers quickly saw the potential of television. The techniques of the American politics, especially the mastery of television, were eagerly embraced. Saatchi and Saatchi produced the publicity campaign while Gordon Reece groomed Mrs Thatcher, ensuring the correct staging, right camera angles, lighting which would bring out her strengths, all to ensure the desired effect, whatever that might be. Her rallies increasingly resembled American presidential conventions, with lavish use of warm-up music, lasers and, above all, Union Jacks. Hecklers were excluded in favour of loyal supporters whipped up almost to a frenzy of adoration and patriotism. Thatcher learned how to trigger applause, which formed the basis of those sections of the speech which were shown on television. The mass media were used, at first to disguise her lack of experience, then to accentuate her prime ministerial qualities and finally to provide the stage on which she could act out her increasingly megalomaniac fantasies.

The Thatcher era saw some important developments in the fraught relationship between politics and the media. She often blamed the broadcasters, particularly the BBC, for broadcasting bad news or for asking awkward questions, something that politicians of all parties have emulated. There were several features to Margaret Thatcher's interview style. She learned to fight interviewers on their terms, by being even more belligerent and learning to hijack interviews by talking without pause to deny her interrogator the opportunity to get the point in. In a tight corner she often took a question as an attack, saying for example, 'You accuse me of so and so'. Until towards the end, this did not appear to have alienated the mass of the listeners or viewers. She also used television interviews to belittle members of her Cabinet, first using the technique to criticise Jim Prior over his handling of the 1980 steel strike.

During her time as Prime Minister there were fierce battles with the broadcasting authorities. As the result of episodes such as the dismissal of the BBC's Director General Alasdair Milne and the threats to the funding both of the BBC and ITV, both organisations kept their heads down and determined to do nothing to offend 'the great editor-in-chief in Downing Street'.[12] Thatcher used both private, behind-the-scenes pressure and more direct methods, such as the laws on secrecy and contempt. During the Falklands crisis there was sustained pressure on the BBC and ITV to broadcast the good news and suppress or minimise the bad; many journalists believed that this pressure was for political rather than strategic reasons. When the BBC tried to broadcast what it saw as the truth about the war (and especially when it allowed the Argentinian view to be heard) this was evidence for Thatcher and her acolytes that the 'Communists' were at it again. When the Prime Minister paid her unannounced visit to the islands soon after the conflict ended, only the BBC had a camera crew still there. Her Press Secretary Bernard Ingham threatened the Corporation with 'incalculable consequences' if it did not pool its film with ITN. The BBC capitulated to this extreme form of pressure and Ingham triumphantly reported to his Prime Minister 'I've won'. But it was not only the BBC which suffered from her attentions. In 1988 she fought the decision of Thames Television to show its documentary 'Death on the Rock'; although the programme was shown Thames later lost its franchise. Mrs Thatcher was the main force behind the broadcast ban of the voices of Irish 'extremists'. The consequences were more to make the government seem foolish than to deny 'the oxygen of publicity' to the IRA, as the Prime Minister had intended.

Yet by the end of her time in office, the public mood turned against the media hype and the triumphalism. Resoluteness and strength became pig-headed arrogance and remoteness. The stage was set for the accession of John Major, whose relations with the media were never as intense as those of his predecessor.

Although when Major became Premier he vowed that the image-makers would not take him over, they soon did. Smart suits replaced the crumpled ones he previously wore, he was fitted with new, non-reflective spectacles and his hair was tidied up. However, he adopted some kind of 'official' tone of voice, which made him seem stilted and unnatural. Bill Jones discussed the three techniques that Major used to avoid answering questions.[13] He tended to give 'wait and see' responses, offering his 'Honest John' personal qualities to inspire trust. He used 'literalisms', answering the question literally in order to sidestep the main thrust. At least in his early days, he was prepared to admit he did not know the answer to some questions. This could come over as naive and disingenuous.

Major did not show the interest in media presentation which so characterised his predecessor. In the 1992 campaign the Conservatives set out to emulate Labour's successful 1987 party political broadcast about the Kinnocks. The film director John Schlesinger was commissioned to make *The Journey*, a film about John Major's rise from humble roots in Brixton. He was successfully projected as an ordinary man made good, a son of the people. Other party political broadcasts featured him with the constantly repeated message of his reassuring niceness.

An example of the complex relationship between television and the marketing approach to politics was seen in the attempt by Conservative Party 'spin doctors' to depict the result of the 1995 leadership election as a vote of confidence in John Major. The final voting figures were 218 for Major, 89 for Redwood, 12 spoiled ballots and 10 abstentions. Argument had been rife in the media about the level of support which would be necessary for the result to be seen as a convincing vote of confidence for the Prime Minister. There was general agreement that a bare victory under the rules would not suffice; Major had to register a much higher level of support if he was to survive and to reassert his tattered credibility as leader. Several commentators speculated that if around 100 Tory MPs failed to vote for Major he would be in deep trouble. However, Major's team used a number of tactics to change the political climate, such as arguing that 200 votes for the Prime Minister was the 'psychologically important barrier'; this enabled them to portray his eventual vote as 'better than expected'. Even more important were the tactics used when the result was declared. 'The objective then was to pre-empt independent analysis of the significance of the voting figure by an immediate display of euphoria . . . The tactic employed was to swamp the broadcast media with pro-Major comments on the results.'[14] Loyal Tory MPs queued before the cameras, several armed with briefing notes supplied by Major's campaign team, to draw comparisons not just with previous contests for the party's leadership, but also with Tony Blair's win in 1994. Major's own reactions were designed to distract attention from the contests and the result by concentrating on the ministerial reshuffle which followed. This exercise in post-election news management was indispensable as a way of projecting the result as a success for Major.

News management and No. 10

Although Prime Ministers still depend on control of Parliament for their continuance in office, the mass media are increasingly important as a way of maintaining and consolidating that control. The communications aspect of the Downing Street office can be divided into several parts:

1 Prime Ministers produce news for the media by their activities and the results of their activities. For example, Wilson made sure of being in the royal box when England won the World Cup in 1966 and Thatcher's advisers made strenuous efforts to ensure that pictures of Mrs Thatcher in the Falklands shortly after the end of the war were carried by both the BBC and ITV.
2 Prime Ministers are public performers, mainly as speech-makers. Despite this, the prime ministerial press conference has not yet become standard. The tendency of Thatcher and Major to come out into Downing Street for impromptu appearances before the cameras has not become part of a system.
3 Managing the government's media relations is another aspect of the job. Attlee left most of the responsibility to his Press Secretary but subsequent Premiers have had to devote ever-increasing time and effort to media management. This has increased the role played by the Press Office and the Press Secretary.
4 News management has become an instrument by which Prime Ministers can manage their Cabinet colleagues. Ministers, immersed in the affairs of their departments, depend to a considerable extend for their knowledge of what is going on in the government on what is released through the various channels operated by the Prime Minister.

To a considerable extent, the task of news management is the responsibility of the Prime Minister's Press Secretary, whose role is crucial and is subject to many cross-pressures. Press Secretaries are generally civil servants, either permanent or temporary, and the balance between partisanship and Civil Service political neutrality is a hard one to achieve. Several Press Secretaries have strayed over the line or failed to perceive that there was a line to observe. The Press Secretary is a classic 'man-in-the-middle': between the Prime Minister and the other members of the Cabinet; between the politicians and the Civil Service; between the Prime Minister and Cabinet and the press. If a Press Secretary becomes too close to the Prime Minister there is a risk of becoming involved in Cabinet disputes and being accused of partisanship, and he or she may lose credibility with the media. On the other hand, if partisan issues are avoided, the usefulness of the Press Secretary to the Prime Minister declines and the press may discount his or her briefings.

The Press Office gradually expanded in size and significance, although as late as 1990 Bernard Ingham only had five assistants plus secretarial staff. Colin Seymour-Ure has divided the role of the Press Secretary into four parts: though the precise content of the job has varied over the years and according to the interpretation put on the task by succeeding Press Secretaries, these four tasks define the task as exactly as possible.

1 Spokesperson: At least in theory, the Press Secretary acts for the Cabinet as a whole. The letter formally appointing Francis Williams as Attlee's Press Secretary said he was to act on behalf of the government generally. Journalists are briefed singly and in groups, usually off-the-record.

2 Adviser on media relations: This means that the Press Secretary is involved with writing prime ministerial speeches unless they are purely of a party nature and with presenting government policy in its most persuasive light. He or she has an important role in helping the Prime Minister prepare for Question Time.
3 Intermediary or agent with the news media: This role involves dealing with journalists, television executives and other media figures about television and press interviews and so on.
4 Co-ordinator of government information services: The Press Secretary liaises with the information services in government departments to try to ensure that they all speak with one voice rather than presenting departmental views and possibly acting for their ministers rather than for the government as a whole.

The most famous (or to some critics, notorious) Press Secretary of all was Bernard Ingham. Thatcher's first Press Secretary, Henry James, was not a success in the post and was quickly replaced by Ingham, a former *Guardian* journalist turned civil servant who had been Press Officer to Barbara Castle and Tony Benn. A former Labour voter, he became a staunch (some would say fanatical) supporter of Mrs Thatcher. He inherited a job which had never been properly defined; its vagueness and secretiveness

> rendered it a source of potentially enormous influence. The powers were there, waiting to be picked up. Given a sufficiently ruthless, determined Prime Minister and an appropriately ambitious, domineering Press Secretary, it was a superb instrument for imposing the views of Number 10 on the media, for pre-empting debate, and for undermining dissident Ministers within the Government. Between them, Mrs Thatcher and Bernard Ingham were to use the Downing Street Press Office in a way her predecessors – even men as astute and manipulative as Neville Chamberlain and Harold Wilson – would never have dared attempt.[15]

Much of the criticism of Ingham centred on allegations that he overstepped the invisible line separating the party political from the Civil Service. As Ingham's time in the job lengthened he sought to increase his control over the whole of the government's information service, becoming in February 1989 Head of Profession for all Government Information Officers. He held weekly meetings of government information officers at No. 10. To some critics, Ingham was a malignant influence on his Prime Minister. Ingham's leaks played a leading role in her quarrels with her Cabinet colleagues. While Thatcher was defending a colleague in the Commons Ingham was putting the boot in anonymously through the 'lobby'. Lobby correspondents realised it was the 'organ grinder' not the 'monkey' whose views they were hearing. He was, in the words of John Biffen, one of the ministers softened-up by Ingham, 'the sewer not the sewage'. Many lobby journalists were offended by the system but were ordered by their bosses to continue the system which suited her and them.

Another criticism centred on Ingham's use of the lobby system to put across the views of the Prime Minister rather than those of the government as a whole. 'The lobby' consists of the political correspondents of the leading London and provincial newspapers and other media organisations who are given privileged access to the Commons and to confidential briefings by the Prime Minister's Press Secretary, ministers and others on condition that the confidentiality of their sources of information is preserved. The key figure was the Press Secretary, who orchestrated the briefings and himself spoke to the lobby twice a day, once for the evening papers and once for the morning. It was during lobby meetings that Ingham is alleged to have rubbished various ministers, including Francis Pym and John Biffen, who had incurred the wrath of Mrs Thatcher. Lobby journalists 'depend on briefings that supposedly never take place with government spokesmen who do not officially exist. In fact the Lobby is the primary conduit for the release by governments of official information. It enables the wheel of Whitehall's news machine to revolve.'[16] Such was the opprobrium which attached itself to the system during Ingham's time that since John Major became Prime Minister, the lobby has been able to source the Press Secretary's remark as coming from Downing Street. This in effect ended the unattributable briefing system.

Gus O'Donnell, Major's first Press Secretary, was prone to various public relations disasters. He had no previous experience either of journalism or of party political warfare, and the lack of control from Downing Street over various scandals and during the 'back to basics' fiasco led some commentators to conclude that the job should not be in the hands of someone who has to play by Civil Service rules of impartiality, something which O'Donnell, conscious of the poisoned chalice left him by Ingham, insisted upon. O'Donnell drew a clear line between Major's political activities and his role as leader of the government. 'Back to basics' came out of the 1993 Tory Party conference, an occasion over which O'Donnell had no influence. O'Donnell appeared uneasy when facing journalists intent on probing the government's political difficulties and his lobby briefings were thought anodyne, especially in comparison with those of his predecessor. Journalists complained about the lack of clear guidance about the direction of government policy and were unsure whether to blame that on John Major or on his Press Secretary. The dinner to mark O'Donnell's return to the Treasury at the end of his three years in Downing Street caused controversy because only ten journalists were invited, mainly broadcasters and political editors from the quality dailies. At the dinner Major was alleged to have threatened to 'f****** crucify' Cabinet right-wingers; this leaked, much to the Prime Minister's anger and embarrassment. O'Donnell was much criticised for allowing Major to have heart-to-heart talks with journalists, when he was particularly prone to outbursts of fury.

O'Donnell's successor, Chris Meyer, also had a Civil Service background. Although he did not stay in Downing Street for a long period, he seems to have had a more successful time than his predecessor. Although lobby briefings remained unattributable during his time in the post, journalists were allowed to use direct quotations and ascribe them to Downing Street. He was able to prevent Major from making the kind of outburst which had previously proved so damaging. However, the difficulties implicit in being a civil servant in an intensely political job have not been solved. Tony Blair appointed the former journalist Alastair Campbell as his Press Secretary.

Other parts of the No. 10 machine are also involved in communication. Most important is the Private Office, whose head, the Principal Private Secretary, is bound to become involved in broad issues of strategy and its communication. The Political Office, staffed by party officials not civil servants, helps prepare political speeches and liaises with party headquarters. The Policy Unit is also involved in public relations matters. Thus, important as the Press Secretary is, the network of communications goes much further, involving the party organisation and a myriad of contacts with the mass media. The part played by No. 10 in advising and assisting the Prime Minister and the other sources of prime ministerial support is the subject of the next chapter.

Notes

1 Peter Madgwick, *British Government: The Central Executive Territory*, Philip Allan, 1991, pp. 178ff.
2 Donald Shell and Richard Hodder-Williams (eds), *Churchill to Major. The British Prime Ministership since 1945*, Hurst, 1995, p. 191.
3 Sarah Hogg and Jonathan Hill, *Too Close to Call. Power and Politics – John Major in No. 10*, Little, Brown, 1995, p. 232.
4 Shell and Hodder-Williams, *Churchill to Major*, p. 194.
5 Colin Seymour-Ure, 'The Media in Postwar British Politics', *Parliamentary Affairs*, Vol. 47, No. 4, October 1994, p. 541.
6 Ben Pimlott, *Harold Wilson*, Harper Collins, 1992, p. 622.
7 Hugo Young, *One of Us*, Macmillan, 1991, p. 510.
8 Quoted in Andrew Neil, 'Blair's Huge New Asset: A Defecting Tory Press', *Sunday Times*, 9 July 1995.
9 Barrie Axford, 'Leaders, Elections and Television', *Politics Review*, Vol. 1, No. 3, February 1992, p. 19.
10 Ibid., p. 20.
11 Quoted in the *Guardian*, 10 October 1995.
12 Ian Gilmour, *Dancing with Dogma. Britain under Thatcherism*, Simon and Schuster, 1992, p. 211.
13 Bill Jones, 'The Pitiless Probing Eye: Politicians and the Broadcast Political Interview', *Parliamentary Affairs*, Vol. 46, No. 1, January 1993, pp. 84–5.
14 Keith Alderman, 'The Conservative Party Leadership Election of 1995', *Parliamentary Affairs*, Vol. 49, No. 2, April 1996, p. 327.
15 Robert Harris, *Good and Faithful Servant. The Unauthorized Biography of Bernard Ingham*, Faber, 1991, p. 82.
16 Michael Cockerell, Peter Hennessy and David Walker, *Sources Close to the Prime Minister*, Macmillan, 1985, p. 10.

8

Sources of advice to the Prime Minister

This chapter considers the various sources of advice and support, such as the Civil Service, special advisers and various types of 'think-tanks', available to the Prime Minister. The role and function of the Prime Minister's Office and of other government bodies will be examined. The argument about whether a Prime Minister's Department should be created concludes this chapter.

Introduction

According to Bernard Donoughue four factors determine the Prime Minister's impact on policy:

1 The personal factor, his or her temperament, background and personal style.
2 The political factor, the Prime Minister's power and standing in relation to fellow Cabinet Ministers.
3 The administrative factor, the scale and competence of the advisory services available to the Premier.
4 The opportunity of events, the big issues which allow the Prime Minister to take the limelight.

The British system is marked by continual inter-departmental warfare in which the various protagonists need a good supply of facts, figures and arguments. Thus the quality of the advice is of central importance because government is not a question of the Prime Minister simply issuing instructions.

The range of advice available to the Prime Minister has expanded since 1945. The Cabinet Office has grown in size and specialisation, while the Cabinet Secretary has evolved, in effect, into the Prime Minister's chief adviser. The Prime Minister's Office in Downing Street now contains around one hundred mainly junior staff and is divided into four sections to reflect the various aspects of the Premier's role. Special advisers from a variety of backgrounds, both official and non-official, are important and their employment has increased since Attlee's time, though the extent to which Prime Ministers use them varies. Some Prime Ministers surround themselves with what can be described as 'kitchen cabinets', small and shifting groups of advisers (official and unofficial), personal staff, cronies, hangers-on and even family members. Of considerable significance as a source of advice and a fount of policy during the Conservatives' predominance of the 1980s and 1990s were the various right-wing 'think-tanks' such as the Adam Smith Institute and the Centre for Policy Studies. Yet these are basically additions to and expansions of the system which existed before the Second World War. Despite the increase in the centrality of the Prime Minister and the growth in his or her power, nothing like a Prime Minister's Department has appeared.

The advice and assistance available to the Prime Minister has not only grown but has become more specialised. Both Wilson and Heath developed what Peter Madgwick has referred to as the 'Downing Street complex' as part of a whole range of institutional reforms, which for Heath consisted of the creation of giant government departments, a new system of policy analysis and the creation of the Central Policy Review Staff, and for Wilson the establishment of the No. 10 Policy Unit. Both Wilson and Heath were former civil servants and both felt comfortable in the company of Whitehall mandarins; this was particularly true of Heath, who relied increasingly on his top civil servants, particularly Sir William Amstrong, then Head of the Civil Service, for advice and information. Heath was one of the most managerially-minded Prime Ministers of the twentieth century and to a large extent approached the problems of government through institutional reform, often tending to ignore the human dimension and the need to woo and conciliate those around him. Margaret Thatcher was more of a 'people-centred' Prime Minister, who emphasised the 'is he one of us?' approach, while Harold Wilson oscillated between the two models. Paradoxically, Heath was accused by many critics, both at the time and subsequently, of having been too reliant on advisers. Armstrong was dubbed the 'Deputy Prime Minister' and criticised for becoming too close to his Prime Minister and of compromising the political neutrality of the Civil Service.

Mrs Thatcher had a curiously ambivalent attitude to Civil Service advice. She deeply distrusted the Civil Service as an institution, suspecting that officials wished to 'educate' ministers to abandon radical proposals and of being wedded to compromise and to a 'do-nothing' attitude, which she saw as having contributed to a generation of Butskellite drift and decline. She began a process of Civil Service reform, one of the aims of which was to ween it away from its emphasis on advice-giving to ministers towards a greater concentration on managerialism and on 'value for money' attitudes. Yet she valued commitment, zeal and what some critics have seen as the inevitable outcome of the 'one of us' test, namely blind conviction about where she was leading her government and the country. Senior civil servants who did not meet the test were given 'early retirement'. Yet other civil servants (who *did* meet the test) were favoured by the

Prime Minister in various ways. Some were given promotion over the heads of more senior men while others, such as Bernard Ingham her Press Secretary and Charles Powell her adviser on foreign affairs, formed part of what came to be seen as her 'court'. The more prominent of the two seemed to be Bernard Ingham, yet Powell's role should not be underestimated, especially in policy towards Europe; his advice helped the Prime Minister towards solutions she favoured and with which he was in sympathy. Both men were accused of having been 'politicised' by their closeness to Thatcher and both chose to leave government service following her resignation in November 1990.

Thatcher was highly eclectic in the sources of advice she used, depending on the circumstances. In terms of presentation, both of government policy and of herself, she relied on help from a wide variety of figures from the media, advertising and show business. People from a range of 'think-tanks', academics such as the economist Sir Alan Walters and many others joined religious leaders such as the Chief Rabbi, Lord Jacobovits, in giving advice to the Prime Minister. The degree to which she relied on outsiders was illustrated by the episode which led to the resignation of the Chancellor, Nigel Lawson, as the result, in part, of her unwillingness to dispense with Walter's help. Although Thatcher stated firmly 'advisers are there to advise, ministers are there to decide', this was clearly an over-simplification; other ministers in her government complained that her advisers frequently second-guessed their decisions and acted in effect as her agents, often to the detriment of any notion of collective responsibility.

John Major adopted a pattern of seeking advice which was more akin to that of Prime Ministers before Margaret Thatcher. He relied less on the 'one of us' model and was more open to advice from his ministerial colleagues. Sarah Hogg and Jonathan Hill give an example of John Major's willingness to consult a variety of sources, both ministerial and non-ministerial. On Saturday 23 March 1991 Major arrived at Chequers for a general review of policy with ministers and advisers 'in a style which would become established practice'.[1] The idea was to familiarise himself with the activities of his ministers, to make progress on various issues and to prepare the ground for the next election, in particular by airing some ideas for the next manifesto.

To some extent accusations of cronyism are levelled at all Prime Ministers, especially when they and their governments run into choppy political water. But all Prime Ministers have close confidants other than their Cabinet colleagues (some of whom are after all potential rivals), and all are to some extent surrounded by the No. 10 machine. The rest of this chapter largely concerns the role of the Cabinet Office and the Prime Minister's Office, although other sources of advice are considered.

The Cabinet Office

The Cabinet Office was established in 1916 by David Lloyd George. Its functions and importance gradually grew and in 1968 it became a separate part of the machinery of government. Following John Major's re-election as leader of the Conservative Party in 1995, the Cabinet Office was reorganised into two sections as shown in Figure 8.1: the Cabinet Office/Secretariat and the Office of Public Service.

The Cabinet Secretariat supports ministers collectively in the conduct of Cabinet business and services the Cabinet and its committees, and is an important link between the departments and Downing Street. It currently consists of six secretariats: Economic and Domestic Affairs and Legislation, Defence and Overseas Affairs, Joint Intelligence Organisation, European Affairs, Telecommunications, and Ceremonial. These deal with the matters coming to the Cabinet and its committees from the departments and other sources. They timetable business, set agendas for discussion and organise committee meetings. The Cabinet Secretariat records decisions of the Cabinet and its committees. These are based on the summing up by the Prime Minister or the chairman of the committee concerned and are binding on the departments. This is an important method of prime ministerial control. The Secretariat is headed by the Secretary to the Cabinet (currently Sir Robin Butler) who is assisted by around thirty-five senior staff, ranked at Assistant Secretary or above. These 'high flyers' are on loan from the various Whitehall departments; although their prime loyalty is to the Cabinet Office, their training comes in useful when they return from secondment. These top officials maintain close links with the departments. Although the Cabinet Office needs the goodwill of the departments in order to do its work, it undoubtedly has enormous influence in the conduct of official business. By the management of the agenda for the Cabinet and its committees, it can slow down or speed up decision-making, help to shut off or open up particular options and its senior staff can guide those who chair the committees.

The post-war trend has been to draw more things into the Cabinet Office, especially those involving cross-departmental matters, thus enhancing the central machinery of government. Sometimes special units are set up to deal with particular items of business, such as the devolution issue of the 1970s, while others are now firmly established within the Cabinet Office, such as economic policy, Europe and intelligence matters. The trend has been to strengthen the position of the Cabinet Office and of those at the centre of the government: the Prime Minister and his or her aides and officials. If the Prime Minister chooses to work closely with the Secretary to the Cabinet, then it becomes an instrument to serve him or her rather than the Cabinet collectively.

In terms of relations with the departments, top officials watch, inform and brief the Prime Minister. They give him or her information about what is being done in the departments and what is likely to come up in Cabinet, and pass on what is being considered at departmental level. These briefs are intended to support and facilitate the work of the Prime Minister, but will have a great impact on what actually happens. The contents of the brief will depend very much on who actually wrote it. Under Thatcher top officials in the Cabinet

Secretariat liaised directly with her rather than with the Cabinet Secretary, briefing her on policy areas for which they were responsible, and this continued under Major.

The Cabinet Office is closely concerned with the flow of information and this gives it considerable influence over departmental business once it enters the Cabinet system. According to some commentators, it gives the Prime Minister the opportunity to slow down or hold back departmental initiatives by preventing decisions being made, although this is a negative power which is not easily exercised. A Prime Minister who wishes to intervene must do so at an early stage and must ensure that the matter goes before a committee chaired by them or on which they have majority support. The Cabinet Secretary (who always sits at the right hand of the Prime Minister during Cabinet meetings) takes the lead in providing briefs for the Prime Minister on matters to come before the Cabinet and the committees he or she chairs. Briefs are also provided for those who chair the other Cabinet committees. The aim is to provide an indication of the business to be covered and on which item decisions need to be made. The briefings give a summary of the various positions being advanced, outline the points of inter-departmental arguments and uncover any hidden options. The Cabinet Secretariat also organises and manages the flow of business through the Cabinet and its committees. The heads of the various secretariats have considerable influence, especially in matters which cross the various departments; they plan and schedule the flow of business and control the distribution of information.

The Office of Public Service (OPS) was headed by the Deputy Prime Minister, Michael Heseltine, who was aided by another Cabinet minister, the Chancellor of the Duchy of Lancaster and Minister of Public Service, Roger Freeman, reflecting the ability of Heseltine to carve out a substantial Whitehall empire as the price for his support of Major in the leadership election. Under the Major government the OPS had wide-ranging responsibilities. It was responsible for the competitiveness agenda and deregulation as well as the Citizen's Charter programme. It had control of the programme of Civil Service reform, including the Next Steps initiative, market testing and so on. It was responsible for a number of Executive Agencies and was divided into a number of sections. The Deputy Prime Minister chaired four Cabinet committees: competitiveness, the co-ordination and presentation of government policy, the environment and local government.

Bernard Donoughue was Senior Policy Adviser and head of the No. 10 Policy Unit from 1974 to 1979. He was in close contact with the Civil Service advisers to the Prime Minister in what was sometimes a harmonious relationship, sometimes not. In his book he discussed the role and functions of the Cabinet Office and the Cabinet Secretary. The original function of the Cabinet Secretariat was to service the mechanics of government policy-making, including providing the secretariat for Cabinet meetings, issuing agenda, providing minutes and so on. However, apart from this purely administrative function, the

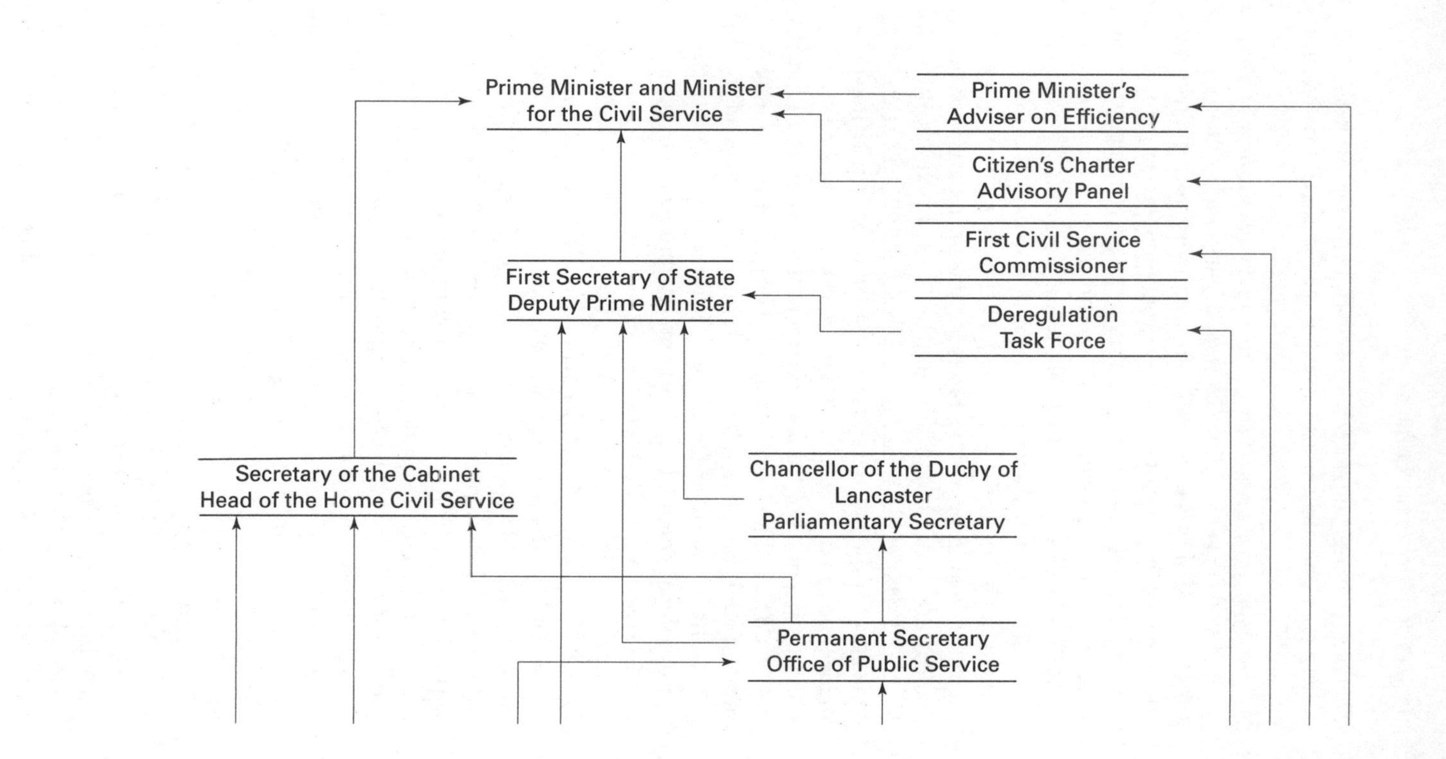
Prime Minister and Minister for the Civil Service
Prime Minister's Adviser on Efficiency
Citizen's Charter Advisory Panel
First Civil Service Commissioner
Deregulation Task Force
First Secretary of State Deputy Prime Minister
Secretary of the Cabinet Head of the Home Civil Service
Chancellor of the Duchy of Lancaster Parliamentary Secretary
Permanent Secretary Office of Public Service

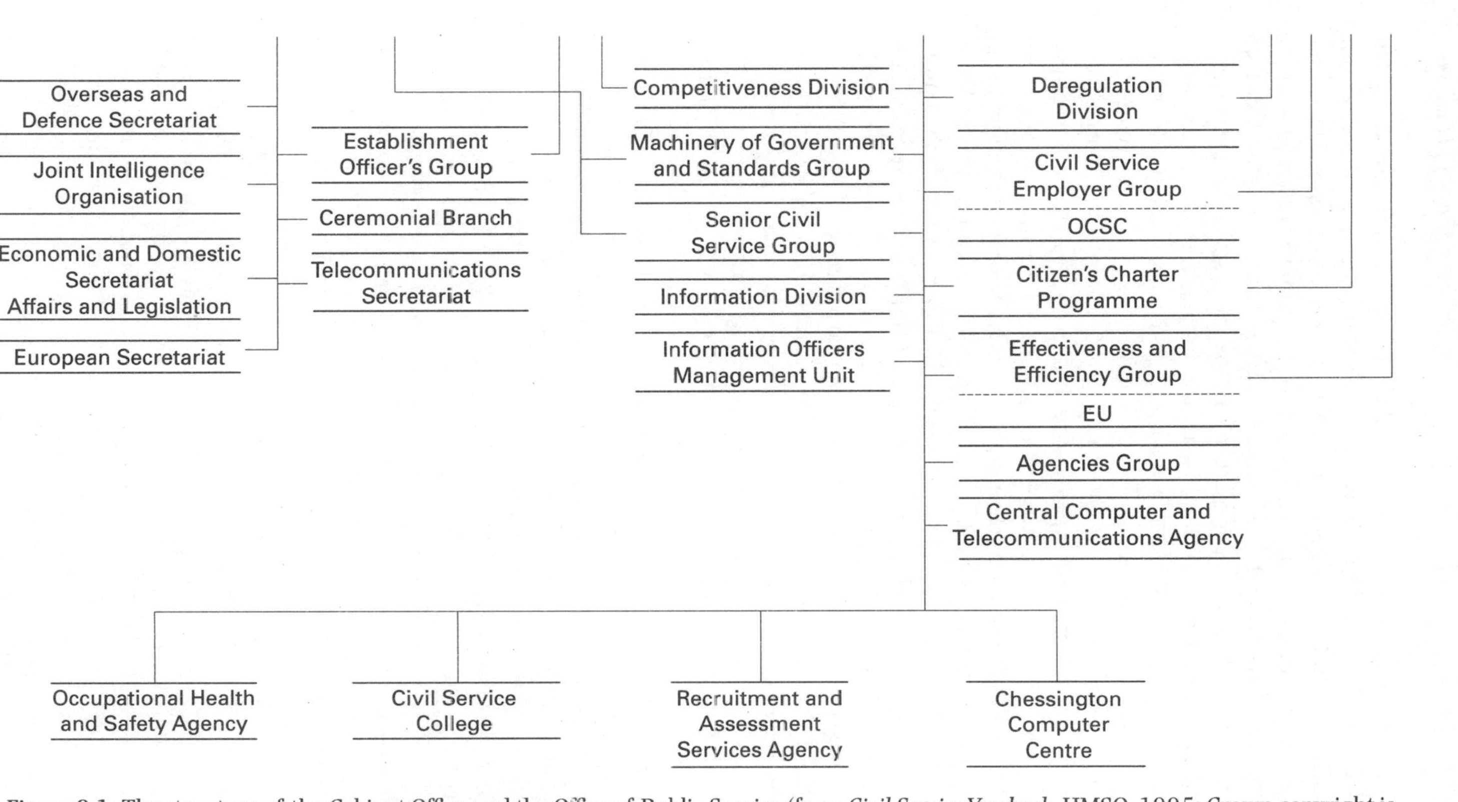

Figure 8.1 The structure of the Cabinet Office and the Office of Public Service (from *Civil Service Yearbook*, HMSO, 1995; Crown copyright is reproduced with the permission of the Controller of Her Majesty's Stationery Office)

Cabinet Office has acquired an independent policy-making function. The Cabinet Secretary is usually the single most powerful official in Whitehall and works closely with the Prime Minister. His or her influence on policy can be seen in the briefing papers which are submitted to the Prime Minister and to the chairmen of the various Cabinet Committees. These 'contain skilful advice on how to conduct the meeting, bearing in mind the interests and preferences of ministerial members. However, they have also increasingly contained arguments steering the Prime Minister towards one policy conclusion rather than another . . .'.[2] The Policy Unit, in an effort to counter the weight of Civil Service advice, began to submit its own briefs relating to the Cabinet Secretary's briefs.

Donoughue also referred to the ambiguity concerning the role of the Cabinet Secretary, often referred to as the Prime Minister's Permanent Secretary, namely whether their prime responsibility lay with the Cabinet as a whole or with the Prime Minister personally. Although in theory there should be no problem, given that the Prime Minister is both the Chairman of Cabinet and a member of that body, the reality is more complex. Premiers' interests may differ from those of colleagues, they may wish to restrain certain members of the Cabinet, to keep things from coming to Cabinet or to influence the composition or activities of Cabinet committees. In all these things they will be assisted by the Cabinet Secretary, who while in theory serving the Cabinet collectively, in case of a conflict is always tempted to give priority to the Prime Minister.

Thus the role of the Cabinet Secretary is crucial: seeing the Prime Minister several times a day on average and advising about important official meetings; taking the chair at meetings of official committees which shadow Cabinet committees; pushing things which he or she thinks important or delaying matters considered unimportant or misguided; helping out a department in difficulties and even having a word with the Treasury to help sort out a problem.

Other institutions have been developed to support the Prime Minister. The Central Policy Review Staff (CPRS), commonly known as the 'think-tank', was established by Edward Heath in 1971 and located in the Cabinet Office. Half the CPRS staff of sixteen to twenty people were 'fast-stream' civil servants and the other half were outsiders from commerce, industry, the universities and other parts of the public service, some of whom had Conservative political sympathies, while others had not. Heath believed that governments quickly lost sight of their original aims and became preoccupied with day-to-day matters so that the emphasis became one of surviving the latest crisis rather than planning for the future. An enhanced planning capacity was needed in British government to allow ministers to take better policy decisions, to establish priorities and to analyse alternative strategies. These, it was hoped, would be aided and facilitated by the new unit. Its first head was Lord Rothschild and during his time it thrived, making a considerable impact on government policy. However, it later ran into difficulties as prime ministerial interest waned under Wilson and succeeding Premiers, and it became increasingly peripheral and concerned with secondary issues. In the 1980s it became involved in politically controversial exercises and was subject to a spate of leaks. In 1983 a CPRS report on the possible abolition of the welfare state got into the newspapers, to the intense anger of Mrs Thatcher, and it was disbanded immediately after the election.

The Prime Minister's Office

The Prime Minister's Office has developed in a gradual and piecemeal fashion, a reaction to the pressure of events rather than as the result of deliberate will. Though in terms of numbers it is still small, the Prime Minister's Office has become a separate part of the structure of Whitehall; in 1977 it was given a designation separate from the Cabinet Office in the *Civil Service Yearbook*, and the functions of its various parts were more clearly defined.

Currently the Prime Minister's Office is divided into four sections, each with a specific set of duties which service the Prime Minister's main roles: Cabinet, party, parliamentary and media.

1 The Private Office conducts the Prime Minister's official relations with Whitehall, Parliament and the public in his or her capacity of head of government. It is staffed by senior civil servants who are on secondment from the various departments.
2 The Policy Unit advises the Prime Minister on all areas of government policy. Its staff are drawn from a variety of backgrounds and are normally sympathetic to the political aims of the governing party, although they have the status of temporary civil servants. Sometimes career civil servants are members of the Unit.
3 The Press Office conducts the Prime Minister's relations with the media and is staffed by civil servants, although it may be led by political appointees.
4 The Political Office manages the Prime Minister's relations with his or her party and deals with constituency matters. It is staffed by people from the governing party and they are not civil servants.

Each section liaises with similar sections in each department, ensuring that the Prime Minister's Office is kept informed about what is happening in and is being planned across Whitehall. The biggest change has been in the number and functions of advisers; the Prime Minister is now better informed about what is going on in Whitehall and more able to initiate policy from the centre. The Policy Unit in particular has made it more possible for the Prime Minister to set the agenda of government and to supervise the general thrust of government policy. Also, the job of monitoring the departments, to ensure that they are working to the guidelines set by the Prime Minister and Cabinet, has been enhanced.

The growth in the effectiveness of the Prime Minister's Office has been one of the most significant developments in British government, especially since 1945, but has been accomplished with a staff far smaller than that of comparable heads of government. The German Chancellor's staff numbers around 450, while that of the American President is 400. The total staff in No. 10

numbers around one hundred, of whom around thirty are key figures. The small size of the Office is an advantage, in that it works in an informal and friendly fashion and operates on the basis of personal contact; 'gossip' is both facilitated and utilised. However, it also has its disadvantages: 'the prime minister has a relatively small personal staff and, while they are undoubtedly loyal and reliable, the sheer weight of business raises questions about their efficiency and effectiveness'.[3] The small size of the No. 10 staff, especially compared with the resources available to departmental ministers, puts a great strain on those who work for the Prime Minister.

Its role grew in scale and significance during Mrs Thatcher's time in No. 10 as she increasingly took over responsibility from the departments for making policy and for scrutinising policy initiatives. This was relatively restrained during her first administration, but gradually a distance grew between Mrs Thatcher and her Cabinet colleagues. Her closest advisers became Bernard Ingham and Charles Powell, with Alan Walters intermittently but powerfully advising on economic and European policy and with Sir Percy Cradock as her foreign affairs adviser. Efforts by ministers and the Civil Service hierarchy to move Ingham and Powell failed. Not since William Armstrong became too close to Heath 'had such a constitutional abnormality been present at the heart of British government . . .'.[4] This tendency aroused considerable discontent; commentators even began to talk of the gradual emergence of a 'Prime Minister's department', although this considerably over-stated both the extent of the changes and manner in which Thatcher departed from precedents set by previous Prime Ministers who had presided over the gradual expansion of the Prime Minister's Office. This trend continued, although in a less confrontational manner, under John Major. A number of initiatives came from No. 10, including the ill-fated 'back to basics' campaign.

The contribution of the various groups who advised and sustained the Prime Minister was illustrated by Sarah Hogg and Jonathan Hill when they discussed the events leading to the 1992 general election. It began in January 1991 when the Party Chairman Chris Patten called a meeting to prepare for the next election. It was attended by Major's Political Secretary Judith Chaplin and Nick True and Sarah Hogg from the Policy Unit. In May the 'No. 12 Committee' was constituted, chaired by Richard Ryder, the Chief Whip, to prepare for the next election. It included the Leaders of the Lords and Commons, Chris Patten or his deputies and senior figures from Central Office. Sarah Hogg, Nick True or Jonathan Hill represented the Policy Unit and Judith Chaplin and Graham Bright, then the Prime Minister's Parliamentary Private Secretary, the Political Office. Gus O'Donnell attended, as did one or more of the Prime Minister's Private Secretaries. The aim was to improve the co-ordination and presentation of government policy. This Committee survived until the reshuffle of July 1995, when it was superseded by a group chaired by Heseltine. The writing of the 1992 manifesto involved a wide range of elements in the government and the party. A team of senior ministers and the Party Chairman was set up and members of the Policy Unit were added to take the minutes and redraft the various proposals and suggestions.

However, Hogg and Hill also illustrate the limits placed on the official side on No. 10. During a general election the officials who staff the Prime Minister's Office fade away to prepare papers for an alternative government.

> At Number 10, the best civil servants behaved with great personal decency, but for most of them the Prime Minister was now someone else's problem . . . To those who had been appointed from outside the system, and whose allegiance to the Prime Minister was personal or political, such apparent indifference was sometimes difficult to understand – but it was a necessary part of maintaining a civil service built on the principle of impartiality.[5]

The heart of the operation became the Political Office team.

The Private Office

The Private Office is the single most important section of the administrative support services in Downing Street and is the main access point to the Prime Minister. It is made up of career civil servants who are the main formal channel for prime ministerial communication with the departments and is staffed by five Private Secretaries, who are Whitehall 'high flyers', plus the Principal Private Secretary, who has the grade of Deputy Secretary, all of whom serve for between two and three years before moving to senior posts in the departments, plus a small support staff. The work is structured; apart from the Principal Private Secretary the other members cover a particular area of prime ministerial business: overseas affairs (for which two secretaries are responsible), economic affairs, parliamentary matters, and home affairs and diary, divisions which closely match those of the Cabinet Secretariat. The Principal Private Secretary oversees the Office and organises the papers which go to the Prime Minister. The Private Office fulfils a number of tasks on behalf of the Prime Minister: organising his or her time and the flow of business and people, briefing him or her on issues and developments and making notes of meetings and conversations. The Private Office also has an important role in briefing the Prime Minister in preparation for Question Time in the Commons and acting as a link with Buckingham Palace. The various Private Secretaries fill the red boxes which are the Prime Minister's nightly and weekend reading.

The Private Office has two main functions as the channel of communication between No. 10 and the departments. Firstly, it selects and comments on the material from departments. The Private Secretaries, based on their experience of central government and knowledge of the Premier's interests and priorities, sift through the flow of communications and decide which to pass on as a matter of urgency, which to delay and which to answer themselves on behalf of the Premier. Secondly, the Private Office communicates to the departments the Prime Minister's views. There are two sources from which material arises: the Cabinet Office and ministers and departments. Civil servants in the Private

Office comment more on material from departments because that from the Cabinet Office has already been filtered and discussed. The Prime Minister's views can be sent back to departments either in a formal memorandum or through the grapevine.

There is unanimity about the quality of those who work in the Private Office. Donoughue felt that the administrative quality of the Private Secretaries was extremely high. They were selected from the cream of their departments and, aided by their experience of Downing Street, were expected to rise to the top positions in the Service. One such was Robin Butler, who had been seconded from the Treasury and who later became Mrs Thatcher's Principal Private Secretary and then Secretary to the Cabinet. Donoughue emphasised how vital it was that the members of the Policy Unit established a close relationship of trust and friendship with the Private Secretaries so that the Prime Minister would be presented with advice which did not conflict. Even more crucial was the relationship with the Principal Private Secretary. Mrs Thatcher, no lover either of the Civil Service or of most civil servants, wrote that she was fortunate to have a succession of superb Principal Private Secretaries. The Principal Private Secretary undertakes a wide range of duties 'from high policy adviser, honest friend and personal nanny. They have to be highly political animals without ever forgetting the canons of Northcote and Trevelyan. It is rather like riding two horses at high speed.'[6]

Although personal chemistry is important, it is likely that the Principal Private Secretary will be one of the group of key advisers which will include the Head of the Policy Unit, Chief Press Secretary and certain special advisers. Under Thatcher, her Parliamentary Private Secretary Ian Gow (in the early years), Ingham, Powell and at times Walters were in this position, while under Major, Sarah Hogg and Gus O'Donnell played this role. Some advisers may develop a set of personal initiatives and interests in line with what they believe to be the wishes of the Prime Minister. This was a particular feature of Downing Street during Mrs Thatcher's time in office. The Private Office returned to its more usual role after the departure of Powell and Ingham. Unlike Thatcher, Major trusted civil servants and worked easily with them.

The Policy Unit

The basic task of the No. 10 Policy Unit is to help in the development of the whole range of short- and medium-term government policies. It was established by Harold Wilson on his return to power following the inconclusive February 1974 general election. Despite the creation by Heath of the CPRS, there was no systematic policy analysis working directly for and to the head of the government. The Policy Unit was designed to fill this gap. It built on the practice of past Prime Ministers who brought in individual advisers to provide policy advice of a more partisan or personal nature than that which could be given by civil servants. In general previous attempts to counter the power and weight of the Civil Service had had little impact on the work of the departments, so the

Policy Unit was larger, more institutionalised and more sensitive to the Prime Minister's needs. It is mainly concerned to provide policy advice for the Prime Minister.

It also has an important role in gathering information. Members have access to the Prime Minister's papers in the Private Office and to information passed through the grapevine of special advisers attached to ministers. Under Wilson and Callaghan its main role was to provide forward policy analysis over the medium to long term, especially on the economic issues which then dominated the policy agenda. Under Thatcher the Policy Unit became much more interventionist regarding the departments, to ensure that they operated according to the policies of the Prime Minister. It later became proactive, originating new policy ideas, which, after approval by the Prime Minister, were developed in the departments. It attempted a general oversight of the government, giving particular attention to proposals which crossed departmental boundaries. Under Major, the Unit became less an initiator of policies and more an evaluator of departmental initiatives, although it was associated with a number of policy ideas.

The Policy Unit is staffed either by outsiders who are in sympathy with the political aims of the government or by civil servants on secondment from their departments. Outsiders are employed as temporary civil servants during their time in the Unit, who although behaving differently from established officials are still subject to limitations, policed by the Cabinet Secretary. One is that they must not become parliamentary candidates. They have no security of tenure and their appointments terminate immediately when the Prime Minister who appointed them leaves office, although they can be retained by the newcomer.

It has always been a small organisation. Under Wilson and Callaghan there were eight or nine members. Initially Thatcher was hostile to its operations and reduced it in size, but following the abolition of the CPRS it was expanded and now consists of around thirteen members, plus a small support staff.

Initially Mrs Thatcher was lukewarm towards the Policy Unit. However, she appointed the businessman Sir John Hoskyns as its first Head and he persuaded her to allow it to concentrate on forward thinking rather than simply reacting to events. He was succeeded by Ferdinand Mount who lasted two years and whose main interest was in family policy; he was also a speech-writer for Mrs Thatcher. The next Head was John Redwood from 1984 until he was adopted as prospective parliamentary candidate for Wokingham in 1985. Under him the Policy Unit grew in size and became more structured and institutionalised. Each member shadowed a group of policies and departments and was responsible for his or her submissions to the Prime Minister; previously they had gone out under the authority of the Head of the Unit. In this way a more collegiate atmosphere was generated. Increasingly the Unit served Mrs Thatcher, it 'was *hers* to its last paperclip. There was no question of its serving other Cabinet ministers or some notion of the wider interest.'[7] Contact with the Private Office became closer to ensure that the Unit only sent her briefings that were relevant to whatever interested her at that time. This new orientation was continued by Professor Brian Griffiths, recruited from the City University Business School, who was Head of the Policy Unit from 1985 to 1990. Soon after becoming Prime Minister Major appointed Sarah Hogg, then a financial journalist, as Head. She remained at No. 10 until 1995, when she was made a life peeress. Under her it was highly influential in four policy areas. The first was in devising a new form of local government revenue to replace the poll tax, acting as a bridge between No. 10, the Treasury and the Department of the Environment. Second, the Unit helped to develop a European strategy in advance of the Maastricht conference in December 1991. The third area was in developing an economic strategy based on non-inflationary growth. Finally, the Unit was highly influential in developing the strategy for the 1992 election, in particular the emphasis on education standards and training and reform of the public services. After 1992 the Unit's drive became more diffuse, but was still felt over a broad range of domestic and European policies. Though she was blamed by some Tory MPs for the disarray over the 'back to basics' fiasco and the ill-fated membership of the ERM, there is no evidence she was pushed out of Downing Street. Sarah Hogg was followed by Norman Blackwell, a senior management consultant.

The Press Office

The work of the Press Office has been discussed in an earlier chapter. It deals with media relations and has a small staff. It maintains its links with Whitehall through a network of departmental information and press officers, and there is a weekly meeting of departmental heads of information, presided over by the Press Secretary or his or her deputy. The Press Secretary has four main roles: spokesman for the government, adviser on media relations, intermediary with the media and coordinator of the government's information services.

It is difficult to generalise about the role of the Press Office as the use made of it differs according to the wishes of the Prime Minister of the day and the style of his or her Press Secretary. The relationship between Harold Wilson and Joe Haines and that of Margaret Thatcher and Bernard Ingham caused much controversy, their roles going well beyond that of press spokesperson for the government. In the case of Ingham, there are a number of reasons why he achieved political notoriety: he served longer than any other Press Secretary, increased television coverage gave him a personal prominence, he had to cover the whole range of the job, partly because Mrs Thatcher did not entrust the task of presentation to any of her ministers, and 'he used his aggressive, bullying style to forward Thatcher's interests'.[8]

During the Thatcher era there was an attempt to extend central control over the government information service, especially after Ingham was appointed Head of Profession in February 1989. The information services were used in a more cross-departmental manner and many critics accused it of acting in a highly partisan manner. After Major became Prime Minister the Press Secretary ceased to be the head of the Government Information Service, although day-to-day responsibility for press and media relations was still highly centralised. Gus O'Donnell was close to Major. Although he came under criticism for presentational failings and for difficulties with handling the press, the continued attacks suggest an element of scapegoating.

The Political Office

The Political Office was first established in 1964 by Harold Wilson. It is a small unit, consisting of the Political Secretary and the Prime Minister's Parliamentary Private Secretary, whose task is to keep in contact with backbenchers from the governing party; the Prime Minister's constituency secretary is sometimes a member. The Office is always funded from party or other external sources, not from public funds. The Political Secretary is not a civil servant and is appointed personally by the Prime Minister. He or she is responsible for links with the party, acts as secretary to the Cabinet when it discusses party political matters (when the civil servants leave the room), accompanies the Prime Minister on tours, prepares political briefings and deal with letters which require a party political answer. 'His overall role is to ensure that while the Prime Minister is busy being Prime Minister, he does not forget that he is also the leader of a political party in whose name he stands for office.'[9] The Political Office has few formal or frequent contacts with Whitehall. It does have close and constant relations with the Whips' Office, which is housed in No. 12 Downing Street. The Chief Whip has specially close links with the Prime Minister, while the whips liaise with departmental ministers about what is happening in their departments and feed the information back to the Prime Minister's Office. The whips are also a channel for the views and concerns of government backbenchers.

Other sources of advice

All Prime Ministers have taken advice from a wide range of sources, both official and unofficial. In some cases the link has been long-standing and has frequently been extremely close. In other cases, advisers have been used to help with a particular difficulty or to deal with a pressing problem. Other significant sources of prime ministerial advice include: special advisers, both official and unofficial, kitchen cabinets, and think-tanks.

Special advisers

The appointment of special advisers to ministers began during the second Labour government of 1929–31. It then lapsed until 1964, when Wilson reinstated the practice to provide a counter-weight to Civil Service advice. Those appointed were to be loyal to the government of the day and to the particular minister. In his second administration Wilson formalised the process by establishing the No. 10 Policy Unit. Thatcher appointed a number of personal advisers on matters including the economy and overseas and defence policy. In some areas they worked with the Policy Unit, in others they had direct access to the Prime Minister, and at one time had eight or nine advisers of various types. Sir Anthony Parsons, for a short time her adviser on foreign affairs, and Sir Roger Jacklin, her defence adviser, illustrate what the Prime Minister needed from these special advisers. 'She looked to them for early warnings of trouble, fresh ideas untarnished by departmental compromise and support for her arguments with ministers.'[10] Parsons will go down in history for one thing. During the Falklands crisis he snapped in exasperation, 'Prime Minister, will you please not interrupt me until I have finished.'[11] Another appointment was the monetarist, free-marketeer economist Sir Alan Walters, whose clash with the Chancellor Nigel Lawson led to the resignation of both men. Under Major, advisers were appointed on foreign affairs and on efficiency questions.

Kitchen cabinets

It is clear that life at the top of the 'greasy pole' can be lonely and that personal relationships can be fraught with many difficulties. Old friends from outside the world of politics may become detached, either through the passage of time or because they fear to intrude on the occupant of No. 10. Political friendships may not last; the relationship will alter once one becomes Prime Minister and the other not. It is more than a matter of form that the mode of address changes; from being on first name terms to being 'Prime Minister' on the one hand and 'Secretary of State for this or that' on the other may alter relationships in all sorts of ways. Old friends may become rivals for the job, and if a Prime Minister has to sack someone he or she was close to that may generate a bitter enmity, as in the relationship between John Major and Norman Lamont.

Prime Ministers have coped in different ways with their eminence. Attlee was highly self-contained and was secure in a happy marriage. Churchill made much use of his family and of a group of 'cronies', most of whom were companions from his war years and who tended to remain close to Churchill throughout his premiership. They helped to cover up his stroke in 1953 and in fact undertook much of the work of running the government in his absence, though in a highly discreet manner. Macmillan suffered from extremes of loneliness, something made ever more isolating by the depression he suffered from for much of his life. Wilson surrounded himself with the archetypal 'kitchen cabinet', which was riven with political and personal animosity. His political secretary, Marcia Williams, had what Joe Haines described as an influence over the Prime Minister unrivalled in his experience, although Bernard Donoughue thought that it was only intermittently exercised and that Haines was much more significant. Heath had few intimates, especially from the world of politics. Douglas Hurd was his Political Secretary but they were hardly on close, let alone intimate, terms. Heath took great comfort from music and sailing, but was notoriously difficult and uncommunicative in social situations. Mrs Thatcher surrounded herself with like-minded advisers from a variety of backgrounds and would quite often relax at the end of the day with small groups of supporters whom she would invite to the flat in Downing Street to relax with a night-cap of her favourite tipple, whisky. A change of Prime Minister often involves a change of advisers. Major replaced Ingham with O'Donnell and Griffiths with Sarah Hogg, while Powell stayed only a few months to see the Prime Minister through the Gulf crisis before departing to the private sector. However, all have needed the support which comes from those who can be trusted and relied upon. '"Friends" enjoy an intimacy with the Prime Minister which goes beyond political advice towards personal support – a quiet chat at the end of the day, feet up, whisky in hand, giving strength in times of adversity and sharing pleasure in success.'[12]

Think-tanks

Since 1979 a number of right-wing bodies known collectively as 'think-tanks' have forged close links with the Conservative Party and have been the source and inspiration for many of the policies with which Mrs Thatcher and her supporters revolutionised first the Conservative Party and then the nation. Sir Keith Joseph was the first leading Conservative to fall under the spell of free-market ideas promulgated by the Institute of Economic Affairs, the Adam Smith Institute and so on, and in turn he converted Mrs Thatcher. These bodies consisted of academics and others, somewhat detached from the political world and not always comfortable with the Conservative Party, then in the grip of consensus-minded figures such as Edward Heath. So Joseph and Thatcher created the Centre for Policy Studies as a way of combating the Conservative Research Department, then dominated by Keynesians. Among its early associates were Alan Walters and John Hoskyns, who later worked for Mrs Thatcher in Downing Street, and Hugh Thomas and Alfred Sherman who wrote speeches for her.

Although the influence of think-tanks on the new leadership of the Conservative Party in the period before 1979 was marked, it waned somewhat after the general election as the predominance of the Civil Service as a source of prime ministerial advice was asserted. However, they came back into prominence in the second Thatcher administration. This was partly because there was something of a policy vacuum as Mrs Thatcher sought for ways to advance her revolution. Several of the new men brought into the Cabinet to replace the 'wets' she was gradually ditching had especially close links with bodies such as the Adam Smith Institute. The same was true of members of Mrs Thatcher's No. 10 staff. The Centre for Policy Studies forged close ties with John Redwood, then Head of the Policy Unit. He became the conduit for CPS papers, sending them to a range of influential policy-makers at the same time as the Policy Unit was extending Thatcher's influence over policy-making in the departments.

Crucially, some of Mrs Thatcher's advisers such as Michael Portillo, John Redwood and David Willets became Members of Parliament and then junior ministers, with one or two graduating to the Cabinet. Willets worked for a period in the Policy Unit and then went on to run the Centre for Policy Studies before entering Parliament. Some of the think-tanks established connections with Tory backbench groups; the Adam Smith Institute used its links with the No Turning Back group to influence the changes to the National Health Service which followed the review by Norman Fowler in 1988–89. Gradually the think-tanks moved from advocacy of change to detailed planning for the implementation of change. In several cases people working for these free-market bodies were seconded to government departments and helped formulate legislative proposals on matters such as housing and education.

During the Thatcher era the influence of the various think-tanks was extraordinary. They fed ideas into the government, provided they were in tune with ministers' thinking, and helped to ensure the success of right-wing, free-market ideas in the Conservative Party. Their success ensured them a direct line to policy-makers and they were able to ensure that their ideas were taken on board by senior civil servants. However, there were limits to their influence. Sometimes their ideas were not taken up by ministers; an example was the failure of bodies concerned with education to sell the voucher system, despite the enthusiastic support of the Prime Minister. In some cases the government did accept think-tank ideas only to find them blow up in its face; the fate of the poll tax, pushed ceaselessly by the Adam Smith Institute, is an example. Think-tank influence began to decline during Thatcher's final years, a tendency which continued under Major. This left the think-tanks in a bind; they could not decide whether to remain loyal to the Thatcherite agenda or to advocate the sort of ideas likely to be acceptable to the new, somewhat less hawkish regime in Downing Street. However, after the 1992 election they made a come-back; the Adam Smith Institute (under Dr Madsen Pirie, said to have been close to the Prime Minister), the European Policy Forum and the Social Market Foundation all made an impact on government policy, although mainly concerning the management of the public sector and relations with Europe.

A Prime Minister's Department?

From time to time there is discussion about whether the creation of a Prime Minister's Department along the lines of the machinery available to the President of the United States would strengthen the British system of government or whether it would produce an unacceptable centralisation of power. This is usually the preoccupation of academic observers but during 1977–78 James Callaghan examined the idea whilst considering a major reorganisation of central government.

Some commentators have argued that the increased responsibilities of the modern Prime Minister have not been matched by a growth in the support given to the holder of that office and have suggested a support system with time to work on problems in some depth across the whole range of government activities. Simon James considered the objections often raised to the idea and found them wanting: 'it is perfectly tenable to argue that, as Cabinet minister with supreme responsibility, the premier needs his own department to brief him and carry out any strategic work that he wants or feels the Cabinet needs'.[13] The first objection was that the establishment of a Prime Minister's Department would forfeit the flexibility of the existing system. This, in James's view, underestimates the adaptability of central goverment bodies such as the Cabinet Office. It is also argued that it would inexpertly challenge the expertise of departments. This ignores the fact that they *need* to be challenged on their policy assumptions. Another argument revolves around the fears that the head of the new department would become over-influential and swamp the Premier. James dismisses this argument, saying that it assumes that the Prime Minister could not control his or her own staff. Constitutional objections that it presages a presidency or undermines the Prime Minister's ability to cultivate consensus are based on a distortion of his or her role. The Premier is not there just to create consensus but to give a lead, to question and query and to make waves. A Prime Minister who does not lead fails, as the premiership of Douglas-Home shows. James concludes that the main argument against its establishment revolves around fears that it would increase the power of the Prime Minister and thus create dissension and suspicion.

Bernard Donoughue takes the opposite line. 'In practice, however, the Prime Minister does under the existing system have all the advisory facilities he needs, even though they may be scattered a little untidily around central government.'[14] The present system avoids bureaucracy, hierarchy and the inflation of numbers that a separate department would create, as the American experience demonstrates. Provided personalities do not clash, the system is flexible and allows the Prime Minister to make what use of it he or she wishes.

Notes

1 Sarah Hogg and Jonathan Hill, *Too Close to Call. Power and Politics – John Major in No. 10*, Little, Brown, 1995, p. 87.
2 Bernard Donoughue, *Prime Minister. The Conduct of Policy under Harold Wilson and James Callaghan*, Cape, 1987, p. 8.
3 Donald Shell and Richard Hodder-Williams (eds), *Churchill to Major. The British Prime Ministership since 1945*, Hurst, 1995.
4 Dennis Kavanagh and Anthony Seldon (eds), *The Major Effect*, Macmillan, 1994, p. 155.
5 Hogg and Hill, *Too Close to Call*, p. 204.
6 Peter Hennessy, *Whitehall*, Fontana, 1990, p. 384.
7 Ibid., p. 658.
8 James Barber, *The Prime Minister since 1945*, Blackwell, 1991, p. 87.
9 Hogg and Hill, *Too Close to Call*, p. 23.

10 Simon James, *British Cabinet Government*, Routledge, 1992, p. 226.
11 Quoted in Hennessy, *Whitehall*, p. 652.
12 Peter Madgwick, *British Government. The Central Executive Territory*, Philip Allan, 1991, p. 119.
13 James, *British Cabinet Government*, p. 241.
14 Donoughue, *Prime Minister*, p. 31.

9

The Cabinet

This chapter examines different perspectives on the nature, role and functions of the Cabinet and scrutinises its part in policy-making. The composition of the Cabinet and the significant role played by non-departmental ministers are analysed, as well as the controvery about collective and individual responsibility and the extent to which these concepts have contemporary relevance. The role of Cabinet committees and the extent to which they are a valuable aspect of the machinery of government are also considered. The part played by highly secret groupings outside the formal machinery of the Cabinet, such as the 'economic seminar', is also a focus.

Introduction: Prime Ministers and the machinery of government

One of the Prime Minister's most important tasks is to determine *how* government is to be conducted. This is a multi-faceted question, involving the organisation of the Cabinet itself, the structure of the various government departments, the use made of No. 10 Downing Street and the Cabinet Office and so on. Post-war Premiers have varied in the extent to which the organisation of government business has been of interest.

Attlee had a well-considered view of the demands of Cabinet government and the problems of running an administration. In Cabinet he was brief, businesslike and highly efficient, ensuring that the agenda was followed. He arranged the machinery of government and managed the Cabinet in a way which suited his style and purpose. By 1947 the government was arranged in the shape of a cone. Attlee was at the apex, overseeing the whole administration and taking the chair at most important committees, including economic policy and defence. Then came the three most important ministers, the Foreign Secretary Ernest Bevin, Sir Stafford Cripps, Chancellor of the Exchequer from 1947 to 1950, and Herbert Morrison who led the House of Commons. On the next tier came other significant ministers, either with particular abilities or with specific responsibilities. Then came a number of departmental ministers who were members of the Cabinet and finally those departmental heads who were excluded from the highest offices. All major matters of policy were brought before the full Cabinet for discussion and approval. This arrangement facilitated the efficient operation of the government machine, enabling the agenda to be reduced in size and thus to streamline the conduct of business. Increasingly, matters were settled by Cabinet committees.

Despite criticisms in opposition of the growth of the state and of the adverse effects of bureaucracy, after 1951 the Conservatives paid little attention to the machinery of government. Churchill himself quickly lost enthusiasm for reform and no other minister was committed to change. Originally Churchill had plans to reorganise the economic departments and especially the Treasury, which he considered excessively powerful, but his interest in the machinery of government quickly faded.

A short-lived and unsuccessful experiment was the appointment of three of his wartime cronies as 'Overlords' to supervise areas of government responsibility. The aim was to reduce the size of the Cabinet and to allow Churchill to run his administration along lines to which he had become accustomed during the war. However, Churchill failed to make it clear precisely what the duties of the 'Overlords' were and how the ministers in charge of the departments being supervised were to conduct themselves. The experiment was abandoned when one of the 'Overlords' announced that the ministers he was supposed to co-ordinate still had complete responsibility to Parliament for the actions of their departments. It was formally ended by the Cabinet reshuffle of September 1953. Later, the problems of Cabinet size and of the co-ordination of the government machine were solved by the wholesale amalgamations of ministries into 'super-departments'.

Eden had little or no impact on how government business was conducted. Under Macmillan there were several changes in the way government was conducted. The burden of work was growing, as was the need for greater co-ordination within the administration. Cabinet committees increased in significance as a way of reducing the burden on the Cabinet; they tended to be chaired either by the Prime Minister or by a senior non-departmental minister. Macmillan chaired the Economic Policy and Defence committees and kept abreast of committee minutes and was in close touch with committee chairmen. If he thought the matter of sufficient importance he would take charge himself. His successor, Alec Douglas-Home, was in office too short a time to make much impact on the organisation of business.

As Leader of the Opposition before 1964, Harold Wilson talked a good deal about the machinery of government and how in Labour's 'first hundred days' in office there would be a new atmosphere in Whitehall. He concentrated on two areas. First, to improve the central direction of government he aimed to strengthen the Cabinet Office and the No. 10 Secretariat. Second, he urged the need for new and enlarged departments. One would counterbalance the Treasury, while others would deal with areas of work Wilson thought of special importance. He accepted the commonly held view that the 'stop–go' economics which were a feature of the closing years of the Macmillan government were primarily due to the over-absorption of the Treasury with the value of sterling and the balance of payments. So Wilson decided to set up the Department of Economic Affairs, which would rival the Treasury and would attempt to stimulate economic growth. A National Plan, with ambitious growth targets, was decided on. However, cuts in government expenditure in July 1966 wrecked the assumptions on which the Plan was based, and the ministry was wound up in 1969. The short and unhappy history of the Department of Economic Affairs typifies the lack of strategic thinking of the Wilson administration. Following the lead of the Macmillan government Wilson established some 'super' ministries: the Departments of Health and Social Security were combined, the Department of Industry was formed by joining the Boards of Trade and Technology, and the Department of the Environment was created out of Housing, Local Government and Transport. Another aspect of Wilson's attempt to modernise the machinery of government was the appointment of a committee under Lord Fulton to examine the working of the Civil Service. However, by the time it reported the Prime Minister had lost interest and little tangible came of the exercise, at least until Mrs Thatcher tackled the problem in the 1980s. In his second term Wilson had more pressing problems connected with the economy and with day-to-day survival to contend with, and so there was little institutional reform, apart from the establishment of the No.10 Policy Unit.

After 1964 Wilson strengthened the staff at No. 10 and set up a special political unit under his secretary, Marcia Williams, later Lady Falkender. Back in office in 1974 he retained the Central Policy Review Staff (known as the 'Think Tank') which Heath had established, and he added the No. 10 Policy Unit, which gave Wilson sufficient control of those areas in which he retained an interest. Wilson also allowed Cabinet ministers to recruit up to two 'special advisers', drawn from outside Whitehall, who would act as temporary civil servants for the remainder of the administration. This regularised a procedure Wilson had begun in 1964.

Heath had an appetite for organisation which was rare in a politician, and in the view of both supporters and opponents he would have been an excellent Permanent Secretary. Heath had become convinced of the inefficiency of Whitehall, which he thought had contributed to Britain's poor economic performance. Institutional changes were seen as a key component in the solution to economic problems. This was wishful thinking which ended in painful disillusion.

Heath's reforms were the most ambitious attempt to change the machinery of government since 1918, although little of the legacy now remains. Four months after his general election victory he issued a White Paper, *The Reorganisation of Central Government*. The three main strands were:

1 The establishment of an efficiency system, Programme Analysis and Review, aimed at looking at long-term policy commitments and at improving policy-making at the micro-level.
2 A change to the structure of departments which involved the creation of super-departments such as Environment and Trade and Industry.
3 The establishment of a Central Policy Review Staff in the Cabinet Office to help produce a clearer long-term strategy for the government as a whole.

Heath claimed that these changes would improve the quality of Cabinet government rather than be a move to a more prime ministerial style of government. It would enable the Cabinet to take strategic decisions, free from day-to-day considerations. Two 'super-ministries', the Department of Trade and Industry and Environment, were set up. The Central Policy Review Staff had only a limited impact on the system.

Callaghan's long experience in Cabinet before he became Prime Minister was a great advantage. He had worked in several departments and knew and trusted the key Permanent Secretaries, who reciprocated. However, he made few changes to the machinery of government apart from re-creating a separate Ministry of Transport in the reshuffle on taking office. Following the sterling crisis in the autumn of 1976, which necessitated seeking a loan from the IMF, he thought of splitting the Treasury into a ministry concerned with finance and a separate section concerned with expenditure matters. However, he postponed the change until overtaken by events in 1979. He retained both the Downing Street Policy Unit and the Central Policy Review Staff, which he regarded as complementary.

Mrs Thatcher's impact on the organisation of government business was surprisingly limited. She was reluctant to alter the machinery of central government and although there were some changes to the structure and organisation of government departments, these were limited compared to those of most of her predecessors. During her time in office, only three new departments were created, and of those abolished only the ending of the Civil Service Department in 1981 created much political controversy. She did not establish anything like a Prime Minister's Department, although the No.10 Policy Unit was strengthened somewhat, being counterbalanced by the abolition of the Central Policy Review Staff. The remit of the Cabinet Office was extended, especially the scrutiny work of the Efficiency Unit, set up under Lord Rayner. These were minor tinkerings rather than revolutionary changes. However, towards the end of her time in office changes to the Civil Service, involving its fragmentation into Executive Agencies, did usher in more fundamental developments which continued under John Major.

Mrs Thatcher continued the trend away from a collective style of government. To a considerable degree, the formal structure was downgraded and became increasingly centred on the Prime Minister. Compared to her predecessors, less time was spent during this period on formal meetings, although the move to one Cabinet meeting a week came in 1975. The really significant change was the fall in the number of Cabinet committees and in their meetings, which declined from 941 in 1978 to 340 in 1989. Several commentators pointed out that she ran the slimmest Cabinet system since before the Second World War. The centre was strengthened and the system became more focused on No. 10, which became more involved in overseeing the activities of government generally, including government information and presentation, and there were sporadic efforts by the Policy Unit to monitor the work of departments.

More business was dealt with through the informal structure, which also came to be more and more centred on Mrs Thatcher herself. She set up a number of working groups, several under her own chairmanship, and including her aides and the departmental ministers concerned, who would work through a policy before presenting it to Cabinet or a Cabinet committee. These were not formal committees. This meant that many matters were predetermined before reaching Cabinet and ministers were presented with issues they had not had the opportunity to consider and which often had such momentum that they were impossible to stop or even significantly alter. During this time, the practice of conducting business by letter or phone call between the relevant ministers continued and grew in volume and significance. But much was also dealt with in *ad hoc* groups, the most important of which was her version of the 'economic seminar', which handled topics like monetary policy and exchange rates. It was a highly flexible group, whose composition changed according to circumstances and the matter under review. Other *ad hoc* groups outside the MISC organisation had a considerable impact, even though they might have had a short life.

Mrs Thatcher conducted much business in this fashion and her ministers felt the need to clear matters with the Prime Minister before developing initiatives. The method varied but generally followed this pattern. Thatcher would ask the Cabinet member concerned to prepare a paper on the issue in question just for her, not for the Cabinet or a Cabinet committee, which helps to explain why the flow of Cabinet papers fell during her time in office. The sometimes hapless minister was then called to No. 10 with his back-up team to be faced by the Prime Minister and her advisers, who might be from the Private Office, the Policy Unit, the Cabinet Office, and probably with some personal advisers. Then, according to a number of commentators, some of them insiders, she proceeded to act as judge and jury in her own cause. It was this, amongst other things, which caused some to speak of a devaluation of Cabinet government and of a 'presidential style'. 'Her highly informal approach was actually very effective in terms of getting business done. The problem was that it was erratic and it raised problems about the co-ordination of policy and the extent to which policy was fully worked out before moving on to legislation.'[1]

Many of the changes she brought about survived her passing, although under John Major they were regularised and made part of the formal structure. He had a very different personality and political style from that of Margaret Thatcher. 'He inherited problems, commitments and policies; his scope for choice has been narrow. But, compared to Mrs Thatcher, he is less insistent on *the* one way, believes in and practices Cabinet government, is more concerned to conciliate and practice agreement, and does not have an agenda so clearly separate from that of his principal Cabinet colleagues.'[2] Major continued the changes to the Civil Service begun by Mrs Thatcher. Several new departments were created, others abolished or merged. Under Major policy originated from two principal quarters: government departments and No. 10. The No. 10 Policy Unit became increasingly important as a source of policy advice, especially under Sarah Hogg, although under Major it was more open, informal and broad-based than during Mrs Thatcher's time.

There was some loosening of the reins of prime ministerial power, with more emphasis on ministers, both as individuals and collectively, and a return to a somewhat more collegiate style in Cabinet which was more of a policy forum, with Major acting as a chairman rather than as a conviction Premier. Major allowed all interested ministers to comment before he summed up the discussion. This practice made it easier to maintain a common line, especially during crisis situations, and helped to bind all ministers to the decision, thus enhancing at least the appearance of collective responsibility. Major worked hard to prepare the ground in Cabinet so that he could carry his colleagues with him and to allow all to have their say. In the view of some commentators, the broad picture was of a restoration of Cabinet government. This meant a move away from *ad hoc* decision-taking outside the Cabinet and Cabinet committees. Major did not fight to keep things off the Cabinet agenda in the way Thatcher did. In his first two years as Premier many final decisions were taken in full Cabinet, although after 1992 the focus switched to Cabinet committees. Matters reached the full Cabinet if they were very important, such as sending troops to Bosnia, or politically divisive, such as the use of Qualified Majority Voting in Europe. Major also reintroduced 'political' Cabinets, whereby party matters were discussed after the regular Cabinet meeting ended. These took place following almost every Cabinet meeting and were markedly less formal in style. There was a 'No. 12 Committee' which reviewed the political and parliamentary aspects of the week ahead. It was chaired by the Prime Minister and included the Chief Whip, Leaders of both Houses and the Chairman of the Party.

In the area of public spending decisions Major increased the involvement of the Cabinet, reverting to the practice of previous governments. A new Cabinet committee (EDX) was created to replace the Star Chamber, the *ad hoc* body set up under Thatcher, following the imposition of tougher controls on the total of public expenditure. This meant that the Treasury had more power over the total amount to be spent, while the Cabinet, through one of its committees, had a say in the allocation of the money. EDX was a standing committee of the Cabinet and its terms of reference were 'to consider the allocation of the public expenditure control totals and make recommendation to the Cabinet'. It consisted of senior figures, several of them non-departmental ministers. Unlike in the Star

Chamber, it was chaired by the Chancellor of the Exchequer and the Chief Secretary was also a member. It was larger and contained more heavyweight figures than was formerly the case. It had a wider remit, in that rather than simply dealing with bilateral matters, it was expected to present a package of decisions on spending allocations within the overall limit established by the Chancellor. Appeals were allowed to the full Cabinet, although the Treasury was still firmly in control of the public expenditure process.

The most noticeable difference between Thatcher and Major was the degree to which he brought senior colleagues into the decision-making process. There was an inner Cabinet, reflecting both Major's more inclusive style but also his relative weakness. Initially it consisted of Major, Hurd, Lamont, Clarke, Heseltine and the Chairman of the party, Chris Patten. It changed over time, especially after the departure first of Patten and then of Lamont. The presence of Hurd, Heseltine and Clarke meant that they remained committed to Major's policies after the exodus from the ERM. It also meant that they helped to prevent the Cabinet moving too far in an anti-European direction. Clarke's position was weakened by presiding over the Treasury in a period when the 'feel-good' factor was absent, by his support for Europe and by his 'one-nation' beliefs. Heseltine became increasingly influential and powerful. His job had five aspects:

1. Chairing four key Cabinet committees, including those on the presentation of government policy and on competitiveness, which had nineteen Cabinet ministers as members.
2. Taking charge of the Office of Public Service within the Cabinet Office, with the Chancellor of the Duchy of Lancaster as his deputy.
3. Acting as a link between the government and Tory backbenchers.
4. Co-ordinating the presentation of government policy.
5. Leading policy initiatives across Whitehall on matters such as information technology.

There was more 'openness' about the operation of government, although the extent to which this was simply a public relations exercise remains a matter of debate. In 1992 the list of all Cabinet standing committees, including their terms of reference and membership, was released, as was the *Questions of Procedure for Ministers*. The diminished control from the centre meant more freedom for ministers, although that led to a reduced sense of direction in the government as a whole.

Although there was an increase in the use both of Cabinet and of Cabinet committees compared to Thatcher, it was slight and was not a reversal to the situation which obtained prior to her premiership. The standing committee system was streamlined. A new committee (EDP), chaired by the Prime Minister, was created to cover the whole of domestic policy.

There are two views about Major's approach to government. His admirers believe that, unlike Mrs Thatcher, Major had a genuine and high respect for Cabinet colleagues. However, to critics it was the product of political weakness. They point out that Major's need to placate the right made government changes resemble those of the Wilson era when every reshuffle was assessed by commentators for the doctrinal balance it revealed. The activities of Portillo, Redwood and Lillie led the Prime Minister to lose his composure in late summer 1993. His failure quickly to sack Lamont and Mellor damaged him in the eyes of the party, which, having got rid of Thatcher because of her divisiveness, found her successor wanting in resolution.

Major had significant effects on the Cabinet system, particularly the greater openness and wider consultation. Yet as Martin Burch pointed out, although to some extent the changes were related to personalities, there are longer-term factors at work concerning the volume and complexity of public business. In addition, there are external pressures and conditioning factors. All leaders are severely constrained, although some have a bigger impact on events than others and circumstances affect an individual Prime Minister's opportunities to exploit his or her role. Both political and economic circumstances constrained Major more than they did Thatcher. The divisions in the Conservative Party and the policy failures of the Thatcher era, the small and declining majority, and the poor state of the economy all contributed to Major's difficulties: 'the central point is this – in explaining changes in the operation of the Cabinet system we need to look beyond factors peculiar to the internal features of the system, to consider the wider context within which it operates. It is a combination of these factors, rather than any one of them, which can help us to make sense of the workings of the Cabinet system.'[3]

The Cabinet: its role and functions

It is impossible to definitely state the role of the Cabinet and what its functions are. A great deal depends on the personalities involved and the political circumstances at any particular time. It is no longer the case (if it ever was) that the Cabinet directs and oversees government policy on a continuous basis. The sheer scale and complexity of governmental responsibilities make this impossible; many crucial decisions, especially those relating to defence, security and key financial and economic issues, are kept away from Cabinet and taken by the Prime Minister and a close circle of colleagues and advisers. The use made by successive Prime Ministers of the Cabinet, the extent to which it has acted in a collegiate manner as opposed to being in a sense a 'rubber stamp' for prime ministerial initiatives, has varied since the war. Thus the Cabinet is best seen as a part of a wider central executive, acting basically as a body to ratify decisions taken elsewhere, receiving reports rather than initiating action. On the other hand, its importance should not be ignored. Although rarely a policy-making body, its consent to major initiatives must usually be obtained and not even the most determined Prime Minister could prevail against the opposition of the majority of his or her colleagues for long.

The first systematic attempt to analyse and describe the role of the Cabinet came in the Haldane Report of 1918.[4] A committee headed by Lord Haldane was appointed 'To enquire into the responsibilities of the various Departments of the central executive Government, and to advise in what manner the exercise and distribution by the Government of its functions should be improved'. The Report concluded that the main functions of the Cabinet were: the final determination of the policy to be submitted to Parliament, the supreme control of the national executive in accordance with the policy prescribed by Parliament and the continuous co-ordination and delimitation of the activities of the several departments of state. Several conditions were necessary if these three functions were to operate:

1 The Cabinet should be small in number, having preferably ten or at most twelve members.
2 It should meet frequently.
3 It should be supplied with all the information necessary for it to make decisions.
4 The Cabinet should consult personally all ministers likely to be affected by its decisions.
5 It should be able to ensure that its decisions were carried out by the departments.

This view of how the system should work became the orthodoxy during the inter-war period, and although the pace of activity gradually quickened under the strain of social reform and economic difficulties, ministerial workloads were still manageable. However, the pressures imposed by the Second World War and by the reform agenda of the 1945–51 Labour government meant that the prewar system was unable to cope and there have been far-reaching changes to the operation of the system.

Besides an enormous growth in the *volume* of work, it has become more complex and detailed, leading to an increase in the size of government departments and to a need for the various parts of the machine to work more closely together. Members of the Cabinet have become more and more absorbed in their own problems to the detriment of the wider interests of the government as a whole, and committees have assumed more and more responsibilities. There have been two significant periods since 1945 in the decline of the Cabinet as a decision-taking body. The first was from 1945 to 1951, when a comprehensive system of Cabinet committees was established. This meant that most decision-taking took place below the level of Cabinet. The second was from 1974 to 1976, when a series of decisions was taken which included the reduction in the number of Cabinet meetings.

Martin Burch analysed the argument that the Cabinet is the main point of decision-making in British government.[5] His view was that the Cabinet is too small, too burdened with a variety of duties and lacking in competence to be really in control of the huge volume of business of modern governments. This means that much policy-shaping and decision-making is done outside Cabinet. Many issues reach the Cabinet virtually in their final form, and although the Cabinet in theory could overturn these decisions, in reality it is unlikely to do so. Burch also took issue with those who believe that the Cabinet will decide all 'major' issues of policy. This depends on what is meant by 'major'; clearly some are never discussed in Cabinet, and important policies such as those dealing with nuclear weapons policy are similarly settled outside the full Cabinet. Matters relating to the security services are not a subject for Cabinet discussion, unless they raise sensitive party political issues. There is also the problem of who decides whether an issue is 'major' or not.

Clearly many significant issues do not come to Cabinet and many of those that do are often pre-determined to the extent that the Cabinet's role is reduced to legitimising and endorsing a policy exercise that has really been carried out elsewhere. This is predominantly a response to the growth in the volume of government business and its increasing specialisation; only partly is it the result of a deliberate attempt by successive Prime Ministers or others to increase their own power. However, the weakening of Cabinet has increased the opportunities for power manipulation. It has become less clear where responsibility for decisions lies. Cabinet meetings do serve several purposes: they are constitutionally necessary, in that Cabinet agreement has to be secured for all decisions; they are occasionally the arena for worthwhile political discussions, and (most importantly) they are the vehicle for keeping members informed of what is happening generally in government. However, while there are some decisions which are genuinely made in Cabinet, they are few. Most are taken in small groupings, which is both reasonable and almost inevitable.

The Cabinet has both executive and political functions, which can be examined under a number of headings.

1 Although its decision-making role has declined, it is still responsible for many matters of high policy and for reviewing and legitimising decisions taken elsewhere in its name.
2 It plans the business of the legislature. Its agreement is required before legislation can be placed before Parliament and it will have an influence on the parliamentary timetable. Members of the Cabinet will also be important in seeking to gain support in the parliamentary party for the government's legislative programme.
3 It arbitrates in the event of a disagreement between two departments or between members of the Cabinet. Arguments which cannot be solved in bilateral meetings or in Cabinet committees may well reach the full Cabinet which will hope to find some kind of solution which will avoid politically embarrassing resignations.
4 The Cabinet provides general oversight and coordination of policy. One of the most important tasks of the Cabinet is to ensure that the actions and initiatives of the government work in harmony and to try to prevent or at least reduce the tendency of the various departments to pursue their own goals and interests at the expense of a co-ordinated strategy. This means that the Prime Minister and his or her non-departmental colleagues have a specially important role in transcending the departmentalism which

several commentators have seen as a significant problem in modern British government.

5 Besides these largely executive functions, the Cabinet is a highly political body, which provides leadership for the governing party, both in Parliament and in the country. This aspect of the role of the Cabinet was given clearer recognition by John Major, who held regular party political sessions following the usual business matters.

The Cabinet at work

Although Cabinet meetings may be called by the Prime Minister at any time and place of his or her choosing, they almost always take place in the Cabinet Room in No.10 Downing Street. The current practice is to hold one meeting a week on a Thursday morning; this is a reduction compared to the period 1945–79, when additional meetings were held as the amount of business demanded. Proceedings are formal, with members being addressed by their titles rather than by name, and seating around the oval table is in an order of precedence decided on by the Prime Minister, who will seat the most important colleagues near by and less significant figures further away. Sometimes the seating arrangements reflect more personal factors; Macmillan felt intimidated by Enoch Powell's accusing glare and had him moved to where he could not be seen. Heath ensured that Mrs Thatcher had to lean right forward in order to make her contributions to Cabinet meetings. Whether this succeeded in stemming the flow has not been recorded.

Simon James examined changes to the working of the Cabinet in the post-war period. Until 1979 it was usual for five or six items to be taken in Cabinet and to be divided into two categories. First came the standing items, parliamentary business and foreign affairs, which were given oral reports by the Leaders of both Houses and the Foreign Secretary respectively. On the whole these were formal reports. Should detailed discussion be necessary, a paper would be tabled and time allocated. However, several purposes were served by such presentations. They allowed colleagues to ask questions and make comments even though introducing new matters was discouraged. An opportunity was provided for ministers to express their concerns and for the Foreign Secretary and the Leaders of the two Houses to assess any political reservations about what was proposed.

Then came individual policy items based on papers tabled by the minister concerned. Some were of sufficient importance to need discussion at Cabinet (even if they had already been discussed and agreed in a Cabinet committee), while others appeared because no agreement had been possible at a lower level. Sometimes matters were raised in Cabinet because of their intrinsic importance or because of the degree of political controversy likely to be caused, either in the country or in Parliament. If difficulties were foreseen in getting a matter through the Commons, a full discussion would be particularly important so that the support of members of the Cabinet could be ensured and their assistance maximised in persuading backbenchers to support the policy. Such full discussions were used by Prime Ministers to ensure collective responsibility. On the other hand, if there was no dissent the matter might go through with little discussion, even though it concerned items of considerable significance. Sometimes a crisis, perhaps necessitating emergency action by the government, would force an item on to the agenda.

In the period 1945–79 the bulk of the agenda was concerned with matters referred from Cabinet committees. From the discussions which followed, a collective view would gradually emerge. This final decision allowed ministers to accept the decision, although with different degrees of enthusiasm, without feeling the need to resign. The Prime Minister would be left with the job of framing the Cabinet's decision, given that it rarely voted. Cabinet in this period was an almost wholly reactive body, rarely initiating policy and largely reacting to initiatives put before it by individual ministers or by the Prime Minister.

Mrs Thatcher radically transformed the Cabinet's role. Faced with resistance from the Tory 'wets', she lost patience and reduced its significance as a policy-deciding and even policy-discussing body. Cabinet met less often and its meetings were shorter, with fewer papers being presented for discussion. Major issues were increasingly kept from the Cabinet and even when they were put on the agenda it was as a *fait accompli*. Increasingly matters were decided in Cabinet committees or by *ad hoc* groups of close advisers, who could be trusted not to upset the ideological apple cart. On the other hand, oral reports increased, adding EC and home affairs to foreign and parliamentary matters. The Cabinet became a stocktaking meeting, being informed of the most important decisions made by committees and individual ministers but with little opportunity for a lengthy discussion and with even less chance of securing their reversal. Few issues were resolved in Cabinet and there were even fewer appeals against committee decisions. Although the new arrangements for oral reports seem to have allowed ministers to bring up matters which concerned them, Mrs Thatcher discouraged dissent from decisions taken outside the full Cabinet. Failure to allow full discussion before final decisions were taken contributed to such policy disasters as the poll tax and was a factor in her eventual downfall.

Size

In the twentieth century, peacetime Cabinets have varied between a membership of sixteen under Bonar Law and twenty-four during Wilson's first administration, with an average size of twenty. Although the wartime Cabinets of both Lloyd George and Churchill were considerably smaller, the experiment has not been repeated in peacetime. Thatcher during the Falklands War and Major during the Gulf War operated with small war Cabinets; both were temporary expedients and did not replace the regular Cabinet.

The Cabinet has to fulfil a number of functions, including decision-making, the discussion of policy issues and the representation of differing interests in the country and in the party. This means that it has to be kept small enough to carry out its various tasks while at the same time including the heads of the various departments, the 'regional' ministers and the small body of non-departmental ministers whose tasks are mainly managerial or concerned with the co-ordination and presentation of government policy.

The size of the Cabinet and the problems caused by the tendency of ministers to become absorbed in the affairs of their own department to the detriment of the general concerns of the government pose problems of fragmentation. Several post-war Premiers have toyed with the idea of a small Cabinet, composed largely of non-departmental ministers and concerned with overall government strategy. Churchill's experiment was not a success and since then Prime Ministers have operated with Cabinets of a conventional size.

There are several arguments against having a formal super-Cabinet. There are political drawbacks, which include the need to balance the various factions in the party and to avoid rivalry and jealousy from those excluded. The precise constitutional relationship between those in the Cabinet and the departmental ministers who would remain answerable to Parliament would be a difficulty, as was the case with the 'Overlords'. In addition, departmental ministers would have a degree of expertise that those in the actual Cabinet would lack; this would lead to bad government if those in day to day charge were to be given instructions by those without the required knowledge and experience.

Since the 1950s ministries have been amalgamated as a way of containing the size of the Cabinet. This tendency increased during the 1960s and 1970s as 'big is beautiful' became the slogan. However, in 1988 Mrs Thatcher was obliged to dismantle the giant Department of Health and Social Security as the strains of running this leviathan gradually destroyed the Secretary of State, John Moore.

Since 1945 several devices have been adopted to try to deal with the problem of Cabinet 'overload', which is said to be a factor reducing the effectiveness of the British system of government. 'Overload' is an imprecise term and consists of a lack of time and expertise to deal with the manifold problems besetting the British state, as well as the departmentalism and inability to focus on the strategic issues and future problems. Attlee set up the structure of Cabinet committees to try to take the strain from the Cabinet itself, while Churchill created the 'Overlord' system. Macmillan strengthened the Prime Minister's Office, Wilson made further changes to the Cabinet committee system and allowed ministers to recruit a small number of special advisers. Heath hastened the move to larger ministries, thus ensuring that each department was represented in the Cabinet. He also created the Central Policy Review Staff in the hope of improving the strategic capacity of British government. Wilson after 1974 established the No. 10 Policy Unit as part of the effort to achieve better coordination of policy and as a way of anticipating political problems. Mrs Thatcher was less concerned with the problem of overload, preferring to bypass Cabinet in favour of small, informal groupings of ministers and advisers. Under Major the emphasis switched to using non-departmental ministers in an effort to improve co-ordination and to avoid 'banana skins'. In July 1994 David Hunt was appointed Chancellor of the Duchy of Lancaster and made chairman of several important Cabinet committees. However, the appointment was not a success, especially as he proved politically maladroit, and he was one of the casualties of the July 1995 reshuffle when Michael Heseltine was given wide-ranging responsibilites for the co-ordination of government action over a wide range of activities.

Composition

There are few formal rules about the appointment of ministers, both Cabinet and junior. Ministers, by convention, must sit in Parliament (with few exceptions) and increasingly in the twentieth century have come from the Commons. A very few people have gone into the Cabinet straight after election to the Commons. Only the trade union leader Ernest Bevin, who was made Minister of Labour in 1940, was a clear success. All Cabinets must contain at least two members of the Lords: the Lord Chancellor and the Leader of the House. Occasionally other Cabinet members may come from the Upper House, but this has become increasingly uncommon in the post-war period.

The ability to make appointments is an important aspect of the power of the Prime Minister and will usually reflect the direction he or she wishes the government to go. Macmillan ensured that pro-Europeans were in crucial posts, while Mrs Thatcher appointed her supporters to the most significant economic portfolios. However, the need to placate powerful figures in the party is a constraint and may lead to possibly disastrous appointments being made, as when Wilson gave George Brown the Foreign Office in 1966. The power of dismissal is also highly significant. Several post-war Prime Ministers have written of their dislike of this aspect of the job. Dismissals create tension which can damage the government, and the human feelings aroused may be very real and deep. Some Premiers such as Wilson intensely disliked sacking people and preferred to move people in what at times seemed an endless game of musical chairs. Sometimes changes are forced on the Prime Minister, for example by the death of Iain Macleod in 1970 and Anthony Crosland in 1977. Resignations are always likely to be a difficulty, as they may expose personal frictions or disagreements on policy or criticisms of the leader. To ask for a colleague's resignation may cause critics to question why the person was appointed in the first place, as when Major dismissed Education Secretary John Patten in July 1994 after only two years in the post. Successive resignations during Thatcher's time were partly related to policy and partly to her style of government and eventually led to her removal from office.

The other factors determining appointment are political and personal. Membership of the governing party is one basic factor, although several appointments have been of people with little or no party background and membership has had to be arranged as a matter of urgency before the appointment could be made public. Political skills and a degree of administrative competence are also factors to be taken into consideration, although one may be more prominent than the other (and in some cases both have seemed to be in short supply). Portfolios may be allocated on the basis of expertise, as with the appointments of Eden, Home and Hurd to the Foreign Office. On the other hand, the reverse may be true and the job given to someone who previously showed little interest in or aptitude for the post, as when Macmillan gave the Foreign Office to Selwyn Lloyd and when Thatcher made Major Foreign Secretary. In both cases the Prime Minister concerned wanted someone who would do as they were told, rather than seeking to make their own decisions.

Seniority in the party, especially when coming into office after a period of opposition, is a factor any Prime Minister has to take into account. To some extent personal relationships affect appointments, although party considerations and the political and administrative capabilities of the person concerned are likely to play a more significant part in whether a post is offered (or sometimes accepted). Sometimes there is a need to appease a disappointed rival. In 1957 Macmillan allowed Butler to choose his position and in 1976 Callaghan gave the same *carte blanche* to Foot. In 1990 Major brought Heseltine back into the fold so as to ensure party unity.

Loyalty to the Prime Minister is an important factor and all Prime Ministers need to have in the Cabinet a core of people on whose support they can rely. In 1964 Wilson brought in several loyal followers to act as a balance against the Gaitskellites whom he feared would be a source of disloyalty and dissent. Sometimes powerful figures in the party have been excluded or sacked, either because of personal or ideological differences or perhaps as a warning to dissident groups in the party: the exclusion of Powell by Heath in 1970, of Heath by Thatcher in 1979 and the sacking of Barbara Castle by James Callaghan in 1976 are examples. On the other hand, the Prime Minister may decide that inclusion of actual or potential critics will reduce the potential for disruption because of the operation of collective responsibility, or because the political risks of not including the person or group concerned are too great. Both Wilson and Callaghan included Benn, and Thatcher felt obliged to include most of the prominent 'wets' in her Cabinet in 1979. The need for party balance is an ever-present constraint on a Prime Minister, even one as apparently dominant as Mrs Thatcher. In the past this has been a significant preoccupation of Labour Prime Ministers, faced with a party at times deeply divided into left/right factions. However, this consideration has not been entirely absent from the minds of Tory Premiers. Churchill's 1951 Cabinet caused some discontent in the party by seeming to favour the left of the party and excluding the more traditional element, especially those seen by Churchill as having been supporters of Neville Chamberlain. Heath left out Powell and those who supported him, while Mrs Thatcher moved quickly to drop the 'wets', although by the end of her time in office she had been obliged to bring in several key figures, such as Hurd and Chris Patten, who were associated with the 'one nation' tradition of

Conservatism. Major's time in office was dominated by the need to keep the various factions in the party in some kind of balance, especially over Europe.

Prime Ministers also possess the power to reshuffle their administrations and in recent years this has become an annual ritual, attended by considerable media attention and arousing all kinds of expectations. They may be seen as the opportunity to clear out dead wood, perhaps tacitly acknowledging that a mistake was made in the original appointment, and to bring in new blood. They may also indicate the balance of power in the Cabinet and show the direction in which the government is moving. Prime Ministers may be criticised for doing too much or too little. Eden was attacked for indecision because of the limited nature of the reshuffle following his appointment in 1955. Callaghan had a reputation for firmness, which he showed by sacking Barbara Castle and William Ross in 1976 and by the boldness of his decision to replace Crosland with David Owen. Although Major retained most of Thatcher's Cabinet he brought back Heseltine with the specific brief of ridding the government of the incubus of the poll tax.

A smooth reshuffle will enhance the Prime Minister's reputation while a bungled exercise will damage it. Macmillan's reputation never recovered from the 'night of the long knives'. Margaret Thatcher had contrasting experiences. For much of her time in office she managed reshuffles smoothly and in ways which added to her power. However, the 1989 reshuffle, affecting Howe, Lawson and Hurd, three powerful colleagues, was a mess. With no consultation she decided to remove Howe from the Foreign Office and make him Leader of the House and Deputy Prime Minister (a post which was publicly stated to have no constitutional significance). At one stage she offered Howe the Home Office, again without informing the incumbent Douglas Hurd. She also deprived Lawson of his official country home, something which gave grave offence to the Chancellor. This antagonised three senior colleagues, caused controversy in the party and the media about the way she treated faithful colleagues and led to accusations that she was acting like a dictator.

In the British system of government specific qualifications and previous occupations are not a significant factor in appointments, except in the cases of the Lord Chancellor, who is head of the legal profession, and the various Law Officers, who must all be lawyers. Cabinet ministers are appointed for primarily political reasons and not for their specific capacities. For this reason ministers are frequently shuffled during their Cabinet careers and undertake whatever task the Prime Minister requires of them. Although Nigel Lawson studied politics, philosophy and economics at university and was a financial journalist before entering politics, it is not a prerequisite for the Chancellor to be a trained economist. It is not even necessary for the Secretaries of State for Scotland and Wales to sit for constituencies in their region; successive Welsh Secretaries in the Cabinets of Heath, Thatcher and Major all sat for English constituencies (most having little if any ethnic connections with the principality) because of the absence of suitably qualified Welsh Conservative MPs. Northern Ireland

Secretaries in both Labour and Conservative governments have not represented constituencies in that part of the country.

Cabinet ministers learn as they do the job rather than being trained for it before taking up the post. None of the Labour ministers elected in 1997 have had Cabinet experience and virtually none ministerial experience of any kind. This makes them the most inexperienced Cabinet in British history; several members of MacDonald's first Labour government of 1924 had been members of previous Liberal or coalition governments. However, British Cabinet ministers share certain characteristics. They are likely to have been members of the Commons for a number of years. On average, they have spent around fourteen years as MPs before entering the Cabinet. Promotion to the Cabinet usually comes after experience as a junior minister; working up the ministerial ranks, often from Parliamentary Private Secretary, is the norm. As already mentioned, entry direct to the Cabinet from the back benches is rare and simultaneous entry to Parliament and to the Cabinet rarer still. Most post-war Cabinet ministers have spent a period in opposition as a frontbench spokesman or woman for their party. In 1951 Attlee formalised the concept of a Shadow Cabinet and subsequent Leaders of the Opposition have used the opportunity to give leading members of their party the opportunity to 'shadow' the real ministers as a way of gaining experience, sharpening their debating skills and generally preparing for office.

Individual ministers vary in the amount of influence they have with the Prime Minister and with their Cabinet colleagues. Most accounts of the working of Cabinet government refer to a hierarchy among ministers. The Chancellor of the Exchequer is usually in a senior position, something deriving from the sheer importance of the office and from the influence this gives him or her over the whole of government policy. Chancellors often have considerable personal and party influence, commonly allied to force of intellect and personality. Between 1974 and 1979 Denis Healey was a major political figure, more than capable of standing up to prime ministerial pressures. However, in the last resort Prime Ministers usually get their way and it will be the Chancellor who goes in the event of a policy clash, as Lawson did in 1989. Sometimes Chancellors will take the blame for a failed policy, as was the case when Callaghan resigned over devaluation in 1967 and Lamont over the forced departure from the ERM in 1992, although it took Major eight months to decide on the replacement, which led to accusations of 'dithering'. Other ministers have different places in the pecking order, partly dependent on the importance of the office, the political and administrative abilities of the minister concerned, his or her ranking with the party and the personal relations of the various protagonists.

Junior ministers not long in Cabinet are on trial. They are judged mainly on their performance as departmental ministers and so tend to avoid involvement in those wider issues which come before the Cabinet, to defer to more senior ministers and to be wary of disagreeing with the Prime Minister. Middle-rank ministers make up a more diffuse group whose status depends on a mixture of length of service, the importance of the office they hold and their political reputation. Then come the top rank, an 'inner circle' or 'partial Cabinet'. This group, of around six people, usually includes the Foreign Secretary and the Chancellor of the Exchequer and may also have as members some non-departmental ministers. One may be designated 'Deputy Prime Minister' even if not actually given the title officially, and collectively they share the leadership of the government.

Yet in many ways this typology is arbitrary. Things such as personality, popularity within the party, perceived success as a department minister and relationships with the Prime Minister and other colleagues affect status within the Cabinet. In some cases, such as those of Healey, Hailsham and Bevin, personality was the key. Others succeed by efficient mastery of their department. Peter Walker's long survival as the only card-carrying 'wet' in Mrs Thatcher's government owed much to his ability to run whichever department she allocated to him, as he showed during his handling of the 1984 miners' strike. Ability counts for much; ministers such as Jenkins and Lawson were marked out from early on by their intellectual skills. However, this counts for little if unaccompanied by a feeling for the political situation. John Patten's ability was not in doubt, but his inability to avoid offending virtually every group connected with education marked him for an early political bath. Some ministers are able to act as a candid friend to the Premier, to take an objective look at the situation and to enunciate sometimes unwelcome truths. Such was the role played by William Whitelaw, which led Mrs Thatcher to lay down one of the iron laws of British politics, namely that 'every Prime Minister needs a Willie'. A record of success as a departmental minister is an important factor, and success within his or her own department often gives a minister greater weight when speaking on matters outside the department's concerns. Thus when 'collecting the voices' in the Cabinet the Prime Minister will give differing weight to the various ministers, depending on the issue.

Sometimes Prime Ministers will be faced with a threat of resignation. Most post-war resignations have been when the minister faced a reversal of his or her departmental policy. There are five factors covering threats of resignation:

1 The minister must be in the Cabinet.
2 The issue must affect his or her department.
3 He or she must be senior or popular enough to cause embarrassment by the threat.
4 The Prime Minister must be able to make the concessions necessary to prevent the resignation.
5 The threat must be used rarely. Brown's failure to understand the importance of the final aspect caused Wilson to lose patience and call his bluff. Brown had no alternative but to go, thus relieving Wilson of a constant embarrassment.

The Prime Minister does not have complete power over the Cabinet agenda but does have the opportunity to display a variety of techniques in order to get his or her own way. Especially if the departmental minister concerned agrees, the Prime Minister may strive to keep a certain policy away from Cabinet. Even if the issue is controversial, ministers may not feel strongly enough to insist on a discussion or may fear the consequences of attempting to push the Prime Minister into a corner, possibly leading to threats of resignation. Wilson was able to keep the issue of devaluation at bay for some time, just as Mrs Thatcher prevented Cabinet discussion of economic policy. A Prime Minister may rush a decision through Cabinet, perhaps by raising the issue at the last minute and demanding an urgent decision. He or she may manipulate the circulation of papers and even, though rarely, refuse to circulate them at all. Mrs Thatcher would ensure that controversial papers were sent to Cabinet ministers the night before the meeting so they had little time to digest them or to develop counter-arguments. Prime Ministers may use the arts of chairmanship to get their own way. In this, much depends on the style adopted by the Prime Minister in question. Some, such as Attlee, have been terse and businesslike, while others dominated by force of personality. Macmillan, in many ways the model chairman, combined efficiency with a relaxed and amusing manner which most colleagues enjoyed, at least most of the time. Heath was silent and aloof, and ministers often were unsure what had been decided until they saw the Cabinet minutes next day. Margaret Thatcher was a poor chairwoman, lacking patience, argumentative and increasingly brutal with those who aroused her anger.

Even the most dominant Prime Minister can be overruled by the Cabinet. Astute Premiers can sometimes disguise defeat by remaining silent on a issue they know they will lose. But sometimes it will be obvious. Wilson lost several arguments in Cabinet, for example over the Cabinet refusal to restore cuts in the overseas aid budget and to send British warships to the Gulf of Aqaba during the 1967 Six Days War. Mrs Thatcher suffered several defeats, sometimes as a reaction against her domineering manner, although most of these were later reversed as she eliminated her opponents from the Cabinet. Sometimes the running can be made by a dominant minority, containing ministers too powerful for the Prime Minister to challenge successfully. One such episode came in December 1996. It was reported that eighteen of the twenty-two members of the Cabinet favoured a shift of policy, involving a commitment not to join a monetary union in the next Parliament.

> The 18, however, do not include the pro-European Mr Clarke. He declared that it would be 'preposterous' to talk about changing the cabinet's policy, reaffirmed at the Tory party conference in October, of not deciding until after the election. Nor do they include Michael Heseltine, the deputy prime minister, who firmly knocked the story down. Faced with their veto, on December 3rd, Mr Major obediently told Tony Blair . . . that the policy would not change.[6]

Every Prime Minister is prone to *hubris*, the tendency to think themselves indispensable and untouchable. The tendency to become remote, unapproachable and at bay, surrounded by real or imaginary enemies, is an ever-present danger. Although some Prime Ministers remained modest about themselves and on good terms with their colleagues, others, such as Macmillan, Wilson, and above all Thatcher, ended their careers convinced of plots and on poor terms with their ministers, their parties and with the electors.

The issue of whether Prime Ministers gather round them some kind of 'inner Cabinet' has been raised by a number of commentators. There is a distinction between an inner Cabinet and an 'inner group'. 'An inner Cabinet is a formal body, properly established and recognised with some degree of authority for taking decisions on behalf of other ministers.'[7] On this definition, there have only been two or maybe three such inner Cabinets since the war. All were established by Wilson in the 1960s and all at times of political weakness. In 1966 Crossman, pressing for devaluation, forced Wilson to set up the Economic Strategy Policy Committee; later Wilson effectively sidetracked it by packing it with his compliant supporters in the Cabinet. The Prime Minister established a Parliamentary Committee, later turned into a Management Committee. Though this did discuss some important issues it did so in an unstructured manner and without a clear agenda. It was beset with problems caused by the jealousy of those excluded and was largely an exercise in prime ministerial gimmickry. An inner group or inner circle is less formal and is a more frequent occurrence. Most Prime Ministers have had a small group of senior colleagues who discuss the issues of the day, help to shape policy and attempt to give coherence to policy.

Collective and individual responsibility

Collective responsibility

This doctrine states that all members of the government are collectively responsible for its decisions. Members must, if required, publicly support and defend these policies and actions, even if they have no personal responsibility for them, whatever their private reservations. If they are unable to do so, they must resign or face dismissal. In this way, the government presents a united front to Parliament and to the electorate, and policy is (in theory at least) that of the government as a whole, rather than of a part. It ensures the accountability of the government to Parliament (in that a defeat on a vote of No Confidence entails resignation) and ultimately to the electorate. It is also a way of ensuring the loyalty of the parliamentary party to one policy and is therefore an aspect of party discipline.

The convention gradually developed from the early eighteenth century to prevent the King from playing off Cabinet ministers against each other. In the course of time it became a weapon used by the Cabinet against Parliament, in that members could collectively stand together against efforts by the Commons to pick off individual ministers. Finally, in the period following the Second Reform Act it became a way of presenting a united front to the electorate, invited to choose between the programmes of the various parties. In the twentieth century the convention is more to do with executive domination of Parliament than with holding governments accountable for their actions, although two minority administrations *have* fallen as the result of No Confidence votes. Thus governments, faced with a rebellion by their own supporters, use the doctrine as a way of putting pressure on dissidents (although this tactic is not always successful). The convention has in recent years been extended to include Parliamentary Private Secretaries, unpaid assistants to ministers. This ability to rely on the votes of something like one hundred members of the government is known as the 'pay-roll' vote.

One of the main preoccupations of any Prime Minister will be to create a corporate entity, a government which will speak with one voice. The need to present a united front in Parliament and to the public is related much more to considerations of political management than to concern for the constitutional position. According to some commentators, Prime Ministers use the doctrine to silence at least public dissent from their ministers and thus ensure that the Cabinet follows their wishes. From this perspective, collective responsibility is more to do with prime ministerial dominance than with the need to preserve a collective voice. This does not mean that ministers no longer resign as the result of policy disagreements. Failure to do so, however, implies public acceptance of the decision, and ministers will be expected to vote for the policy in Parliament, to defend it on public platforms and to refrain from criticism, except in private.

However, in recent decades the force of the doctrine has considerably weakened. Starting with Harold Wilson's administration of 1964–70 there has been an increasing tendency for ministers to express dissent, albeit in veiled or oblique ways. In 1966 Frank Cousins, while Minister of Technology, expressed support for union criticisms of government policies regarding prices and incomes policy and support for American action in Vietnam; subsequently he resigned from the government. In 1969 Callaghan's statements to the PLP and the NEC in opposition to 'In Place of Strife' were widely reported in the press, as Callaghan intended. During the Labour ministries of 1974–79, dissent by left-wing ministers, especially Benn, was barely hidden. This dissension threatened the existence of the government and in 1975 Wilson was obliged to officially suspend the convention to allow ministers publicly to adopt opposing positions regarding the referendum on continued membership of the EC. Wilson relied on the precedent of the 1932 episode, when members of the National government were given permission to 'agree to disagree' over the imposition of tariffs. However, in the 1975 case the permission did not extend to statements made in Parliament, and Eric Heffer was sacked for departing from the official line in a speech to the Commons. In 1977 the convention was again suspended when Callaghan allowed ministers to vote against the Second Reading of the European Assembly Elections Bill. The aim again was to avoid a serious party split. Callaghan showed his commitment to the convention when he said that the doctrine should apply, except in cases where he announced that it did not.

During the Thatcher era, Britain had 'government by leaks', in which ministers used their contacts with the press to air their views. They also made obliquely worded speeches to make their real opinions known, a tactic freely used by both Tory 'wets' and the Prime Minister's 'dry' supporters. Mrs Thatcher used the weapon of leaks to isolate her opponents (and, at times, to distance herself from government policy as a whole). The medium was the 'lobby system', where Bernard Ingham, her Press Secretary, used unattributable briefings to put her views across. This tactic was used to isolate John Biffen, described as a 'semi-detached' member of the Cabinet. The bitter battles over Westland also concerned in part the nature of collective responsibility. This tendency was somewhat less marked under John Major, whose successive Press Secretaries were more traditional civil servants.

In Mrs Thatcher's time, some ministerial resignations were more to do with power struggles within the Conservative Party than with arguments about constitutional niceties. Although Heseltine claimed that his departure from the government over the Westland affair was partly the result of a dispute between himself and Mrs Thatcher over industrial policy and partly to do with the manner in which she led the government, it also concerned a personality clash between the two, which in turn was related to Heseltine's long-term ambitions to lead the Conservative Party. Similarly, Sir Geoffrey Howe presented his resignation as the result of a dispute about collective responsibility, with the Prime Minister increasingly ignoring its conventions and seeking to pursue an essentially personal policy, especially towards Europe. However, the clash of personalities was a significant, perhaps decisive, factor; Howe's resentment at the way he was treated had been growing since he was shifted from the Foreign Office and sidelined into the Leadership of the House with the empty title of Deputy Prime Minister. Although Howe had no aspirations to lead the party, the timing of his resignation was calculated to provoke a challenge to Mrs Thatcher. Thus collective responsibility can be used by dissident ministers to challenge and perhaps unseat the Prime Minister.

Some commentators have suggested that the doctrine should be buried and that disagreements should be openly acknowledged. They say that the public is likely to be less cynical if it is openly admitted that ministers genuinely disagree. It is also felt that the public have the right to know much more about the processes of government and the factors which affect policy decisions. However, despite the weakening of the convention, others claim that it still has an important role to play. The confidentiality of Cabinet discussions facilitates free discussion and the candid exchange of views; this might be inhibited by premature disclosure. In certain situations ministers might be compelled to support a policy they were known to have opposed in Cabinet. Public dissent among ministers would weaken the authority of the government, could lead to a loss of confidence at home and (perhaps more crucially) abroad, and could lead to the view that ministers who are deeply divided yet who do not resign will do anything rather than forego the privileges of office. Serious public divisions create a poor image, giving the impression that not only is the government divided but that it is unsure what to do; this uncertainty may spread, with a consequent lowering of national morale. Collective responsibility allows ministers to voice their objections before agreement is reached, while supporting the matter in public once a decision has been taken. This point is made in *Questions of Procedure for Ministers*, a document handed to ministers when they take up their position, which states that the doctrine depends on free and frank discussion, which would be put in peril if made public prematurely.

Individual or ministerial responsibility

In constitutional theory each minister is responsible for his or her own personal conduct, the general work of his or her department and the acts or omissions of the civil servants in that department. Ministers, both of Cabinet and more junior rank, will answer for their department, will explain and defend its actions, and will provide information about it. Thus a politician will take responsibility; civil servants will be shielded from political controversy, thus ensuring their neutrality and anonymity.

However, it is clear that reality is very complex, especially when allocating praise or blame. It used to be argued that resignation should follow disclosures of *misconduct*, *mismanagement* or *misconceived policies*. However, in all these categories the doctrine is somewhat imprecise. It is clearest in the case of *personal misconduct*, and several examples will be considered later.

In the case of *mismanagement* the doctrine is very unclear. It used to be said that a minister should be held responsible for the mistakes of his or her civil servants. The growth of government responsibilities has meant that in reality ministers cannot know all that is going on in their departments and the generally accepted doctrine today is that ministers are not liable for the actions of their civil servants except where there is a 'direct connection between ministerial involvement and the requirement of resignation'.[8] Thus ministers may be required to resign for departmental errors or misjudgements in which they were involved, or of which they knew or should have known. Resignations for departmental errors are rare; there were less than twenty between 1855 and 1955 and few if any *clear* examples since.

However, since 1979 ministers have increasingly sought to make a distinction between matters of 'high policy' for which they will accept responsibility, and the administration of that policy, for which they will not. Ministers increasingly seek to avoid responsibility by referring to advice given by civil servants and other advisers when errors, some of considerable significance, have occurred. This is constitutionally incorrect, as ministers do have choice and should be required to accept responsibility for the consequences of their actions. It also means that civil servants and others may be named as responsible without having the opportunity (or the necessity) to defend themselves, as was shown by the Scott Inquiry into arms sales to Iraq. This is another example of the way in which relations between ministers and civil servants have changed in recent years. This supposed distinction between policy and administration can be seen in episodes such as the IRA escape from the Maze Prison in 1983 and the Brixton escape in 1991. It was also the defence adopted by the Home Secretary, Michael Howard, after he dismissed the head of the Prison Service, Derek Lewis, following a damning report on escapes from various prisons. Increasingly the House of Commons (or at least the Conservative majority during the 1980s and 1990s) seems to accept this highly dubious distinction.

In cases of *misconceived policies* the question is, who decides whether the policies are *in fact* misconceived? The Cabinet as a whole may support the policies which are being criticised and may shelter the minister through the doctrine of collective responsibility. Such was the situation when Defence Secretary John Nott was under pressure over the Falklands War. Alternatively, it may be politically expedient to sacrifice a minister whose policies, although perhaps previously agreed, cause a political storm, as when Norman Lamont was under attack over his handling of the economy and over his private financial problems. A minister may be allowed to resign in order to deflect criticism from the Prime Minister or the government as a whole. The resignation of Lord Carrington in 1982 is a case in point.

Robert Pyper, in considering the period since 1964, has outlined five circumstances in which ministers have resigned or been dismissed.[9]

1. Changes in government structure and personnel (i.e. reshuffles).
2. Electoral defeat of a minister.
3. Miscellaneous personal reasons, such as age, health, family circumstances and pursuing a career outside politics.
4. Factors associated with the convention of collective responsibility.
5. Factors associated with the doctrine of individual ministerial responsibility.

Most ministers who have left government since 1964 have done so because of reshuffles, sometimes willingly, sometimes not. The next largest category includes those who have gone for miscellaneous personal reasons. Then comes matters relating to collective responsibility. Except in the case of a change of government due to defeat in post-war general elections up to and including the 1992 contest, only ten ministers have resigned since 1964 because of rejection by the voters, including four after the 1992 election, of whom the most notable was Chris Patten.

Pyper divides cases of individual ministerial responsibility into role responsibility and personal responsibility. Depending on the precise circumstances, a minister might resign because of failings in a political role in his or her department or because of personal misdemeanours involving moral lapses or breaches of the law.

The issue of role responsibility is complicated because in some cases resignations have occurred in order to conceal wider failings in government policy or actions. Examples include the resignations of Jim Callaghan over devaluation in 1967, the Foreign Office team of Lord Carrington, Humphrey Atkins and

Richard Luce over the Falklands in 1982, Leon Brittan over Westland, and Norman Lamont over the management of the economy. As all ministers in theory 'resign', there is an additional complication in deciding whether a resignation is voluntary or forced, a matter of 'constructive dismissal'. Lamont decided not to leave the matter in doubt by declining to send the customary letter 'thanking' the Prime Minister for the 'privilege' of being allowed to serve in the government to be followed by a letter of 'appreciation' for services rendered.

Pyper listed seven cases of resignations over matters of personal responsibility between 1964 and 1993. In 1972 Reginald Maudling resigned as Home Secretary as details of his financial dealings with the architect John Poulson, jailed for corruption, gradually became public. Lord Brayley resigned as Minister of State for the Army in September 1974 while under investigation for fraud. In May 1973 two junior ministers in Heath's government, Lord Lambton and Earl Jellicoe, resigned over sex scandals, with the Conservative Party still acutely nervous over the Profumo Affair. Cecil Parkinson initially attempted, with the support of the Prime Minister, to cling to office after revelations about the affair with his secretary. However, growing publicity soon forced his resignation, although he later returned to Mrs Thatcher's Cabinet. Patrick Nicholls resigned as junior Environment minister after he was convicted of a drunk-driving offence in September 1990.

David Mellor initially survived the reports of his affair with an actress; Major gave his strong support and with Parliament about to go into recess critical backbenchers lacked an opportunity for public criticism. However, his luck ran out when a family friend, Mona Bauwens, sued a Sunday newspaper for libel. During the trial it emerged that Mellor had accepted a holiday at Miss Bauwens's expense; other details of Mellor's financial affairs emerged later. Errors of financial judgement were added to the lurid stories of his sexual interests. Parliament was called into emergency session to discuss the national economic crisis, giving Tory backbenchers the chance to consider the political damage being done by the Mellor affair. Opinion in the 1922 Committee was turning against Mellor and with Major too politically weak to support him, he had to go. Then followed a string of ministerial resignations for various reasons; these included Tim Yeo, Michael Mates, Neil Hamilton, Tim Smith, Allen Stewart and David Willets. This led to a storm of criticism over 'sleaze', which forced John Major to set up the Nolan Committee into standards in public life.

Two conclusions can be drawn. One is that resignations are influenced as much by political considerations as by the nature of the event. The other is the importance of 'sanctions-holders', the people or bodies who can bring pressure to bear on the Prime Minister to remove the transgressors. Several factors combine to determine the outcome of a scandal. Whether the minister goes depends on the degree of support received from the Prime Minister, Cabinet and backbench colleagues. When support from these quarters begins to seep away or when a personal scandal means that the minister is unable to function effectively as a member of the government, the person will be in serious trouble.

Prime Ministers tend to seek to protect ministers who come under pressure to resign, either for role or personal reasons. Resignations temporarily weaken prime ministerial authority, as they reflect on the leader's judgement in appointing that person in the first place. They may also indicate that outside forces, such as media pressure, may have an impact on the composition of the government. Hence, the party may rally behind a minister who is under pressure, as (initially) in the case of Lamont and later Heseltine over the pit closure policy. However, the protection can be withdrawn if criticism continues and the Prime Minister and the government are put at risk. The cases of Leon Brittan and Edwina Currie are examples. A minister is more likely to survive a misjudgement if the House is in recess or if he or she can postpone accounting for the matter until then. An example is the inquiry ordered by Kenneth Baker as Home Secretary into the escape from Brixton prison in July 1991. The long-running saga of the Matrix-Churchill case and the Scott Inquiry into arms sales to Iraq is another example of successful stalling tactics by the government.

The significance of party opinion is seen in several recent cases. The most important body in the case of the Conservative Party is the Executive Committee of the 1922 Committee. This body was crucial in the cases of Brittan, Currie, Ridley and Mellor and significant in Carrington's decision to go.

The importance of the media lies not so much in the opinions expressed as in 'the length of time ministerial misjudgements remain headline news, the nature of the coverage and the extent to which they distract attention from news that the party managers wish to see featured'.[10] The sexual and financial indiscretions of ministers generally make better headlines and sell more newspapers than do the dry and often complex details of departmental errors and miscalculations. This may help to explain why ministers are more likely to survive departmental scandals than personal ones. Diana Woodhouse concludes, 'Thus whether or not a minister finally resigns finally depends on pragmatic considerations about government and party interests, with wider political considerations sometimes being influential'.[11]

Commentators have pointed out that in many respects the two conventions make it easier for ministers to avoid taking the consequences for errors both of policy and administration, unless they are deserted by their colleagues or annoy their backbenchers beyond a certain point, as in the case of Edwina Currie. They also allow civil servants to escape the consequences of incompetence or high-handedness; the doctrine of Civil Service anonymity means that it is hard to discover the advice given to ministers by officials and the extent to which decisions are taken in reality by officials rather than by ministers. In recent years efforts have been made to throw light on this relationship; the new departmental select committees have probed more deeply than had previously been possible. But they have been frustrated in their efforts as both ministers and civil servants feel that their joint interests are served by maintaining the fiction of ministerial responsibility. This was most clearly seen in the Westland affair.

Nowadays few ministers are prepared to resign, however strong the initial pressure. They rarely accept either a moral or a constitutional obligation to go. Rather, they hang on and try to 'tough it out', only resigning when the lack of support becomes overwhelming. Concerns about probity in government have grown. Resignations may be a way of avoiding explanations, as in the case of Brittan and Currie. They involve the avoidance of giving full explanations to the House and to the public. The failure of some ministers to resign under Major 'weaken[ed] the force of resignation as a symbol of integrity and honour, and suggest a weakening of the values which underpin British government . . . It would seem that . . . years in power has produced ministerial complacency and a carelessness with constitutional constraints and obligations.'[12] This leads to some worrying conclusions about modern British government. 'It is the failure of the House of Commons, or more accurately the government backbenchers, to extract accountability that is most disturbing. Ministers, it might be suggested, will always try to get away with minimal accountability. The real danger occurs when Parliament allows them to do so.'[13]

It is clear that the precise outcome of any particular controversy about ministerial responsibility will depend on a number of factors, with the support or otherwise of the Prime Minister as the most important single aspect. Yet the doctrine remains important, in that ministers are answerable for the work of their departments. The possibility of being forced into resignation remains a significant sanction, however infrequently it happens. The House of Commons can damage a reputation or bring about the discreet removal of a minister even if it can only seldom directly lead to a resignation. It seems that both collective and individual responsibility continue to exist, but as essentially political rather than constitutional doctrines. The survival of the Prime Minister and the government, rather than constitutional rectitude or democratic accountability, is *the* key factor.

Cabinet committees

The significance of Cabinet committees has grown and there is much controversy about whether they are a valuable aid to the system in the sense of taking the load off the Cabinet and allowing it to concentrate on essentials, on the 'major' decisions, or whether they are a device used increasingly to bypass the Cabinet, to present it with decisions already made and generally to bolster the power of the Prime Minister. Cabinet committees are committees served by the Cabinet Secretariat and recorded in the Committee Book, maintained by the Secretary to the Cabinet, thus distinguishing them from the numerous inter-departmental committees which are not within the scope of the Cabinet system. The number of Cabinet committees and Cabinet committee meetings has tended to fall in recent years, especially under Mrs Thatcher. The reduction in the number of meetings began under Wilson and Callaghan, although both made extensive use of the system as a way of handling business.

Under Thatcher the trend away from Cabinet intensified and there was less use of committees. The total number of meetings of all kinds of Cabinet committees was less than half that of Heath. Although Major made more use of committees than Thatcher, the general decline continued.

Cabinet committees are composed of Cabinet and non-Cabinet ministers, usually from those departments having an interest in the matter under consideration, and chaired by a senior Cabinet minister, in a number of cases the Prime Minister. Details of the system are (in theory) a closely guarded secret; until recently the very existence of Cabinet committees was denied. Successive Prime Ministers have relied on the wording of paragraph 17 of *Questions of Procedure for Ministers* to justify refusal to divulge details of the system. The internal process through which a decision has been made, or the level of committee by which it was taken, should not be disclosed. Decisions reached by the Cabinet or its committees are binding on all members of the government. This refusal was to avoid giving the impression that decisions taken by committees have less authority than those made by the full Cabinet. It was also thought that announcing their existence might lead to suggestions that there were divisions in the Cabinet or that some things were of sufficient importance to rate a committee, while others, which might be dealt with in some other manner, did not. It was also feared that disclosure might lead to demands for information about other parts of the Cabinet system. However, in July 1983 Thatcher acknowledged the existence of the four main standing committees and following the 1992 general election John Major published a full list of ministerial committees and their membership. The position as of July 1995 is given in Table 9.1.

There are several types of committees. Peter Hennessy divides them into five categories.[14]

1 Standing committees, which are set up for the duration of a Premier's term of office. The standing Cabinet committees, usually designated by letters such as EDP, are divided into three broad categories: overseas and defence policy, economic and domestic policy, and legislation. The legislation committees are largely concerned with questions of the handling of business in Parliament. They construct the legislative programme and examine the bills drawn up by the parliamentary draftsmen. Only the legislation committees can take decisions on these matters; the policy committees cannot interfere. Overseas and defence policy committees are normally highly specialised and with a small membership.

2 *Ad hoc* committees, which are established for a particular purpose, such as the decision to purchase Trident or the so-called 'Star Chamber' which under Thatcher adjudicated in the event of a dispute about public spending. They are called GEN groups in one administration and MISC in the next, regardless of a change of the party in government. For example, in 1994 GEN 24 was establish to deal with refugees from the former Yugoslavia.

Table 9.1 *Ministerial committees of the Cabinet and their chairs, July 1995 (committees on which the Deputy Prime Minister sits are marked with an asterisk)*

Committee	*Chair*
Ministerial Committee on Economic and Domestic Policy*	Prime Minister
Ministerial Committee on Defence and Overseas Policy*	Prime Minister
Ministerial Committee on Nuclear Defence Policy*	Prime Minister
Ministerial Committee on Northern Ireland*	Prime Minister
Ministerial Committee on the Intelligence Services*	Prime Minister
Ministerial Committee on Competitiveness*	Deputy Prime Minister
Ministerial Committee on the Coordination and Presentation of Government Policy*	Deputy Prime Minister
Ministerial Committee on the Environment*	Deputy Prime Minister
Ministerial Committee on Home and Social Affairs*	Lord President of the Council
Ministerial Committee on Local Government*	Deputy Prime Minister
Ministerial Committee on Public Expenditure*	Chancellor of the Exchequer
Ministerial Committee on The Queen's Speeches and Future Legislation*	Lord President of the Council
Ministerial Committee on Legislation	Lord President of the Council
Ministerial Sub-Committee on Health Strategy	Lord President of the Council
Ministerial Sub-Committee on European Questions*	Foreign Secretary
Ministerial Sub-Committee on Terrorism*	Home Secretary
Ministerial Sub-Committee on Drug Misuse	Lord President of the Council
Ministerial Sub-Committee on Women's Issues	Lord President of the Council
Ministerial Sub-Committee on London	Environment Secretary

Source: The Cabinet Office

3 Ministerial committees, at which the civil servants present take the minutes but do not participate. They can be either standing or *ad hoc*. Some of the ministerial committees have sub-committees, which are mainly concerned with co-ordination and presentation in their particular areas, rather than with the formulation of new policies, which are considered by the parent committees. Ministerial committees either prepare business for decisions at a higher level, possibly in Cabinet, or reach decisions on matters of policy on their own account on behalf of the Cabinet.

4 Official committees are purely made up of civil servants and can be either standing or *ad hoc*. They prepare papers and clarify issues for ministers. Some shadow ministerial groups, while others service standing ministerial committees, with others being established to handle a specific problem.

5 Mixed committees are those in which both ministers and civil servants participate. These were much favoured by Heath, who saw them as a way to

improve the working of the Cabinet system. They did not work particularly well, as officials were generally reluctant to argue with ministers.

Cabinet committees are rarely chaired by departmental ministers, who may be involved in the matter under discussion, but by a neutral chairperson. In matters of domestic policy, this is likely to be a minister without portfolio. The Prime Minister decides the membership and Simon James has outlined the six reasons for appointing a particular minister to a committee.

1 Functional reasons. The minister or ministers with a direct interest in the matter being dealt with must be included, which means that a number in effect choose themselves. A Treasury minister, though not necessarily the Chancellor, will attend because most decisions have spending implications, and one of the Law Officers will be a member of those committees which have legal implications.
2 Collegial reasons. 'The principles of collegiality and collective responsibility require that any committee, because it acts on the Cabinet's behalf, should represent the main interests at stake.'[15] Failure to ensure this may mean that appeals to the full Cabinet occur. The Prime Minister is likely to add some ministers who are not directly involved in order to give an outsider's view and to prevent the matter degenerating into a departmental battle.
3 Personal reasons. Ministers may be added because of their personal knowledge of the matter under discussion or because of their closeness to the Prime Minister. Some ministers have membership because of their government or party roles, as in the case of successive party chairs under Mrs Thatcher.
4 Regional representation. Committees dealing with Welsh, Scottish and Northern Ireland matters must include the Secretaries of State for the respective regions.
5 Political balance. There is less need to ensure political balance in the British single-party system than in the coalition systems found in most European countries. However, it is still an important consideration for any British Prime Minister, given the often wide ideological differences within Cabinets. Wilson made sure that both the pro and anti Europe factions inside the Labour Party were represented on the committee dealing with the 1975 referendum, and Mrs Thatcher made sure that one 'wet' was included on the economic committee.
6 Political weighting. Prime Ministers commonly 'weight' a committee to ensure that its decisions reflect his or her wishes. Mrs Thatcher on most occasions ensured that committees contained a clear majority of her 'dry' supporters and so ensured that her views triumphed.

Cabinet committees perform several functions. The official view is given in paragraph 4 of *Questions of Procedure for Ministers*:

> The Cabinet is supported by Ministerial Committees which have a two-fold purpose. First they relieve the pressure on the Cabinet itself by settling as much business as possible at a lower level; or failing that, by clarifying the issues and

> defining the points of disagreement. Second, they support the principle of collective responsibility by ensuring that, even though an important question may never reach the Cabinet itself, the decision will be fully considered and the final judgement will be sufficiently authoritative to ensure that the Government as a whole can be properly expected to accept responsibility for it. When there is a difference between Departments, it should not be referred to the Cabinet until other means of resolving it have been exhausted, including personal correspondence or discussions between the Ministers concerned.

Thus there are three basic reasons why a matter may be dealt with in committee: because departments cannot agree, because the issue is intrinsically important, or because it is politically controversial.

The aim is to deal with an issue in a way that the Cabinet as a whole can accept, that avoids resignations or the threat of resignations or an appeal to the whole Cabinet. However, consensus at any price is not enough, and the committee must be aware of all the consequences of its decision. Sometimes reference to a committee fails to prevent a policy shambles. The poll tax had its own Cabinet committee, which did not prevent it proving the most disastrous single decision of the Thatcher government.

Cabinet committees: the controversy

It is clear that in reality many vital decisions are taken in Cabinet committees (or in even more informal groupings of ministers close to the Prime Minister and a number of official and unofficial advisers). As Martin Burch pointed out 'it is the Cabinet *and* its committees which must be considered the main forums for decision-making'.[16] Attlee's decision to manufacture the atomic bomb and Eden's to invade Suez were both taken in small and highly secret committees, and vitally important matters such as the banning of trade unions at GCHQ and the purchase of Trident were taken by Mrs Thatcher and small groups of ministers without reference to the full Cabinet. Mrs Thatcher's preference for taking significant decisions entirely outside the Cabinet structure was a feature of her time as Prime Minister. The 'economic seminar', in which vital economic policies were made, was a small group in which officials and advisers outnumbered ministers and bypassed the Cabinet's economic strategy committee. Many commentators and some ministers regard this as the negation of Cabinet government; they feel that overall the consequences of this development has been to remove much of the responsibility for formulating and taking decisions from the Cabinet to bodies which cannot be held accountable for their decisions and which put an ever-increasing amount of power in the hands of the Prime Minister and his or her advisers. However, other observers feel that the criticisms are over-stated. By saving the time of the Cabinet and allowing it to focus on crucial issues, Cabinet government is strengthened. Cabinet committees are essential if the whole system is to avoid becoming overloaded.

As much business as possible must be settled outside the Cabinet. Despite the fall in the use made of committees, more business is settled below Cabinet level, much of it in correspondence between ministers in the form of memos or informal meetings. The efficiency of Cabinet committees has increased; more decisions are reached and less is passed on to other bodies or postponed to another meeting. However, there are disadvantages to this development. Since 1974 the Cabinet has been downgraded as the central decision-maker. This reflects much more fundamental and long-term factors than the style of any particular Prime Minister. While the speed and efficiency of decision-making is aided, the collective nature of the system is downgraded and the influence of those at the centre of the system, such as the Cabinet Secretariat and the Prime Minister's Office, has been enhanced. 'Yet the position and resources of these central institutions have not been enhanced to the extent required to enable them to handle these steering and leadership tasks adequately. Moreover their right to act in these areas, as against the interests of the collective executive and the prerogatives of individual departments, remains strongly contested.'[17] Burch saw two disadvantages in this style of government. 'First, there is the risk that the operation of the central machinery of government is not subject to clear lines of control and, therefore, when something goes amiss, blame is hard to apportion . . . responsibility is obscured and accountability rendered ineffectual . . . Secondly, the standards and thoroughness of policy-making may be compromised.'[18] The need is for an executive system which is both effective and responsible; we are in danger of ending up with neither.

Notes

1 Martin Burch, 'The Prime Minister and Cabinet from Thatcher to Major', *Talking Politics*, Vol. 7, No. 1, Autumn 1994, p. 29.
2 Dennis Kavanagh and Anthony Seldon (eds), *The Major Effect*, Macmillan, 1994, p.14.
3 Burch, 'The Prime Minister and Cabinet from Thatcher to Major', p. 33.
4 Ministry of Reconstruction, *Report of the Machinery of Government Committee*, Cd 9230, HMSO, 1918.
5 Martin Burch, 'Power in the Cabinet System', *Talking Politics*, Vol. 2, No. 3, Spring 1990, and Martin Burch, 'Cabinet Government', *Contemporary Record*, Vol. 4, No. 1, September 1990.
6 *The Economist*, 7 December 1996. I am indebted to Bill Jones for this reference.
7 Simon James, 'Cabinet Government: A Commentary', *Contemporary Record*, Vol. 8, No. 3, Winter 1994, p. 500.
8 Diana Woodhouse, 'Ministerial Responsibility in the 1990s: When do Ministers Resign?', *Parliamentary Affairs*, Vol. 46, No. 3, July 1993, p. 280.
9 Robert Pyper, 'When They Have to Go . . . Why Ministers Resign', *Talking Politics*, Vol. 5, No. 2, Winter 1993.
10 Diana Woodhouse, 'Ministerial Responsibility in the 1990s', p. 285.
11 Ibid., p. 286.
12 Ibid., pp. 290–1.
13 Ibid., p. 292.
14 Peter Hennessy, *Cabinet*, Blackwell, 1986, pp. 26ff.

15 Simon James, *British Cabinet Government*, Routledge, 1992, p. 63.

16 Martin Burch, 'Prime Minister and Cabinet: An Executive in Transition', in Robert Pyper and Lynton Robins (eds), *Governing the UK in the 1990s*, Macmillan, 1995, p. 23.

17 Ibid., p. 25.

18 Burch, 'Cabinet Government', p. 8.

Select reading list

Books

Bagehot, Walter, *The English Constitution*, Fontana, 1963 (Introduction by R. H. S. Crossman).

Barber, James, *The Prime Minister since 1945*, Blackwell, 1991.

Blake, Lord, *The Office of Prime Minister*, Oxford University Press, 1975.

Burch, Martin, and Ian Holliday, *The British Cabinet System*, Prentice Hall, 1995.

Butler, David, and Gareth Butler, *British Political Facts 1900–1994*, Macmillan, 1994, 7th edn.

Chrimes, S. B., *English Constitutional History*, Oxford University Press, 1967, 4th edn.

Cockerell, Michael, *Live From No. 10*, Faber, 1988.

Cockerell, Michael, Peter Hennessy and David Walker, *Sources Close to the Prime Minister*, Macmillan, 1985.

Crossman, Richard, *Inside View. Three Lectures on Prime Ministerial Government*, Cape, 1972.

Denver, David, *Elections and Voting Behaviour in Britain*, Harvester Wheatsheaf, 1994, 2nd edn.

Donoughue, Bernard, *Prime Minister. The Conduct of Policy under Harold Wilson and James Callaghan*, Cape, 1987.

Foley, Michael, *The Rise of the British Presidency*, Manchester University Press, 1993.

Hennessy, Peter, *Cabinet*, Blackwell, 1986.

Hennessy, Peter, *Whitehall*, Fontana, 1990.

Hennessy, Peter, *The Hidden Wiring. Unearthing the British Constitution*, Victor Gollancz, 1995

Hennessy, Peter, and Anthony Seldon (eds), *Ruling Performance. British Governments from Attlee to Thatcher*, Blackwell, 1989.

Hogg, Sarah, and Jonathan Hill, *Too Close to Call. Power and Politics – John Major in No. 10*, Little, Brown, 1995.

James, Simon, *British Cabinet Government*, Routledge, 1992.

Jones, George (ed.), *West European Prime Ministers*, Frank Cass, 1991.

Jones, Bill (ed.), *Political Issues in Britain Today*, Manchester University Press, 1994, 4th edn (Chapter 1, Bill Jones, 'John Major's Style of Government').

Jones, Bill, and Lynton Robins (eds), *Two Decades in British Politics*, Manchester University Press, 1992 (Chapter 7, F. F. Ridley: 'What Happened to the Constitution under Mrs. Thatcher?').

Jones, M. P., *The Prime Minister and the Cabinet Under Margaret Thatcher and John Major (May 1979 to May 1993)*, PARC, 1993.

Kavanagh, Dennis, *Thatcherism and British Politics. The End of Consensus?*, Oxford University Press, 1990, 2nd edn.

Kavanagh, Dennis, and Anthony Seldon, *The Thatcher Effect. A Decade of Change*, Oxford University Press, 1989.

Kavanagh, Dennis, and Anthony Seldon (eds), *The Major Effect*, Macmillan, 1994.

Keir, Sir David Lindsay, *The Constitutional History of Modern Britain from 1485*, A. & C. Black, 1969, 9th edn.

King, Anthony (ed.), *The British Prime Minister*, Macmillan, 1985, 2nd edn.

Lawson, Nigel, *The View from No. 11. Memoirs of a Tory Radical*, Bantam Press, 1992.

Mackintosh, John P., *The British Cabinet*, Methuen, 1981, 3rd edn.

Mackintosh, John P. (ed.), *British Prime Ministers in the Twentieth Century, Vol. I Balfour to Chamberlain*, Weidenfeld and Nicholson, 1977.

Mackintosh, John P. (ed.), *British Prime Ministers in the Twentieth Century, Vol. II Churchill to Callaghan*, Weidenfeld and Nicholson, 1978.

Madgwick, Peter, *British Government: The Central Executive Territory*, Philip Allan, 1996, 2nd edn.

May, G. H. L. le, *The Victorian Constitution. Conventions, Usages and Contingencies*, Duckworth, 1979.

Norton, Philip, *The Constitution in Flux*, Martin Robertson, 1982.

Pyper, Robert, and Lynton Robins (eds), *Governing the UK in the 1990s*, Macmillan, 1995.

Rhodes, R. A. W., and Patrick Dunleavy, *Prime Minister, Cabinet and Core Executive*, Macmillan, 1995.

Riddell, Peter, *Honest Opportunism. The Rise of the Career Politician*, Hamish Hamilton, 1993.

Seymour-Ure, Colin, *The British Press and Broadcasting since 1945*, Blackwell, 1996, 2nd edn.

Shell, Donald, and Richard Hodder-Williams (eds), *Churchill to Major. The British Prime Ministership since 1945*, Hurst, 1995.

Shepherd, Robert, *The Power Brokers. The Tory Party and its Leaders*, Hutchinson, 1991.

Thatcher, Margaret, *The Downing Street Years*, Harper Collins, 1993.

Thatcher, Margaret, *The Path to Power*, Harper Collins, 1995.

van Thal, Herbert, *The Prime Ministers Vol. I, Sir Robert Walpole to Sir Robert Peel*, Allen and Unwin, 1974.

van Thal, Herbert, *The Prime Ministers Vol. II, From Lord John Russell to Edward Heath*, Allen and Unwin, 1975.

Young, Hugo, *One of Us*, Macmillan, 1991.

Young, Hugo, and Anne Sloman, *The Thatcher Phenomenon*, BBC, 1986.

Articles

Alderman, R. K., and Martin J. Smith, 'Can British Prime Ministers Be Given the Push by their Parties?', *Parliamentary Affairs*, Vol. 43, No. 2, July 1990.

Axford, Barry, 'Leaders, Elections and Television', *Politics Review*, Vol. 1, No. 3, February 1992.

Barber, James, 'Finding the Leader. The Party and the Prime Minister', *Politics Review*, Vol. 1, No. 2, November 1991.

Burch, Martin, 'Power in the Cabinet System', *Talking Politics*, Vol. 2, No. 3, Spring 1990.

Burch, Martin, 'Cabinet Government', *Contemporary Record*, Vol. 4, No. 1, September 1990

Burch, Martin, 'The Prime Minister and Cabinet from Thatcher to Major', *Talking Politics*, Vol. 7, No. 1, Autumn 1994.

Cockerell, Michael, 'Prime Ministers on Television', *Contemporary Review*, Vol. 2, No. 5, Spring 1989.

Cockerell, Michael, 'Armchair Fever', *Independent*, 14 March 1992 (Magazine Section)

Donoughue, Bernard, 'The Prime Minister's Day. The Daily Diaries of Wilson and Callaghan, 1974–79', *Contemporary Record*, Vol. 2, No. 2, Summer 1988.

Dunleavy, Patrick, and R. A. W. Rhodes: 'Core Executive Studies in Britain', *Public Administration*, Vol. 68, No. 1, Spring 1990.

Dunleavy, Patrick, G. W. Jones and Brendan O'Leary, 'Prime Ministers and the Commons: Patterns of Behaviour, 1868–1987', *Public Administration*, Vol. 68, No. 1, Spring 1990.

Hailsham, Lord, 'Elective Dictatorship. The Richard Dimbleby Lecture', *The Listener*, 21 October 1976.

Hailsham, Lord, 'Prime Ministers and Near Prime Ministers', *Contemporary Record*, Vol. 1, No. 3 Autumn 1987.

Hennessy, Peter, 'The Quality of Cabinet Government in Britain', *Policy Studies*, Vol. 6, No. 2, October 1985.

Hennessy, Peter, 'The Condition of Cabinet Government (Introduction)', *Contemporary Record*, Vol. 8, No. 3, Winter 1994.

James, Simon, 'The Cabinet System since 1945: Fragmentation and Integration', *Parliamentary Affairs*, Vol. 47, No. 4, October 1994.

Jenkins, Roy, 'Changing Patterns of Leadership. From Asquith via Baldwin and Attlee to Mrs Thatcher', *Contemporary Record*, Vol. 2, No. 2, Summer 1988.

Jones, Bill, 'The Pitiless Probing Eye: Politicians and the Broadcast Political Interview', *Parliamentary Affairs*, Vol. 46, No. 1, January 1993.

Jones, George, 'Cabinet Government and Mrs Thatcher', *Contemporary Record*, Vol. 1, No. 3, Autumn 1987.

Jones, George, 'Mrs Thatcher and the Power of the Prime Minister', *Contemporary Record*, Vol. 3, No. 4, April 1990

Kavanagh, Dennis, 'Prime Ministerial Power Revisited', *Social Studies Review*, Vol. 6, No. 4, March 1991.

King, Anthony, 'The Prime Minister and Cabinet', *Contemporary Record*, Vol. 4, No.1 , September 1990

Lawson, Lord, and Lord Armstrong of Ilminster, 'Cabinet Government in the Thatcher Years', *Contemporary Record*, Vol. 8, No. 3, Winter 1994.

Madgwick, Peter, 'Prime Ministerial Power Revisited', *Social Studies Review*, Vol. 1, No. 5, May 1986.

Madgwick, Peter, 'Prime Ministers and Parliament', *Talking Politics*, Vol. 5, No. 2, Winter 1993.

Norton, Philip, 'Prime Ministerial Power', *Social Studies Review*, Vol. 3, No. 3, January 1988.
Norton, Philip, 'Collective Ministerial Responsibility', *Social Studies Review*, Vol. 5, No. 1, September 1989.
Norton, Philip, 'Chosing a Leader: Margaret Thatcher and the Parliamentary Conservative Party 1989–90', *Parliamentary Affairs*, Vol. 43, No. 2, July 1990
Norton, Philip, 'Parliamentary Behaviour since 1945, *Talking Politics*, Vol. 8, No. 2, Winter 1995/96.
Pyper, Robert, 'When They have to Go . . . Why Ministers Resign', *Talking Politics*, Vol. 5, No. 2, Winter 1993.
Seldon, Anthony, 'The Cabinet Office and Coordination, 1979–87', *Public Administration*, Vol. 68, No. 1, Spring 1990.
Seymour-Ure, Colin, 'Prime Minister's Press Secretary', *Contemporary Record*, Vol. 3, No. 1, Autumn 1989.
Seymour-Ure, Colin, 'Political TV: Four Stages of Growth', *Contemporary Record*, Vol. 4, No. 2, November 1990.
Seymour-Ure, Colin, 'The Media in Post-war British Politics', *Parliamentary Affairs*, Vol. 47, No. 4, October 1994.
Wakeham, Lord, 'Cabinet Government', *Contemporary Record*, Vol. 8, No. 3, Winter 1994.
Woodhouse, Diana, 'Ministerial Responsibility in the 1990s: When do Ministers Resign?', *Parliamentary Affairs*, Vol. 46, No. 3, July 1993.

Index